About

The media and the politicians are always screaming at us about horrifying, end-of-the-world threats, and also about miraculous new technologies that will save us and transform our lives. These are the two main types of Hype—Fear Hype and Hope Hype. They work together to befuddle our minds and keep us on edge.

Both forms of Hype, according to Arnold Schelsky are overblown, exaggerated to the nth degree, and scientifically worthless. Climate change does not threaten us with extinction, machines can never conspire against their human creators—and on the other hand, "global governance" cannot solve any of our serious problems, while most of the miraculous expectations for quantum physics are scientific nonsense.

AI is a focus of both types of Hype, with provably false predictions that machines will be able to think and create, provably false predictions that machines will replace employees causing mass unemployment, and provably false predictions that machines can conceive purposes or intentions hostile to humans.

Medical Hype reigned supreme during the Covid episode, when the authorities pursued one disastrous totalitarian measure after another, culminating in the deadly pseudo-vaccines, which did nothing to stop the spread of the virus but did inflict serious injuries on millions of people gullible enough to get multiple shots.

Fear Hype justifies the move toward a permanent State of Emergency, where we will willingly swallow appalling intrusions into our lives, while Hope Hype titillates us with wild dreams which can never be realized.

The political result is a system Schelsky calls "neo-feudalism." The psychological result is a rapid oscillation between extreme, unwarranted Fear and extreme, unwarranted expectations of salvation and bliss.

In the life of any animal, overactivity is short-lived and restricted to emergency situations. No living being can sustain overactivity for longer periods without self-harm. Hype is a form of toxic overactivity of entire societies. Today the West is in an accelerated Hype Cycle, hyping ourselves from one peak of excitement to the next.

"Arnold Schelsky warns us in The Hype Cycle *against exaggerated fears and hopes, so one must be careful to avoid exaggerations in praising the book. I believe, though, that it is indeed an important book which challenges conventional views on many subjects. I found*

the discussions of global warming, quantum computing, and scientism especially valuable. The author has an acute philosophical mind and an unusually wide knowledge of many different fields, both scientific and cultural."

—DAVID GORDON, Senior Fellow, The Ludwig von Mises Institute

"Hypes have a huge impact on our lives. They can be artificially triggered to manipulate and fanaticize people and they can lead to irrational and catastrophic decisions. If you want to understand how Hypes work, who triggers them, who benefits from them, and why we're not defenseless against them, you should read this excellent analysis by Arnold Schelsky, a book that may become a standard work."

—HANS GEORG MAASSEN, former head of the BfV, German counterpart of the FBI, removed from office by Angela Merkel in 2018 after contradicting her on uncontrolled immigration

"An exciting, entertaining book, filled with bold insights which are often unexpected, thought-provoking, and yes, sometimes infuriating."

—RAY SCOTT PERCIVAL, Enlightenment Defended podcaster and author of The Myth of the Closed Mind: Explaining Why and How People Are Rational (2011)

"Arnold Schelsky distinguishes many different types of Hype in his ambitious, novel, and very welcome attempt to survey, describe, and evaluate contemporary follies all of which involve the vice of chronic exaggeration or worse. The variety of contemporary Hype cannot be understood or evaluated without taking into account many different bodies of knowledge and disciplines—physics, mathematics, economics, biology, medicine, and philosophy, in particular social and political philosophy—a daunting task. But Schelsky, who is something of a polymath, is not daunted."

—KEVIN MULLIGAN, Professor Emeritus, University of Geneva, Switzerland

The Hype Cycle

The Hype Cycle

Uppers and Downers in Our Bipolar Culture

ARNOLD SCHELSKY

OPEN UNIVERSE
Chicago

To find out more about Open Universe and Carus Books, visit our website at www.carusbooks.com.

Printed and bound in the United States of America. Printed on acid-free paper.

The Hype Cycle: Uppers and Downers in Our Bipolar Culture

ISBN: 978-1-63770-055-6

This book is also available as an e-book (978-1-63770-056-3).

Library of Congress Control Number: 2023942185

*This book is dedicated
to my wife and children.*

Contents

A Time of Hype

We live in a time of vast, all-encompassing Hype. That statement isn't Hype! It's sober reality.

Hype is the extreme exaggeration—and in most cases emotional exploitation—of some topic's importance. We have Climate Hype, Virus Hype, AI Hype, and War Hype, to name but a few. Hype is an exaggerated collective emotional valuation of a natural or cultural process. Victims of Hype are emotionally disturbed because they attribute to Hyped topics an emotional importance un-warranted by what's really going on.

Hyped objects may be positive or negative, inspiring admiration and hope for amazing new developments, or dread and anxiety about issues represented as horrendous problems. So there is Hope Hype and Fear Type, though generally Fear attracts more Hype than Hope. Hope Hype and Fear Hype typically lead to action. But Despair Hype and Panic Hype, unlike mere Fear Hype, lead to resignation and passivity.

Hyped topics receive enormous attention in the media and lead to strong collective, shared emotions. For example, the climate changes we can observe since the middle of the nineteenth century, a natural process returning global temperatures to what they were a few hundred years ago, are Hyped as 'man-made climate catastrophe' and arouse collective fears among hundreds of millions of people in Western countries. Victims of Climate Hype, like the unhappy Greta Thunberg, sometimes become super-spreaders of the Hype and quite pointlessly transmit their unhappiness to countless new victims.

A Time of Hype

Another example is the Covid virus endemic, falsely described as a 'pandemic'. Its factual pretext was an infectious flu-like disease of very low mortality, like the common rhinovirus responsible for the common cold. Covid Hype aroused intense Fear, sometimes approaching despair, in many millions of people worldwide, not only among academics, who always tend to be a bit unbalanced, but also among many ordinary folks, and this collective terror led to policies that seriously damaged personal happiness, public health, and economic well-being.

This book describes the Hype phenomena we're facing, debunks the exaggerations (or pure inventions) involved, and tries to hint at some elements of a possible explanation for why we live in a time of Hype.

Hype is everywhere, all around us, and encompasses many topics of public and private life. The emotions Hype stirs up lead to discord and conflict, and campaigns of vilification against those people who keep their cool and don't participate in the collective frenzy of the Hyped-up mob. These conflicts rip through families and friendships, pitting numerous groups and individuals against each other. The Hype phenomenon sadly and needlessly divides Western societies into antagonistic camps.

The Types of Hype

We observe two basic forms of Hype: Hope Hype and Fear Hype. Hope Hype exaggerates the expected benefits of a natural or cultural process. Fear Hype exaggerates the expected dangers of a natural or cultural process.

Hype can also be classified as scientific or cultural. Science is of course a part of culture, but in this context I use 'cultural' in the narrow sense to describe Hype trends that do not evolve from scientific topics, but are based on narratives formulated by the interpreting class, such as academics in the humanities, teachers, pundits, religious ministers, hack writers, or media talking heads—the people Orwell called "the Outer Party."

Hype of the scientific kind is described in the first part of the book. I cover important examples such as Medical Hype, Artificial Intelligence Hype, Climate Hype, Transhumanism Hype, Food Hype, and Quantum Hype.

The second part describes cultural Hype with phenomena such as Diversity Hype, Gender and Transgender Hype, Death Hype, Globalism Hype, Migration Hype, and War Hype.

This book reviews the most important postmodern Hypes we are facing and argues that they are irrational, anti-scientific, and just filled with factual inaccuracies. I use classical scientific arguments from physics, mathematics, and biology for the scientific Hypes. The book then turns to the Cultural Hypes, using arguments from philosophy, history, sociology, anthropology, and economics.

Both Parts rely on the modern, pre-postmodern view of science formulated between 1880 and the 1960s before postmodernism with its anti-scientific and anti-metaphysic views and Popperian anti-scientific irrationalism (leading to thinkers like Paul Feyerabend) became mainstream.

The Modernist View of Reality

There is a reality external to humans. We can perceive and adequately describe this reality using our mind and language. Language allows us to create scientific knowledge, of which there are three kinds: positive knowledge (physics and other sciences), philosophical knowledge (the humanities), and theological knowledge (frequently challenged since Feuerbach and not discussed in this book). Positive knowledge is not waiting to be falsified (Popper), but a solid structure of contradiction-free true propositions which can be used to engineer machines and reliably shape our natural environment into a technosphere (which is not free of risks). I make use of positive scientific knowledge in the first part to reject science Hypes.

Philosophical knowledge is context-dependent and changes, but we can be certain that there are universals such as 'house' or 'tree' which we obtain from experience, and that there are a priori ideas (essences) which are mind-dependent and man-made, such as the circle, the number π, or the idea of justice.

Homo sapiens sapiens has genetically encoded properties which produce trans-cultural behavioral regularities that we can observe and determine in all cultures and societies. Among them are archaic patterns such as the eyebrow flash for greeting, the (often unconscious) inspection of the female back by males to determine reproduction capacity, or the fundamental differentiation between own and foreign (Eibl-Eibesfeldt 2017). These anthropologic patterns are the building blocks of sociology and the science of history, which add culture to the basic anthropologic patterns to describe and interpret society and the events of the past.

This is my position. It is rationalist, metaphysical in the sense of Aristotle and Kant, and science-affirming. I'm against postmodernism. I use philosophical knowledge in the second part of the book to debunk cultural Hypes. I f y o u s ubscribe to postmodernism, I don't expect you to agree with the second part, but unless you reject the validity of physics for the mesoscopic (mid-sized, from molecule to our galaxy) realm, you'll find it hard to disagree with the first part.

Some Things This Book Does and Doesn't Discuss

There are several very important questions about the origins and effects of Hype, such as: Why do humans accept Hype? Which groups accept what type of Hype? Where does the Hype come from, what is its function, and why do we see so much Hype in our time, while there was much less Hype in the 1970s or 1980s (though there was some)? What are the psychological consequences when millions of people are kept in a constant state of unrealistic Fear, only alleviated by equally unrealistic doses of Hope?

This book does not try to answer the questions why humans swallow Hype, or which groups of people believe which types of Hype, or how the incessant bombardment by Hype affects people emotionally. These are questions of psychology, especially mass psychology, and media theory. I will simply offer a few broad observations here.

Hype is created by one-way media, by the educational system, the churches, PR firms, press spokespersons, the government, public resolutions, petitions, rallies, and demonstrations as well as other channels of public communication. It is propagated to the masses via social media, which are 'n-way' because everyone can (theoretically) talk to everyone in public. Theoreticians of mass psychology such as Gustave Le Bon, Hippolyte Taine, Gaetano Mosca, Vilfredo Pareto, Max Scheler, José Ortega y Gasset, Elias Canetti, and Hannah Arendt have tried to explain how collective emotions form and spread among the masses.

An important aspect is that individuals in anonymous mass societies become prone to Hype and indoctrination by propaganda if they are *lonely, devoid of sense in their lives, and suffering from free-floating anxieties,* as the psychologist Mattias Desmet (Desmet 2022) proposes. While Desmet's popular book has many flaws (Ludwig 2022), it's a useful starting point for the reader interested in mass psychology.

The main human property that enables Hype waves is foolishness. Unlike stupidity, which is the inability to grasp what is perceived due to lack of intelligence, foolishness is the inability to control the impact of emotions on the cognitive system of our mind. Foolishness allows emotions to control our behavior, as when the fox says that the grapes are too sour because he is unwilling to acknowledge that he is unable to reach them (Mulligan 2016). In all the anti-rational, anti-scientific and anti-humanistic Hype waves we will read about in this book, human foolishness is the key to understanding why so many of our contemporaries get caught in the nonsense and let it dictate their behavior.

While this book says nothing further on mass psychology, it does try to answer the question of the origin and function of Hype in the last chapter, which suggests that Hype is a technique of political control and the exertion of power by ruling elites.

To understand this, we have to see that the various forms of Hype are embedded in an Orwellian framing of reality. Today, we hear messages similar to the propositions that "War is peace, Freedom is slavery, Ignorance is strength"—the slogans which George Orwell famously formulated in his novel *Nineteen Eighty-Four*. Lies are now recognized as truth, and our modern Ministries of Truth tell us that we're facing a man-made climate catastrophe (which we're not facing), that terrible pandemics grip us with their sinister, deadly and invisible stranglehold (though there are none, just normal endemic viruses), or that we are threatened by a new Hitler named Vladimir Putin, who is indeed a brilliant rival of the Western political classes and a power-optimizer, but not a madman who invades without provocation.

Like the Outer Party members in *Nineteen Eighty-Four*, we also have a hate Hype with daily hate ceremonies as Orwell describes. For example in Germany, at the time of this writing, there are demonstrations each weekend attended by millions of participants who protest against a conservative party, the AfD (Alternative for Germany). The AfD strictly abides by the Constitution, and has a political program comparable to the program that the formerly conservative party CDU (the Christian Democrats established after World War II and comparable to the UK's Conservative Party) published in the year 2000. But the AfD is now painted as a new Nazi Party, and at the rallies, the protesters carry signs and banners with texts such as 'Everyone in Germany hates the AfD' or 'Kill AfD supporters' (Such slogans are formally illegal under present German law, but the DAs take no action). The protesters' faces are distorted with hatred as they scream that AfD members and voters, currently more than a fifth of the voters on average and more than a third in Eastern Germany, should be killed. They are called to these rallies by the government and praised as 'defenders of democracy' (though the AfD has absolutely no intention to attack or limit democracy).

This book's last chapter explains the Hype phenomena from the point of view of the rule by a permanent state of emergency. As we will see, in essence, the Hypes are created by a complex process by which parts of our society serve the goal of rule and control of the masses via Fear and Hope. Instead of legitimate rule via democratic participation in political will formation and the rule of law, we face a ruling power that pushes the interests of a tiny minority against the interests of the vast majority by means of Hype and propaganda.

I don't in this book propose any way in which the sad state of affairs we are confronted with can be changed. Like Edmund Burke, I believe in the spontaneous evolution of human political affairs. The collective folly we are witnessing will fail, but no one can predict after what specific type of struggle or in what precise period of time. History shows that illegitimate, arbitrary rule usually doesn't persist for more than a few decades. And so, there are good grounds to keep calm and carry on.

I

Science Hype

Artificial Intelligence Hype

Intelligence is the power of making a meaningful response in the face of a new situation.

—MAX SCHELER, 1927

There is now a major Hype around so-called Artificial Intelligence (AI). We're told by prophets of doom that machines will soon become conscious and intelligent and then surpass human intelligence, a fateful moment called the Singularity. Then, these machines will use their vast and continually expanding intelligence to completely control humans, for their own anti-human ends, or even destroy all humans, if this appeals to them.

This term 'Singularity' is often used by a well-known pioneer of 'applied stochastic AI', Ray Kurzweil, who informs us that "The Singularity is near." Another prominent figure in this camp is Nick Bostrom, who believes that mathematicians and philosophers should now work exclusively on preventing "superintelligence" from being born.

The philosopher of zombies and fashion, David Chalmers, also believes in the Singularity; he even believes he has proved that it must occur. Another of these hyperactive Hypers is the highly gifted con man Elon Musk, who made his money obtaining subsidies based on Climate Hype and who believes that we are now threatened by the specter of "AI overlords."

All these intoxicated visions assume that machines will not only become conscious and intelligent, but will also develop a will of their own, and a lust for power; they will deliberately pursue their own goals, in other words, they will be ethical subjects capable of autonomous actions. At the same time a trillion-dollar tech bubble of AI investments is being pumped up under the illusion that AI will replace most human blue- and white-collar workers. As with many other topics in this book, we observe Fear Hype and Hope Hype, but the Fear is far stronger than the Hope and the Hope is fueled by financial interests.

Based on speculations not grounded in any scientific reasoning or facts, AI hysterics such as Nick Bostrom call for intrusive state regulation of AI research. Furthermore, many acolytes of the AI creed are also transhumanists. They believe that human cognition can be enhanced by merging mind and machine, and that we can achieve both physical longevity and digital immortality (see my chapter on Transhumanism Hype).

All of these predictions, fears, and hopes, including the economic AI dreams, are seriously misconceived. Nothing like these speculations can ever come to pass. There will be no Singularity, not ever. The argument for this conclusion takes a bit of thought, and a bit of math, but I will try my very best to keep it simple.

The AI faith is a neo-religion confounding a marketing slogan with reality. The phrase 'Artificial Intelligence' was coined at a Dartmouth Workshop in 1956 mainly with the intention of attracting more funding for applied mathematics and computer science research. There is literally no possibility of 'artificial intelligence', there are no conscious or cognitive machines, and such imaginary machines will never be built. Neither will there ever be any machine with a consciousness, a will, any understanding of what's going on, or any sense of morality.

Why am I so certain? Before explaining this, we briefly need to understand what it is that we're talking about when we use words like 'intelligence', 'consciousness', or 'will'.

Although I insist that there can be no such thing as artificial intelligence, I will sometimes use the expression 'AI' to refer to actually existing applications, simply because to describe it more accurately every time I mention it would be extremely cumbersome. There is something real, a type of technology, called 'AI', but it isn't in the least bit intelligent and can never become so.

Properties of the Human Mind

The human mind is a non-separable component of the mind-body continuum. It cannot be understood in isolation. In this continuum, there constantly occur many biological processes in parallel which create energy from inanimate matter and spend it on highly complex activities. The human brain is the organ in which the processes that cause our mental experiences occur. It is the most complex biological system we know of.

Processes occur in systems. Understanding a process means being able to describe how the elements of the system which cause the process interact. We understand some natural processes quite well, for example the celestial mechanics of our solar system which we can describe using Newton's laws.

But we don't understand at all how the mind-body continuum generates our mental experiences: consciousness, emotions, intentions, or cognitive capabilities. We can merely experience them, observe them through introspection into our own private experience, and then compare our conclusions with observations of other people.

Now what are these mental experiences? I will pick out the three that matter most to this discussion.

Consciousness is the "state of awareness or sentience during the waking hours" (John Searle). This is only basic consciousness (*Bewusstheit* in the terminology of the philosopher Hermann Cohen); there's also higher consciousness (*Bewusstsein*), our ability to describe ourselves and our position in the world. Despite attempts of contemporary philosophers to divide even basic consciousness into subcomponents or of neuroscientists to identify its biological substrate, it is indivisible to us, as Kant pointed out in 1790. And this is still true today.

Intentions are acts of resolution or planning to achieve a goal, they are the smallest units of the formation of our will, which is driven by our person, the center of our acts.

Intelligence, which we can observe in animals and humans is the ability to spontaneously find a solution to a novel problem. This solution must be meaningful or useful for the individual. The individual need never have seen a similar situation before and may not have been trained to find a solution. Both animals and humans are capable of such behavior. But only humans can combine it with abstract, propositional thinking to see the world as made of objects. We understand them as individuals of classes at different levels of abstraction. For example, we can see a group of beeches as plants, trees, and individual beeches, and we can count them. Non-human animals just can't do any of that.

Given these definitions, *what is AI?* We can only obtain an AI if we can model consciousness, intentions, will, and intelligence and then engineer them. And we can only obtain transhumanism, such as the enhancement of cognitive capabilities of the brain, if we have models of these capabilities.

This is because everything that we engineer is made of components for which we have a model. A model is a representation of an aspect of reality using abstract symbols that is created to describe, explain, or predict the aspect of reality in question. This reality can be man-made, which is always the case when we engineer something. If we do not aim to emulate a natural system, the model merely needs to be adequate to the requirements which the machine we're designing is supposed to fulfil.

But if we want to emulate the behavior of a natural system, we need a *synoptic* model. A synoptic model is a model that can be used to engineer a machine replicate of a given natural system or to emulate its behavior.

And so, to obtain real artificial intelligence, we would need to model the mind. For example, if we want to model the intelligence of a bee, we need to model the bee's mind. If we want to model human intelligence or improve it using brain implants, we need to model the human mind. Can we do that? No, we can't.

Why We Can't Obtain Synoptic Models of the Mind

The mind is a 'complex system' in the sense of thermodynamics. That's why we have to apply this science to understand the limits of our inquiry and of the scope of our engineering. Thermodynamics is the part of physics dealing with physical properties depending on heat. It describes the phenomena which occur when thermal exchange happens or energy is transformed from one form into another.

Thermodynamics was initially conceived to describe macrostates (the physical mode of being of an aggregated system), such as the effect of heat on a gas, but very soon was adapted to also describe miscrostates, using statistical mechanics. A microstate in a thermodynamic system is the complete microscopic description (using one or more variables) of an element (a point) of its phase space. The phase space is the co-ordinate system used to mathematically model the behavior of the system's elements. So a microstate is a mathematical model of a system element modeled as a point. This is of course only an approximation, as a point in the mathematical sense is infinitely small, whereas real matter cannot be like that.

What is a system? A system is a totality of dynamically interrelated physical elements participating in a process. Systems are usually delimited by humans for a certain purpose, though systems may also have natural boundaries. For example, a cook, when engaged in his professional activity, delimits the system 'kitchen' for himself to produce meals. A scientist might select a single bacterium as a system or instead look at an entire colony of bacteria as a system made of millions of individual systems. When we delimit a system, we select a level of *granularity* of its elements, from particles to groups of galaxies.

The mind-body continuum is a system with a natural boundary, our skin and corneae, that delimit our body from our environment. We don't have the slightest idea of how our higher mental properties come about, because the mind-body continuum enabling intelligent behavior is a complex system which we cannot fully understand and will never understand to an extent that would allow us to reproduce its function artificially.

This is true because we know very well from thermodynamics that we cannot mathematically model such complex systems to an extent that allows their replication. Therefore, we cannot replicate consciousness and the higher properties of the human mind.

All we can do is model and engineer logic systems such as the combustion engine, a nuclear reactor, or a nuclear magnetic resonance device, for instance an MRI machine (which is based on quantum mechanics).

Complex systems have natural properties that make it impossible for us to model them in their totality. We are essentially limited to formulating models of parts or aspects of such systems only. We have many such partial models, for example of the various regular patterns displayed by living systems, such as breathing, the heartbeat, or the monthly female fertility cycle. We also have basic models of the function of some of our sensory organs; this is why we can build cochlear implants, for example.

Here are three of seven thermodynamic properties of complex systems (more details can be found in the book by Landgrebe and Smith, *Why Machines Will Never Rule the World*) that prevent us from modeling them in a synoptic fashion:

1. **their evolutionary character,**
2. **the drivenness determining their behavior, and**
3. **their irregular and non-ergodic phase space.**

1. Their *evolutionary character* means that complex systems can add or remove elements and element types from their components at any time. There is no way for mathematics to model this, because mathematical models have fixed sets of element types. There is no possibility to overcome this at all.

2. Their *drivenness* means that complex systems constantly transform energy from one type into another. For example, when a jet of water flows into the basin of a fountain, mechanical energy is dissipated by turbulence, taking the form of heat. In the basin, you can observe many gyres and vortexes which perform this energy transformation. It has been shown that there is no way to model this mathematically. The same is true for all types of energy flows determining the behavior of complex systems.

3. Their *irregular and non-ergodic phase space* means that the location of elements of the system within it constantly change. The likelihood of finding a given element at a certain spot is always different. For example, any wave that ever reached any shore of the Atlantic Ocean is different, at the microstate level, from every other.

It follows that we can never gather enough infomation about the nature of the formation of the waves by sampling waves. Even if we sample them infinitely, we do not get any information that allows us to predict the microstates of the next wave. We will see that this property prevents us from engineering artificial intelligence using the most important method we have today, which is statistical sampling.

But why can't we model complex systems in a way that allows us to reproduce their function? Because the math we have cannot capture the relationships between their elements that would allow us to replicate them.

We don't understand how these elements work together to create the behavior that complex systems display. For example, though we have a complete wiring diagram of the way the 302 neurons of the worm *Caenorhabditis elegans* are connected, we cannot model how the millions of biomolecules inside each neuron work together to co-ordinate the complex behavior of this simple animal, which can forage, avoid danger, and reproduce in a dynamical environment such as a compost heap.

Neurobiology has almost no mathematical models, and those we have are at a rather high level, for example to model the generation and conduction of action potentials in neurons. Some are very detailed and describe the physiology of a molecule using partial differential equations. But there are no mathematical models of the functioning of the neuron as a whole, let alone how neurons interact.

Incidentally, the word 'ergodic' is a technical mathematical term which can't be explained briefly. Roughly, 'ergodic' means 'simple', in a technical sense. The bottom line, however, is that only ergodic systems, like a toaster or a cellphone, can be adequately modeled and can therefore be designed. Non-ergodic systems, like an intelligent mind, cannot be adequately modeled and therefore can never be designed and engineered.

But can't we just copy some existing non-ergodic system? No, because we can't understand it well enough to copy it. The human brain contains a hundred billion neurons, and each neuron is itself an unbelievably complicated ergodic system. It's just hopeless.

Explicit and Implicit Mathematical Models

We can create mathematical models of nature in two ways—explicitly and implicitly, and both methods can be combined. Most mathematical models used in physics, chemistry, biology, and engineering are *explicit*. Physicists like Newton or Einstein created them by thinking about relations in data or between abstract entities (such as spacetime). In physics, explicit models are usually expressed as differential equations. Such equations describe how the elements of the system we are modeling interact in time and space.

Implicit models are generated via statistical modeling which is also called statistical learning. The machine does not learn anything, but identifies regular patterns in sampled data. It does this by computing a human-defined algorithm for pattern identification. Only relationships that are regular in the data and that occur with sufficient frequency can be mapped into stochastic models. *They cannot identify the non-ergodic patterns created by complex systems.* The use of such massively pre-configured models in computer systems has nothing to do with intelligence, which is the ability to react to a novel situation without prior experience.

Neither type of model, nor a combinations of both, are able to provide holistic, synoptic models of complex systems. This has been proven in thermodynamics. Because consciousness, the will, or intelligence are capabilities that result from highly complex processes, we cannot model them. Therefore, we cannot build them. This is why there will never be artificial consciousness, artificial intelligence, or an artificial person. Mathematics is not going to change so fundamentally that we might suddenly be able to model complex systems in a synoptic fashion. For a more detailed elaboration of this claim, see the book by Landgrebe and Smith.

Because of this, we can't create AI, and we can't realize any of the goals of transhumanism either. To merge the mind and technology, for instance, in the way transhumanists dream of, we would need models of the mind we cannot possibly acquire. We can certainly build ever better prostheses of sensory organs. But we will never 'chip the brain' beyond substituting basic functions, such as treating Parkinson's disease by electrical stimulation or enabling control of a computer using electromagnetic patterns of the cortex. We will never be able to upload our mind to a computer, or to somebody else's body, and we will never achieve significant Methuselah-like longevity.

What about Machine Evolution?

A frequently encountered argument among AI proponents is that machines might spontaneously evolve to become conscious or intelligent. Here's why this is also impossible. Evolution is a long-term process run by systems of complex systems interacting in complex ways. Though we have a good idea of the high-level principles of evolution, we do not know the details. Let's start with the origins of life.

As James Tour has shown, we do not have the slightest idea how organic molecules formed from inanimate matter and how they then assembled to form the first life forms. We don't understand, in sufficient detail to replicate the process, how evolution brought about the properties of higher organisms. But only by replicating it could we drive machine evolution. We do not have the models to do it.

In the absence of an evolution model, can machines somehow spontaneously evolve? Certainly not. Like everything else, machines are subject to the second law of thermodynamics, which states that heat cannot be transmitted from a colder to a warmer body spontaneously, and that spontaneous processes are not reversible. This means that machines spontaneously tend to states of lower energy and higher entropy (reduced order). Mental abilities are the expression of the highest order we know in nature, and because of the second law, they cannot spontaneously occur. They would need to be engineered using an energy-creating and energy-consuming, directed process. Evolution is such a process. But we can't model it and therefore we can't engineer it.

Taken together, the 'AI' which actually exists is just a branch of mathematics concerned with the identification of patterns in data and the exploitation of regularities in

data for automation purposes, usually employing computers (Turing machines). Phenomena emanating from complex systems like humans are fundamentally irregular and
consequently outside the scope of AI.

What Does This Mean for Us?

First of all, it means that AI proponents and transhumanists make one big mistake: They assume a linear or even
exponential extrapolation of the technological progress of
the last 150 years into the future, without looking at the
results of physical theory. But the growth we have seen was
based on an exploitation of the positive insights of physics
(including chemistry) in electromagnetism and quantum
mechanics, many of which are now fully exploited. The
negative results from thermodynamics are rarely looked at
and usually not taken into account.

Secondly, it means that we do not have to worry about
artificial consciousness, artificial intelligence, or artificial
subjectivity. These will not happen and we do not need
tests for this, because it is essentially impossible. Machines
are performing syntactic operations on symbols which
humans have defined. The machines don't understand
what they do, and these operation only make sense to
humans, never to the machines themselves. For all other
living systems, machine output is meaningless, as it is for
the machines themselves. This means that we never have to
worry that switching off a machine may be immoral, as
some misguided AI philosophers attributing personhood
to machines do. But it also means that machines will never
develop a will, or personhood, or intelligence, thus they
will never attempt to rule the world or become dangerous
for us as subjects. There cannot be any machine subjectivity.
Machines will not become moral actors.

Thirdly, it means that the dreams of transhumanists are
not founded on science and will never be realized. They
are in contradiction with the findings of thermodynamics,
biology, and neuroscience. We know that we cannot model
complex living systems in a synoptic way to enhance
their higher capabilities beyond the natural level. Digital
computers, including (so far non-existent) quantum computers are just machines, logic systems. Humans are com-

plex systems. Those systems are incompatible when it comes to higher properties of the latter.

Fourthly, it means that the economic impact of AI won't be as great as it is currently estimated to be. We have seen that only regular patterns can be automated using AI. At first glance, it may seem that many human activities are highly repetitive and therefore will be automated using AI, in the mid to long term. But a more detailed consideration of the processes humans are involved in reveals that many apparently regular processes contain irregular patterns—this shows up in many of the activities that constitute these processes, for example skiing, sailing, or flirting. This is true whenever language needs to be interpreted or uttered, when visual situations have to be interpreted to derive an adequate activity, or when the rapid fine-tuning of motions is required.

Though animals and humans perform sensorimotor coordination for movements or perception all the time, it is a highly irregular activity, and we do not know how it is generated at a neuronal level. Our models may become better, but it seems unlikely that the connection of sensorimotor perception, consciousness, and intelligent decision-making will ever be modeled. Thus, we won't be able to replicate it, and lacking this fundamental skill of all moving animals, machines will never be able to take on a high proportion of motion-bound human activities.

Those who invest in AI-based full-automation projects such as driverless cars or transhumanist projects such as supposedly cognition-enhancing brain chips are facing, or have already realized, heavy losses. It is not financially healthy to confound science and science fiction.

Lastly, AI is a powerful tool, a result of the industrial revolution which has been transforming our world for two hundred years. Like all tools, it can be used for good and bad purposes.

Good purposes include the rationalization of human toil to free up time for more interesting work and activities, or the use of AI as a tool in scientific research.

Important examples of bad purposes are the abuse of AI for coercive political rule: to attack our privacy, to conduct mass surveillance, to manipulate and censor free speech, or to use AI as a weapon of mass destruction.

This last example is the most worrying, and we have already seen it in action in the Ukraine war. We need binding international treaties for the regulation of AI in warfare, as we have them for ABC weapons of mass destruction. AI can be used to build terrible automated mass-destruction weapons. These could be used on innocent civilians as carpet bombs were used in Europe during World War II or in the Vietnam war. But such AI weapons of mass destruction would be much more efficient than carpet bombing.

Abuse of private and public actors to employ AI for illegitimate ruling and exertion of power also needs to be regulated and forbidden. Certainly, small groups of domestic or international terrorists can do harm using AI; digital systems have to be protected against cyber-attacks that can exploit AI to be more effective. But as history shows, we mainly have to be afraid of those (humans) who control the infrastructure.

Because AI does not understand texts, dialogues, conversations, pictures or movies, its employment for surveillance purposes is limited. While some regular language patterns can be identified using AI, it will always generate many false positives, for example when someone says 'I would never say that the Nazi rule in Germany had positive aspects', the AI could erroneously classify this as a problematic utterance, though it certainly is not (leaving aside that commenting positively on the Third Reich, as disgusting as this may be, is covered by freedom of speech).

But more importantly, due to the non-ergodic character of human utterances and behavioral constellations, AI will overlook many signals that a human observer would reliably identify. Therefore, automated mass surveillance and censorship are hard to realize, especially when humans are aware that the machines are listening in. For example, during the pseudo-pandemic, Google took down YouTube videos criticizing the vaccination campaign or other government measures. Critical journalists and commentators who became aware of this avoided key words such as 'vaccine damage' or 'plandemic' to prevent the automated deletion of their contents or their demonetization or de-platforming. As the Twitter files showed, public officials and the managers of private internet corporations worked closely together to suppress freedom of speech. But most of this censoring could not be fully automated because machines do not understand human language.

Rather, civil liberties are threatened by the surveillance and manipulation possibilities and mechanisms enabled by digitization. Digitization not only encompasses our use of the Internet, in which our behavior can be completely registered and observed, and where our perception can be influenced by selecting the content that is suggested to us. But digitization also covers an increasing proportion of our physical life—via cameras, sensors in the public space, and in our cars, and the Internet of Things by which private and public objects are linked to the Internet.

All of this allows techniques of control along the lines imagined by Jeremy Bentham, who thought that the control of perception, behavior, and people in institutions like prisons, would contribute to the maximization of total utility in a society. Thus AI is not the problem; the problem is its abuse in the context of digitization by those who control the digital infrastructure.

The West ought to avoid China-like applications of digitization to suppress us, the free citizens living under the rule of law. Our big corporations and the state must be prevented from using digitization and AI to control our movement, perception and the free expression of our thoughts. The strength of the West was based on individual freedom and the rule of law. We need to regain this strength.

2

Planet Hype

Controlling carbon is a bureaucrat's dream. If you control carbon, you control life.

—Professor RICHARD S. LINDZEN

The media are boiling over with horror stories about climate change, global warming, climate emergency, and climate crisis. We're constantly told that humans have caused the roughly one degree Celsius increase in global average temperature, observed since 1850, by emitting greenhouse gases, mainly carbon dioxide which results from burning wood and fossil fuels containing carbohydrates (gas and oil-based fuels) or carbon (coal-based fuel).

The Fear Hype now being ferociously disseminated around this topic is omnipresent and overpowering. You can't spend a day exposed to media without getting stories about the climate emergency. Whenever there's a spot of bad weather, no matter if it's heat, a tropical storm, hail, a snowstorm, heavy rain, or unseasonably cold weather, we're told that this weather is due to the climate crisis—and this despite the admission by the IPCC that extreme weather events are not becoming more frequent or severe. We're warned that if we don't stop burning fossil fuels altogether, life on Earth will become impossible because of the temperature rise and resulting weather catastrophes.

The media, politicians, and numerous private and corporate activists tell us we're destroying the planet. We need to 'save the planet'—yes, they really do come out with this—a statement which can hardly be surpassed for its

17

absurdity. The mood among activists is hysterical and completely anti-rational. Facts, rational methods, and careful scientific considerations are angrily dismissed and designated 'climate denial'. Denial is a term from religious cultural wars to anathematize theological opponents as heretics. Indeed, the climate movement has reached a cultish state of pseudo-religious, sect-like excitement comparable to the mood in Bhagwan Shree Rajneesh's ashram in Oregon, but with the addition of radical aggression against those who do not share this faith.

The idea that the rise in global temperature since 1850 must be entirely attributed to human activities—so-called anthropogenic climate change—and that this development is terribly dangerous and threatens to destroy life on Earth is now widely accepted by conventional opinion. The media and politicians are continually calling for policies to achieve what they call 'climate change mitigation', a preposterous phrase that has now become totally accepted and normalized.

Like the talk about 'viral pandemics' which are biologically impossible, it can be seen as a symptom of collective idiocy. These policies are mainly directed towards a reduction in the combustion of fossil fuels and wood. Broadly speaking, the following main goals are declared:

1. **To lower energy consumption per capita,**

2. **to produce all of the electricity we consume by using so called 'renewables', directly or indirectly based on solar energy,**

3. **to replace combustion engines used for the transportation of passengers and goods by engines which do not use fossil fuels,**

4. **to make the heating of houses fossil-fuel free,**

5. **to make industrial processes free of the emission of carbon dioxide, and**

6. **to stop eating meat, in order to reduce methane and nitrous oxide emissions from agricultural production.**

These goals are often summarized under the Hype term 'zero carbon'.

I will now explain why there is no climate crisis, no climate emergency, and no biologically relevant anthropogenic climate change; why the 'zero carbon' plans are technically not feasible; the real reasons for the Climate Hype; and what the real tasks of environmentalism should be.

There Is No Climate Crisis

Since 1850, the relative amount of carbon dioxide in the atmosphere has increased from 280 to 420 parts per million (ppm), that is from 0.028 to 0.042 percent. The last time we had such levels of carbon dioxide was three million years ago in the Pliocene. Carbon dioxide is a trace gas: The main components of the atmosphere are nitrogen (78.08 percent), oxygen (20.95 percent), and argon (0.93 percent).

At the same time, global average temperature has risen by a bit more than one degree. It rose 1.5 C on land, but only 0.8 C over the oceans which cover 71 percent of the Earth, so that the average increase over the entire surface of the Earth is very close to one degree Celsius. Climate crisis proponents claim that this increase is solely caused by human activity. They contend that the combustion of fossil fuels has led to the increase of carbon dioxide in the atmosphere and that this is the sole cause of the warming. They believe that this warming is dangerous and about to accelerate furiously due to the reaching of 'tipping points' in the climate system, after which we will have 'runaway climate change' with irreversible catastrophes. They go on to say that this warming is very dangerous even before we reach their 'tipping points' because it causes a melting of ice, an unprecedented rise in sea levels, more extreme weather, and 'climate damage' affecting biodiversity, agriculture and humans ('heat deaths').

With the exception of the warming by one degree of the Earth's surface since 1850, and the resulting net melting of some of the Earth's ice, none of this is true.

The Source and Effect of Carbon Dioxide

First, let's look at the claim that the rise in carbon dioxide which we observe was solely caused by human activity.

Certainly, human combustion of fossil fuels on a large scale which started in the middle of the nineteenth century has contributed to a part of the increase of the trace gas. But we don't know to what extent. Recent findings by Skrable and co-authors using radioactive 14C-carbon as indicator for natural exchange-reservoir derived carbon dioxide show that by 2018, only 12 percent of the accumulated atmospheric carbon dioxide originated from the combustion of fossil fuels. This is not enough at all to cause climate change. Rather, the increase in carbon dioxide since 1850 seems to have been caused by warming and not vice versa.

Thus the warming must be attributed to an increased activity of the Sun, which leads to a release of carbon dioxide from natural, mainly oceanic, reservoirs. Henrik Svensmark has spent his life developing a convincing theory which shows that the activity of the sun and of cosmic radiation influence the climate of the Earth decisively (Svensmark and Calder 2007).

As Svensmark and many others show, the climate changes in cycles. During past cycles, the warming caused an increase in the carbon dioxide levels by warming-induced chemical reactions releasing the gas from its main inorganic depositories, which are bicarbonate, carbonate and to a small extent (approximatively one percent) carbon dioxide in solution. Warmer water can store less carbon. To some extent, which we do not know, this released carbon dioxide may historically have contributed to a self-reinforcement of the warming in the sense of a positive feed-back loop. For the last couple of decades, we have good data. We know that each year, approximately 120 billion tons of carbon are exchanged between atmosphere and Earth via photosynthesis. Another 80 billion tons are exchanged at the water surface. Humans add 10 billion tons of carbon each year via the combustion of fossil fuels and the production of cement. In total, we currently add a bit less than 40 billion tons of carbon dioxide to the atmosphere, which corresponds to a relative increase of 4.7 ppm each year. The ocean and the plants absorb more than half of it, so that we add a net relative amount of 2.1 ppm to the atmosphere per year.

What is its effect on the climate? We don't know.

From laboratory experiments, we know that carbon dioxide is a greenhouse gas. This means that it prevents solar energy that has entered the atmosphere from going straight back into space. It is certain that, as such, it contributes to the climate of the Earth, though it is actually the distant second most important greenhouse gas, after water vapor. The most important others are: ozone, nitrous oxide, and methane. From experiments, we estimate that with a doubling of the concentration of carbon dioxide in the atmosphere, we should obtain a temperature increase of one degree. Given that we live in an interglacial period, during which we have had historical averages of 300 ppm of carbon dioxide concentration, which we can take as the norm, an increase from this norm to 600 ppm would only give us an increase of one degree Celsius.

But it seems that the greenhouse effect reaches saturation at the greenhouse gas concentrations we currently observe (van Wijngaarden and Happer). These authors argue that 'the forcings from all greenhouse gases are saturated'. The results by Wijngaarden and Happer mean that a further increase in carbon dioxide concentrations will not increase the flux, so that more of the gas has no additional effect on the climate anymore.

The IPCC, on the other hand, maintains that there is a reinforcement of the primary carbon dioxide effect: according to them, a doubling of the concentration from the interglacial norm to 600 ppm could lead to a 2.5 to 4.5 degree increase (AR6, the sixth assessment report). But if van Wijngaarden and Happer are right, the effect is even lower than one degree and it would not matter very much how much more carbon dioxide we emit. This debate is called the carbon dioxide climate sensitivity question (equilibrium climate sensitivity, ECS) which is scientifically unresolved. However, there is more and more empirical evidence that the ECS is 2, 1.5, or even lower. This would mean that mankind has all the time it wants to reduce carbon dioxide emissions via technical progress.

Hot Climate Ahead?

We often hear that some current or recent year, or even month or day, is 'the hottest on record'. Sometimes it's 'the hottest ever'. The first statement is misleading, the second is false and is presumably based on a misunderstanding of the first statement. 'Hottest on record' refers to the thermometer record. A precision thermometer was invented in 1714 by Daniel Fahrenheit, but it took a while before there were enough continuous temperature records of widely separated locations on the Earth to make a global estimate, so there is no good record of global temperatures until somewhat less than 150 years ago, a fleeting moment in the life of the Earth. We know from various different geological measurement techniques (which all give roughly the same results) that the Earth has been much, much warmer than today, sometimes for thousands of years at a stretch, without any catastrophic effects.

Now, let's look at the claim that we're heading towards an exceptionally hot climate that will make life on Earth impossible. Five hundred and fifty million years ago, the level of carbon dioxide was 7,000 ppm, which is seventeen times higher than today, though still an extremely tiny component of the atmosphere. It was much hotter (ten to fifteen degrees) than now, and it was an exceptionally productive period of evolution. Obviously, there were no humans, so there was no human activity influencing the climate. Later, the temperature and carbon dioxide levels dropped. Whenever the temperature drops, the carbon dioxide level drops as well (with a certain temporal offset), as the oceans can store more carbon when they cool down. When the climate gets warmer, carbon dioxide is freed from its inorganic stores, with a certain delay.

Now, we live in the Holocene, which is a warm period that started approximately 11,700 years ago ending a period of glaciation, the Pleistocene. During that ice age, North America and northern Europe were covered by an ice sheet of more than 1 km thickness. But in a sub-period of the Holocene, during a 5,000-year-long interval called the Northgrippian *period, which lasted from 9,800 to 5,700 years ago, it was roughly three degrees warmer than today.* That time is called the Holocene Thermal Maximum. At the time, there was much less ice on Greenland than today and the glaciers in the Alps were much smaller than now. Animals and humans did very well during this time. Then the climate cooled down. From 250 B.C. to 400 A.D. the climate was at least as warm as it is now, or a bit warmer, before it cooled down in the early Middle Ages (the so-called Dark

Age). Then, there was another warm period from 800 to 1300 A.D., the Medieval Warm Period (MWP), which coincided with a high solar activity. When the sun's activity dropped, the Medieval Warm Period ended and the Little Ice Age (LIA) started. It was the coldest period since the end of the Pleistocene roughly 14,000 years ago. The Little Ice Age was a bad period for mankind, leading to a decline in the world population due to the shorter growth periods for edible plants. During the warming periods of the Holocene, the rate of climate change was as fast as today or much faster. Often, the climate rose by up to one degree in a few decades, an increase which is much faster than what we observe today.

When the Pleistocene ended, the sea levels were 120 meters below the current level, the water was stored in the form of ice. When the ice melted, the sea levels rose at a velocity of 10–20 mm per year, a process which ended 5,000 years ago. Since then, they rose and sank again, over the last 150 years they rose by 0.4 mm per year on average. This pace is 25 to 50 times slower than from the end of the Pleistocene to 3,000 B.C. Compared to that period, the sea level is not really changing. In some places, sea levels have been continuously dropping. For example, in Sweden, the sea level decreased by 3.7 mm a year on average from 1880 to 2020. This could not happen if we were looking at a massive global increase in sea levels.

By historical standards, there is nothing special about the current rate of increase in global temperature and sea levels. The temperature increases more slowly than during the last warm period before the Little Ice Age, and the sea levels are rising very slowly and not globally. We are still far away from the temperatures of the Northgrippian. Because of this the climate emergency proponents claim that while the temperature is still moderate as compared to then, we will soon get there, and much faster than ever before. I look at this speculative proposition below when I consider climate models.

The Causes of Global Warming

The historical massive climate fluctuations we know of have been caused by the varying energy intensity of the sun itself, which in addition is modulated by interstellar radiation (Svensmark and Calder)—intense cosmic radiation reduces the net solar energy flow to the Earth. The amount of the sun's energy arriving on Earth is the ultimate cause of most energy sources on Earth. Fossil fuels and wood which we burn contain solar energy which was turned into carbon or carbohydrates by plant photosynthesis. The so-called renewable energies are directly driven by the sun (photovoltaic power) or indirectly enabled by it (wind results from the energy of the sun). Merely geothermal energy and nuclear fission power are not based on solar activity, but on terrestrial inorganic resources.

The energy provided by the sun undergoes massive variations. Once the Earth cooled down to an extent that the water became liquid, the levels of oxygen rose and the Earth cooled and solidified, life started to emerge (roughly two billion years ago), the climate has become more and more determined by the energy of the sun that makes it through the varying levels of cosmic radiation. Since at least a billion years, the surface of the Earth is so cold that if the sun were to be switched off, the Earth would get into a thermal equilibrium between the temperature of outer space and the heat emanating from the Earth's core, which after a short time would be far below freezing point.

The Sun has short and long term cycles of radiation intensity: There is the Hale cycle (22 years), the Gleissberg cycle, the Suess-DeVries-cycle, the Eddy cycle, and the Hallstatt cycle (2,300 years), and there may be more. All of them overlap and create non-linear complex patterns of variation, modulated further by varying levels of cosmic radiation, which changes as our solar systems orbits around the center of our galaxy (which takes 240 million years, that is one galactic year). The effect of the Sun is further complicated by the position of the Earth in relation to the Sun which also varies over time. Our modeling abilities are insufficient to create causal or predictive models of these highly complex and ever changing non-ergodic overlaying effects. But we can measure the intensity of the Sun via its spots—their number is proportional to its energy level. We can also measure the strength of the Sun's electromagnetic field, which varies over time in proportion to its energy. The field strengths of the past are proportional to the presence of radioactive isotopes in iron cores, sediments, dripstones, and tree rings. From these data, we know quite well how the energy of the Sun has changed over time.

But we do not know exactly the physics of the transmission of solar energy into climate events. First of all, the total irradiance of the sun does not vary very much over time, certainly not enough to explain the evolution of the climate. But the Sun's electromagnetic field and its ultraviolet radiation vary strongly over time. The atmosphere's ozone layer may convey the variance in UV radiation to lower levels thus heating up the air in the lower troposphere close to the surface. The troposphere is the part of the atmosphere up to 12 km. A stronger Sun has a stronger electro-magnetic field. This protects the Earth more strongly from cosmic radiation. *Cosmic radiation leads to the formation of condensation cores for water molecules, which form clouds.* Less condensation nuclei in the atmosphere cause less clouds and more heating by the rather constant solar irradiance; this is the mechanism proposed by Svensmark by which cosmic radiation modulates the energy contribution of the Sun. In the short term, all of these effects are so complex that we cannot model them using partial differential equations, which are the core models for the explanation of natural phenomena in physics.

Nevertheless, with some delay, the medium-term climate must always be dependent on the level of energy which the Sun provides, the amount of cosmic radiation, and the position of the Earth in relation to the Sun. We know quite well that changes in solar energy levels have driven the historical climate evolution, there are multiple studies about this relationship (documented by Vahrenholt in his books and his contribution to the Clintel report in chapter 6). The short-term climate is also determined by temperature cycles in the oceans, the amount of water and its positions in the atmosphere (cloud formation, density and position) and the activities of the wind. All these phenomena are indirectly driven by solar energy.

The ocean water temperature cycles which we know, the Pacific Decade Oscillation, the Atlantic Multi-decade Oscillation, the North Atlantic Oscillation, which is an air pressure cycle, as well as other cycles, contribute to the short-term climate evolution. Cloud formation is another climate-factor which we do not understand at all. Because

the ocean, air pressure and cloud formation processes interact with each other and with further causal factors of the
climate, the resulting system processes are too complex for
our causal models in physics. And thus, unfortunately, the
effect of the Sun, ocean cycles and cloud formation are not
modeled or insufficiently modeled by the climate models,
as we will see below.

Modeling and Prediction Issues

The climate models are failing. Criticism of them falls into
two categories: empirical and theoretical. While there is a
lot of the former, there is rather little of the latter. We look
at each in turn.

The models are systems of partial differential equations
which model different aspects of the climate. For example,
General Circulation Models use (drastically simplified)
Navier-Stokes equations to model fluid motion and energy
convection in the sea and in the atmosphere. Over thirty
different models for temperature, precipitation, wind
speed and snow depth were combined in the CMIP6 research effort used to compile the IPCC AR6 report.

Empirically, the climate models are failing. How's that?
First of all, they cannot model the climate evolution of the
Holocene, and they can only partially reproduce the period
since 1850. But they cannot model the global temperature
oscillations with a range of 15 degrees which occurred since
end of the Pleistocene: They still show the evolution of
global temperature as flat since the birth of Christ and then
suddenly rising with the beginning of the industrial era
(1850), a pattern called the hockey stick (Figure 1a in the
IPCC's 'Summary for Policymakers' published within AR6).

The model thus fails to model the MWP and the LIA,
the coldest period of the Holocene. If the models were cal-
ibrated to describe these correctly, they would not show
relevant temperature increases in the future. *This is because the models are constructed to show that carbon dioxide
is the dominating factor of the climate evolution we see.* But
the trace gas played no major role in the historical evolution of the climate; it was certainly a co-factor, but the
main factor was the change of energy levels of the Sun.
This effect is not included in the models underlying the AR6.

Attempts to model the LIA using volcano activity have failed. Over the last two millennia, the models misestimate the surface temperature of the oceans by a factor of 50. The models are also incapable of simulating the Antarctic climate. Especially, it is highly unlikely that the ice shield of the Antarctic will melt—it even persisted throughout the massive warmth of the Pliocene four million years ago. The models also fail to simulate precipitation. Models that cannot capture the basic climate evolution of the past are necessarily invalid. But the models of the last decades also failed to predict the radical slowdown of global warming at the turn of the century. This was probably due to ocean cycles which were not sufficiently taken into account, but also due to more fundamental modeling issues.

What about the latest models used in the AR6? In the Clintel report (May and Crok) McKitrick shows that the climate models' temperature simulations for the tropical troposphere deviate massively from the real observations. The models give much hotter temperatures than what we measure. If the carbon dioxide forcing postulated by the IPCC modelers is taken out of the models, they give results very close to the real measurements. *This totally invalidates the models and proves that they have no predictive power at all.* Carbon dioxide does not seem to have a forcing effect in the troposphere at today's concentrations, which is in line with the results of van Wijngaarden and Happer. Furthermore, the lower and mid-troposphere models of AR6/CMIP6 for the entire globe and the tropics deviate from real temperature trends by massively overestimating the heating. If the carbon dioxide climate sensitivity (ECS) is set to a low value (1 or lower), the models can explain the warming trends much better, indicating again that the sensitivity against carbon dioxide is very low at the current (or higher) concentrations. The CMIP5 models used for the previous IPCC report modeled the sea surface and the tropical troposphere as being much hotter then they actually were. These models show too much warming for the entire lower- and mid-troposphere. The models are invalid as they are unable to describe the phenomena we measure.

What about the *predictions*? First of all, it makes no sense to trust a model that cannot describe the past about which we know. Secondly, the AR6 advertises highly

unlikely climate predictions as 'business as usual' consequences. However, these predictions (models SSP5-8.5 and
SSP3-7.0), which predict an increase in global temperature of 4
to 5 degrees by 2100, are highly unlikely. They assume a totally
unrealistic ECS (carbon dioxide effect on climate) and also a
massive increase in annual carbon dioxide emissions. Using a
moderate ECS around 1 or lower, the global temperature
will not rise by more than 2 degrees until 2100. The IPCC's
predictions are unscientific and unrealistic; they seem to be
intended to drive policy makers into radical decisions.

Tipping Points

In 2000, a well-known German climate alarmist, Hans
Joachim Schellnhuber, introduced the idea of climate tipping points. In biological ecosystems, a tipping point is
"reached when minor changes in the driver (for instance,
environmental change) lead to large changes in the state
of the system" (Scheffer 2001).

The concept was very popular at the time, but quickly
lost support when biologists recognized that change in biodiversity is gradual and slowly accumulating over time and
not exponentially evolving after a 'tipping point' or threshold is reached. Also, pressures on populations are delayed
through the inertia of natural systems and tend to wash out
unless a massive pressure persists over a long time period.
The same seems to be true for the climate system.

According to the alarmists, once climate tipping points are
reached, we get into 'runaway climate change'; catastrophes
occur from which we cannot recover, life becomes impossible in
some regions of the Earth. A crazy Fear Hype is presented to
us. What are the tipping points in our climate system supposed
to be? The IPCC AR6 has not learned from past mistakes in
Tipping Point Hype and still keeps an entire list of them, for
which we give the expected global temperature impact in
degrees Celsius in parentheses: A collapse of the Greenland
Ice Sheet (+0.13), a collapse of the West Antarctic Ice Sheet
(+0.05), a collapse of the Labrador-Irminger Seas/SPG Convection (a cold water circulation West of Greenland, -0.5), a collapse of the East Antarctic Subglacial Basins (+0.05), a crippling
'dieback' of the Amazon Rainforest (+0.2), a collapse of the
Atlantic Meridional Overturning Circulation (-0.5), a collapse

── Sidebar: Theoretical Reasons for Failure ── of the Models

Theoretically speaking, the models fail because they can never be really valid. The global climate is a complex system with all of the properties of complex systems listed in the AI chapter: It is evolutionary, as it can change radically and obtain new element types. This is because animate systems, which have evolutionary properties, interact with the climate system. This happened, for example, when aerobic organisms consuming oxygen emerged two billion years ago and started to produce carbon dioxide.

The system also has highly complex interactions which overlay each other, for example in the modulation of solar energy by cosmic radiation or the formation of clouds. Also, the interaction patterns differ depending on the type of the elements involved in the interaction.

The processes which occur in the climate system are non-ergodic. This means that although there may be (and indeed are) regular patterns and cycles in the system, there is no overall regularity. Each climate situation is unique, and even by collecting fine-grained data over a long time, we cannot identify a regular pattern which enables mathematical modeling and prediction. Statistically speaking, it's not possible to draw an adequate sample from a non-ergodic process. Therefore, statistical models of the system as a whole are impossible, even if we can model partial aspects of it.

The climate system is also driven: there is a constant flow of energy through the system caused by the energy of the sun. This means that the radiation and thermal energy dissipate into mechanical energy via turbulence and other dissipation processes. Such processes are outside the scope of mathematical modeling.

The system is also context-dependent, which means that symmetries and time-reversibility of physical laws do not apply. Last but not least, deterministic chaos is relevant for the climate system. This means that the measurement errors we have when we determine a system state lead to exponential model deviations as the system evolves with time, even though it is completely deterministic.

All these complex system properties make it theoretically impossible to obtain predictive climate models. While partial systems with period character can be modeled to a certain extent, a holistic modeling that allows us to make reliable predictions is impossible due to the properties of the system. A detailed analysis of this problem applied to another complex system, the human mind-body-continuum, can be found in Chapters 8 and 9 of Landgrebe and Smith's book, *Why Machines Will Never Rule the World.*

of the Arctic Winter Sea Ice (+0.6), or a collapse of the East
Antarctic Ice Sheet (+0.6).

All of these are supposed to occur suddenly, though some
only in more than a thousand years. But the most impactful
ones, we are told, will occur very soon, during the next 5 to
50 years (a range of sufficient length for the proponents of
these ideas never to be held accountable for them). Furthermore, we are told by the Climate Panic Hypers that coastal
cities will drown and droughts of Biblical dimensions will hit
once the points are reached.

Let's review the most important of these predicted horror events.

The Greenland Ice Sheet has been stable over the last
three million years, and was certainly continuously present
over the last million years. The last four interglacial warming periods (we have lived in an ice age for 34 million
years) over the last 350 thousand years were all much
warmer than the Holocene, but the ice stayed in place.
Some of the ice was melting, but it did not contribute
very much to sea level rise.

According to climate panic leader Al Gore, the Arctic
Winter Sea Ice was supposed to be gone by 2013. As of today,
the Arctic sea still carries ice in summer. If it would melt
completely, this would not impact the sea levels because the
ice is already swimming in the water. But it does not.
Instead, like biological ecosystems, it seems to have a lot of
inertia and resilience so that it is growing very quickly in
cold winters.

Antarctic collapse was seen as a danger by many alarmists,
but since the late 1990s the Antarctic has been cooling and
gaining more ice. There has been no warming trend in
Antarctica over the last 100 years. Nevertheless, the West
Antarctic and the Antarctic peninsula are losing some ice
which is not fully compensated by the ice gain in the East.
This loss of ice mass contributes roughly 20 percent to the
very moderate increase in sea levels we measure.

Forests, among which the Amazon rainforest and the
Boreal forest are the most strongly hyped candidates, are
supposed to wither away due to climate change. But this
is not happening. Where humans do not interact with
the forest by lumbering, fire-clearing, the erection of
water dams or mine dams, forests benefit from the

increase in carbon dioxide, which acts as a plant fertilizer (see below).

Overall, there is no empirical evidence at all for tipping points in the climate system. The concept should be discarded, it has no scientific, but merely political value.

Climate Change Induced Dangers

What about the other dangers which Fear Hype climate alarmists raise? The main ones are: rising sea levels, an increease in extreme weather events, and extinction of animal species induced by climate change.

Sea levels vary globally over time and space. Most of what we have observed since 1980 is related to the small warming that has occurred since the Little Ice Age ended. There is a trend of slightly increasing sea levels in some areas, but in Scandinavia, for example, sea levels are falling. We observe an overall slow trend in rising levels which is similar to cycles we have seen before. Mankind does not have a sea-level problem.

On weather-related disasters, it has to be pointed out that damages to infrastructure have to be normalized with regard to "inflation, population growth, economic growth, and affluence" (Clintel). If more land surface has buildings, roads, and other infrastructure, then an unchanged incidence of tornadoes will lead to greater damage. Careful analyses normalizing the weather-induced infrastructure damage show a decline of relative damage from 0.25 percent to 0.2 percent of GDP between 1990 and 2021. The losses are decreasing.

Over the last fifty years, there has been no increase in landslides, lightning frequencies, floods, or droughts. There is also a slight decline in the total area destroyed by wildfires—at least there has been no increase since the early 1990s. There are markedly fewer heat waves than in the recorded maximum, which occurred in the 1930s. Neither is there an increase in periods of extremely cold weather. In accordance with these findings, the number of climate-related deaths caused by floods, droughts, storms, wildfire and extreme temperatures have dropped from half a million per decade in 1920 to a few thousand per decade in the 2010s.

At the same time, non-climate related deaths which were caused by earthquakes, tsunamis, and volcanic eruptions have remained at the same level. Certainly, the main explanation of this is that industrial civilization allows a better protection from climate-related events, while protection from the second category of natural disasters is impossible. But altogether, there is simply no increase in catastrophes due to climate change.

Carbon Dioxide Is a Fertilizer

With the increase in atmospheric carbon dioxide, the Earth has become much greener over the last forty years, the increase in surface of green biomass on Earth since 1982 is twice as big as the area of the United States. This has led to a massive increase of photosynthesis on the surface of the Earth and also in the oceans, which now absorb 55 percent of the emitted carbon dioxide. This capacity is still increasing and would only saturate at an atmospheric carbon dioxide concentration almost four times higher than today's levels, at 1,500 ppm. Carbon dioxide is an effective fertilizer used in greenhouses. We know from experiments that adding another 300 ppm to the atmosphere—which is likely to occur over the next 100 years—will increase plant growth by at least 30 percent, for some species even more.

Under higher carbon dioxide concentrations, plants produce more fruit and these contain more vitamins and nutrients. The levels of phytoplankton in the seas also increases, leading to more fish of higher quality. The increase of carbon dioxide since 1850 has augmented global crop yields by 15 percent in addition to all other measures taken by humans. Carbon dioxide helps us to feed the global population. Furthermore, plants need less irrigation under higher carbon-dioxide concentrations.

The exponential growth of green biomass since 1982 occurred with a linear growth in water consumption of the plants. Carbon dioxide allows plants to grow on soils with less nitrates and phosphates because their utilization of these compounds becomes more effective. The gas also helps against oxidative stress, heat stress and UV-radiation induced stress and makes crops more competitive against weeds. We should eagerly look forward to carbon dioxide concentrations of 700 ppm which we may reach by 2100.

Zero Carbon Is Absurd

Zero carbon is an absurd ideology. The idea that we should reduce our carbon emissions to 'net zero' by off-setting unavoidable emissions is unnecessary, unfeasible, and damaging. Why?

First of all, we do not have a climate emergency or problem. As we have seen, the whole idea is not supported scientifically; it's a mere fantasy. Secondly, carbon dioxide is good for the planet, we should continue to emit enough to get to 700 ppm—which is likely to happen anyhow given the plans of the BRICS countries. But if we continued to burn all the carbohydrates we can obtain, we would run out of them sooner or later. It would then become necessary to make benzene rings we need for organic chemistry from carbon by hydration, which is cumbersome and costly. Therefore, we should start using less oil for combustion to have more of it for organic chemistry later.

Thirdly, given that CO_2 is good for the planet, we do not need an aggressive reduction of carbon dioxide emission, but in the mid-term it would be good to reduce the use of fossil fuels for combustion and to adapt the energy mix. The highest yielding energy source which we can use today is nuclear fission. As we will see at the end of this chapter, the global average per capita energy consumption is increasing and will continue to do so. We can only meet this demand by using nuclear power.

But instead of pursuing a rational policy for energy production and consumption, we are vainly trying to electrify our economies. By doing this, we're destroying our energy infrastructure while increasing the harm to the environment. The main reasons are:

1. **Poor effectiveness and poor efficiency of renewables**
2. **limited chemical storage capacity for electricity using batteries**
3. **massive energy need to mine the metals for the renewables and the batteries**

4. pollution related to mining, production of batteries and renewables.

The total primary energy needed in modern societies cannot, in most countries, be obtained solely from solar, wind, and water power. The total amount that can be obtained is insufficient to meet the total need for electricity—electricity is roughly one third of today's primary energy consumption, more in countries with a higher contribution of electricity to house heating such as France. But the total primary energy consumption is three times higher and comprises transportation, industrial production, and heating.

In Germany, for example, the available kinetic energy of the wind combined with solar power could meet less than twenty percent of the primary energy need because there just isn't more wind and solar radiation available. Furthermore, these energy sources are fluctuating and would require storage capabilities to be set up as reliable energy sources. Batteries are very expensive to make, do not provide big storage capacity and are dangerous in routine operations (see below). Therefore, electricity from renewables would have to be stored using power to gas technology to create hydrogen via hydrolysis or methane using the hydrogen. These processes are technically feasible, but lead to energy losses via dissipation and heat, making the electricity much more expensive (5 to 10 times more than today's prices). Even if the electricity were to be produced in countries with more wind and solar energy and then transformed and transported, the costs would be exorbitant. *There is not enough renewable energy in the world to cover our needs, and it is too ineffective and expensive.*

It's rarely considered how expensive it is to make solar panels, wind turbines, electrical switching gear and batteries. But it is also massively polluting. Today, we do not have enough mining capacity to obtain the metals we need to make the gear which would be required to realize the goals set by the EU in its Green Deal policy scheme. *To obtain them, we would need to mine so aggressively that the required energy would necessitate huge amounts of fossil fuel utilization offsetting the gains from using renewable energy sources.* It's unclear how mining, which would involve a massive increase of technically very demanding and not yet fully elaborated deep-sea mining, is to be scaled up to the required amounts.

Furthermore, mining regularly leads to environmental devastations when mining dams break. The toxic mud which is freed from such failures is so enriched with heavy metals that the surface covered by it will never recover. The boom in renewable energies has already led to the release of large quantities of sulphur hexafloride which is 25,000 times more potent as a greenhouse gas than carbon dioxide and stays in the atmosphere 150 times longer (1,000 years). An electrification of the entire energy consumption of modern nations will also fail because it is too costly to build the required distribution networks. We simply do not have the amounts of metal required to do it and cannot obtain them.

The production of batteries, a chemical method to store electricity and currently the main approach in most countries (those which can use natural water level differentials excluded), is not only highly toxic, they are also extremely hard to dispose of and to recycle. Furthermore, they can self-ignite and cause massive damage, for example when batteries of electric vehicles self-ignite in garages or on ships. Wind turbines are detrimental for birds and insects and the infra-sound they produce is damaging to humans living nearby. The zero carbon idea is not feasible and de-stroys our environment instead of saving it. Renewable energy would be better called neotoxic energy.

Overall, we will not be able to electrify our energy use and we should not try to achieve this. Even if we did, we would not save the planet, but worsen the environment because we would need to burn huge amounts of fossil fuels in the attempt to do so. We would merely drive billions back into poverty without any benefit for our natural environment. Carbon dioxide is not our problem.

Energy Control as a Means of Political Rule

If the climate emergency is a neo-religious myth and the de-carbonization agenda is bound to fail, why do we have them?

In industrial societies, energy has the role which the land had in the agricultural age before the industrial revolution. Energy is used for every product that we consume, even in the water we drink and the air we breathe: Water needs energy to be purified and transported to our homes, and exhausts need to be cleansed of nitrogen, sulfur oxides, and other pollutants, an energy-consuming process built into modern fossil fuel burning power plants and combustion engines in cars.

The per-capita use of energy will continue to rise thanks to digitization, automation, and ageing of our population. A reduction of energy use can only be achieved via diminishing the quality of life. If energy usage drops drastically, there will be famines, people will freeze to death and there will be public unrest and serious political instability. As Arnold Gehlen pointed out in "The Soul in the Age of Technology," modern populations will not accept deindustrialization, with a return to the chronic mass hunger and destitution of the pre-industrial age.

The Earth can easily support 8–10 billion human beings and allow them to live in an equilibrium with nature if we produce enough energy to recycle the by-products of our metabolism and the products at the end of their life cycle. This is possible, but we need cheap energy to do it. Of course, this costs energy-bearing materials, but we have an unlimited supply of them on Earth if we consider nuclear fission and fusion which will be realized long before all other sources of energy will be exhausted (see next section). Today, we're witnessing a major pollution of the environment and a reduction of biological diversity, which is very worrying. With more energy use, we could reduce both to physiological, pre-industrial levels.

In feudal societies, power was based on control over the land, which provided the main foundation of wealth (mines played a certain role as well from the late Middle Ages onwards). When it was impossible to conquer the land of an enemy, military campaigns often targeted the agricultural infrastructure by burning down barns and farms or by poisoning wells to make it impossible to use the land for a certain period. Today, political power depends on control over the production and distribution of energy because it is the foundation of wealth in industrial societies. Per capita energy use is directly proportional to the standard of living.

Since the early 1970s when the Club of Rome published *The Limits to Growth*, a growing movement to reduce energy consumption has developed. This neo-Malthusian ideology has been put into effective policy since the early 2000s, when governments in Germany, Switzerland, and other very rich countries started a program to replace fossil fuel derived energy sources by so-called 'renewables', which are, as we saw, neotoxic forms of energy production.

Although these forms of energy are unreliable and insufficient to cover the permanent energy needs of modern societies, fanatical political ideologues continue to call for 'de-carbonization' or 'zero carbon' policies in order to 'save the planet'. As we have seen, even if this de-carbonization were to take place, it would not change the climate at all. We are now facing a situation in which the lack of cheap energy has started to de-industrialize Europe, and the US and Canada are also under threat due to the spiraling of energy prices.

For the oligarchic elites of the West, which possess 70 to 90 percent of the means of industrial and agricultural production, the climate and renewable energy policies result in an increase of their power based on the emerging scarcity of energy resulting from it. With lower amounts of energy available, the power of those who control its production and distribution increases. This does not imply that the policy is consciously malign—it is rather a natural policy in a situation of extreme wealth concentration.

The political power direction of the energy policies can be recognized from the following observations:

- There is a massively financed climate emergency campaign to keep the scientifically invalid climate narrative alive. It involves research funding for the nonsensical climate models, funds for NGOs and activism and massive climate emergency publishing and propaganda. Among the activists, there are neo-religious sects supported by public and private funding. Propaganda is one of the four fundamental modes of power described by the sociologist Heinrich Popitz: authoritative power.

- Scientists and journalists opposing the climate myth are suppressed and removed from social media, which are controlled by the handful of oligarchs owning them. This is another mode of power: instrumental power.

- Private corporations, such as the investment funds Blackrock or Vanguard, have formed a global alliance with sovereign wealth funds, the United Nations, the World Economic Forum, the EU, and many other organizations to promote the so-called 'sustainable development' policy which is a social credit system for private companies to enforce the carbon reduction policy via the control of bond emissions and other forms of corporate financing. This network is a private-public-partnership controlled by the Western oligarchs. This is again a form of instrumental power.

- Many countries are implementing carbon reduction policies although they directly reduce industrial output and hurt societies. These policies are justified with propaganda that tries to instil fear in the population. The policy changes the infrastructure of society. It is a mixture of three modes of power: instrumental, authoritative, and data-setting power.

The ideological foundations of this policy are (i) the Malthusian belief in overpopulation shared by many members of the elite and (ii) the aim of maximizing power via introducing energy scarcity. We see that these policies are pursued in the open, the actors and their motives are publicly visible. Therefore, this is not a conspiracy, but the evolution of a global power enhancement process. However, non-Western global players do not follow this policy. In the medium term, countries with a rational energy policy will prevail over those which choose the insane zero-carbon agenda.

Real Environmentalism

Real environmentalism is achieved by protecting the environment from pollution damage to maintain species diversity and nature. But mankind will need more energy. How can these goals be reconciled?

We need more energy for growth to defeat poverty, and for automation and digitization to continue shaping our high-density civilization. This also includes relieving the burden on our ageing population. New technology costs energy. For example, in 2022, Bitcoin alone required approximatively 100 terawatt hours of electricity per year worldwide for its algorithms, which is roughly as much as a fifth of Germany's electricty consumption in that year.

Between 1990 and 2008, world energy demand increased by 39 per cent, and the growth continues to accelerate. In the words of Arnold Gehlen, the mechanization of all our lives will continue to broaden and deepen, and as a result we will need more and more energy. We are talking about a short-term increase in per capita consumption compared to today (in one generation) by a factor of 2.

How do we cope? Europe is a world leader in neotoxic (so-called renewable) energies at a very high cost, and yet these provide significantly less than ten percent of our current total energy needs, which are yet still modest compared to the future. We still get most of it from the use of covalent bond energy in the oxidation (burning with oxygen consumption) of fossil fuels. In principle, this is a primitive form of energy generation through ignition. With natural gas and coal, this may still be acceptable, but with oil, combustion is a real sin because it destroys valuable aromatics such as benzene instead of using their potential for the synthesis of polymers.

Our descendants will curse us for this, because they will then have to extract the oil under adverse conditions or synthesize the aromatics using energy from coal and hydrogen like the Nazis did in the hydrogenation plants of Leuna. In addition to the combustion of fossil fuels, we also get energy from the use of nuclear bond energy through nuclear fission.

But if we need two to ten times more energy per capita, where is it supposed to come from? Certainly not from neotoxic (so-called renewable) energies. Their energy yield is already far too low for today's demand, and it will be even more insufficient if demand continues to rise. Then we need energy sources with a high energy content. Let's take the hard coal unit (HCU) as a reference, which is the energy released when burning one kilogram of hard coal, by definition 7,000 kcal. Burning one kilogram of wood produces half a HCU, 1 kg of crude oil 1.4 HCU.

By contrast, nuclear fission of one kilogram of 235U (uranium) yields 2.7 millions of HCU, and enriched natural uranium, which is used in nuclear reactors and contains only about 5 per cent 235U, about 15,000 HCU, depending on the degree of enrichment. Enriched uranium thus has an energy content 15,000 times higher than coal and 10,000 times higher than crude oil. This is because the binding energy in the nucleus is much higher than the covalent bond between atoms of a molecule that is released during combustion.

The sun and all stars in the universe generate energy through nuclear fusion. The fusion of two hydrogen nuclei releases thousands of times more energy than the fission of enriched natural uranium. This is because the fusion product, helium, has a lower mass than the two initial atoms, and the difference is released as energy according to Einstein's formula for the ratio of mass and energy. The technology is not yet available, but a fusion reactor would use deuterium and tritium, which are hydrogen atoms each with one proton and one or two neutrons. The fusion of one kilogram of deuterium-tritium mixture in a nuclear fusion reactor would provide a thermal energy of 12.3 million HCU, or twelve million times a kilogram of hard coal.

Energy production through nuclear fission or fusion has the advantage over the burning of fossil fuels that no carbon dioxide is released during energy production and that the supplies are de facto inexhaustible. What problems do we have to overcome before we can use these highly promising forms of energy to meet the growing demand for energy in the foreseeable future?

The main problems of energy production by nuclear fission are operational safety, waste storage, and raw material deposits.

As a result of the serious accidents at high-pressure/boiling-water reactors built in the 1960s and 1970s (Harrisburg, Chernobyl, and Fukushima) with core meltdown or high release of radioactive material, the impression has arisen among Western populations that the residual risk in operating nuclear power plants is too high. This is certainly true for this now completely outdated generation of reactors—the technology has too many pre-determined breaking points. One can say that an immature technology has been put into operation. In the meantime, however, reactor types have been developed that promise to be sufficiently safe or have already proven to be safe enough: the gas-cooled fast reactor, the high temperature gas reactor, the supercritical water reactor, the sodium-cooled fast reactor, the lead-cooled fast reactor and the molten salt reactor. Some of these, such as the sodium-cooled reactors, have been in operation for a long time, and all or a subset of these types will become commercially viable. These reactors are not only much safer in operation than the old high-pressure water reactors, some of them can also use nuclear waste as fuel. This brings us to the waste problem.

When enriched uranium is used in a high-pressure water reactor, numerous low-level, very long-lived nuclides remain as waste after the reactive nuclides have been consumed. This waste remains radioactive for tens of thousands of years and is difficult to store safely. The minor actinides neptunium, americium, and curium are particularly long-lived. However, these and others can be transformed into short-lived nuclides by transmutation. This can take place in modern breeder reactors, which are capable of producing more fissile material than the amount of material that enters the breeder reaction. Step by step, this will enable us to use the spent fuel rods from the high-pressure water reactors as fuel. This creates a complete cycle of utilization of natural uranium, in which considerably more energy (50–100 times) is extracted from it than in the utilization pattern of light-water reactors. At the end of the cycle, the result is a waste that cannot be further utilized, whose nuclides are strong gamma radiators with a short half-life of 50 to 60 years—after only 300 years, this waste no longer emits radiation. The problem of final storage is thus solved.

It is often not considered that other industrial production processes also produce highly toxic waste such as heavy metal waste, but it never decays and must be stored safely until the end of time. The amount of this waste is much higher than the nuclear waste from classical high-pressure water reactors.

Critics of nuclear power often argue that there are not enough uranium reserves. In fact, there are at least 10 to the 13th power tonnes of uranium deposits on Earth whose mining costs increase over time, but this is not a problem in a market economy—as can be seen from oil production and the oil price: There only has to be demand, then the production facilities will be built. In addition, we still have two to three times the amount of thorium on Earth, which will soon be used commercially in molten salt reactors. These reserves would last a practically infinite time even with 10 times the per capita consumption we have today and 10 billion people living on earth.

Nuclear fusion is much more attractive than nuclear fission because the energy yield is about 1,000 times higher than natural uranium and 10–20 times higher than the full breeder cycle of natural uranium. In addition, the deuterium deposit in water is practically unlimited. Tritium can be produced from lithium, but this lowers the energy yield of the fusion reaction somewhat. Nuclear fusion works by heating deuterium and tritium so strongly that a plasma forms in which the atomic nuclei are separated from the electrons and move quickly due to the thermal energy. If two nuclei then meet, the exothermic fusion reaction occurs, which can be self-sustaining (as in the sun) if enough new fuel is added and the waste (the helium) is removed. Today, a plasma temperature of 150 million degrees Celsius is the target. Since no vessel can withstand this temperature, the plasma must be held together by means of a magnetic field (fusion with plasma confinement).

So far, only short fusion reactions could be generated in experimental facilities. Many technical problems still have to be solved, and it will take several decades or centuries to get fusion reactors whose energy output is permanently greater than the plasma ignition energy. But since it is physically possible and feasible, we will get these reactors.

Soon, therefore, mankind's energy supply problem will be solved: on the one hand, with the complete fuel utilization in nuclear fission in safe reactors and the solution of the waste problem through transmutation, the commercial breakthrough of which is already foreseeable, and on the other hand, with nuclear fusion, whose technical and commercial breakthrough is only a question of time. Humanity will thus have at its disposal two technologies that can generate practically infinite amounts of energy from resources available on Earth. This will enable us to protect ourselves effectively from climate change—even if the ice age we are currently living in ends or is exacerbated by a new glaciation.

The problem of living in the technosphere in harmony with other living beings, on whose well-being our existence depends, will then be reduced to dealing with civilization's waste. The Earth offers enough space for coexistence with the other species and an almost infinite amount of resources for our needs. Therefore, *the 'limits to growth'*, which have been hailed time and again since the Club of Rome report of 1972, *are real only in the limits of waste we can afford*. We need to achieve the required minimization of waste and its safe storage. We need economic incentives to achieve these goals. For example, if we consider a certain kind of waste that should be avoided, we need a tax with otherwise free energy markets—renouncing an 'energy transition' that wants to force neotoxic energy production with miserable efficiency and a 'nuclear phase-out' that leaves this highly efficient form of energy production to countries that are less capable with complicated technology. Then, despite the foreseeable increase in per capita energy demand, we would soon have managed the conversion to a low-carbon dioxide economy—through nuclear power and later also through nuclear fusion.

The same applies to other forms of waste: we need incentives to avoid them or to re-use them, then we can also afford further growth in production.

3

Transhumanism Hype

Hope is such a bait, it covers any hook.
—OLIVER GOLDSMITH

Transhumanism is the atheist billionaires' religion. It's one of the strongest Hype trends among Western elites, naturally trickling down from the rich elites to the masses. Its aim is to transcend the natural limitations of human biology using genetic engineering and neural man-machine interfaces. With these tools, we can acquire the gift of eternal life, especially if we start out with high personal net worth.

We see transhumanism all over the media and even in the plans and actions of government. It's rarely questioned despite its absurdity and the dangers its pursuit would entail. Transhumanism is an insane ideology which is bound to fail because its goals are unscientific and infeasible. Proponents of transhumanism, including Yuval Harari and Klaus Schwab (rumored to be the real-life original for "Dr. Evil"), but sadly also the recent US administration, have endorsed ideas such as these:

- that we can improve the human body to create cyborgs, fictive organisms in which human organs and technological gadgets are seamlessly combined;

- that properties such as human intelligence can be genetically enhanced by germ-line genome manipulation;

45

- that mRNA technology will soon allow us to "write circuitry for cells and predictably program biology in the same way in which we write software and program computers" (as worded in President Biden's Executive Order on "Advancing Biotechnology and Biomanufacturing," September 12th 2022);

- that we will soon cure cancer using genetic or even nano-mechanic (tiny machine) therapies;

- that we can achieve longevity using pharmacology including somatic gene therapy;

- that we will soon be able to engineer life from scratch;

- that machines will shortly be able to read thoughts;

- that soon we will obtain digital immortality by 'uploading our minds to the cloud';

- that artificial intelligence (AI) will soon lead to machines more intelligent than humans;

- that AI will make most humans useless to society because all their work will be taken over by machines;

- that we'll be able to genetically reprogram the sex of adult humans in the near future,

—to name just a few of the preposterous notions espoused by adherents of this ridiculous cult.

Why do I say that all of this is unscientific nonsense? And why do so many—including clever people like the shrewd billionaire Elon Musk or the highly intelligent Russian president Vladimir Putin—say they believe in it? What are the roots and goals of this movement? Let's answer these questions by starting with the goals of transhumanists.

What Are Transhumanists' Goals?

There are two groups of transhumanists.

The first group sees transhumanism as the ultimate method of self-actualization (self-realization), supposedly allowing the super-rich to afford this costly road to self-improvement, transcending the biological limits of their bodies. For example, the transhumanist Martine Rothblatt (whose cells have the XY karyotype but who 'became' a trans woman using hormones and surgery) says that self-defining your gender is just the first step on a path that will lead to a cure for cancer and other lethal diseases, to Methuselah-like longevity and ultimately to digital immortality.

Related to this goal, but of lesser importance, is the idea that transhumanism could promote universal equality of outcomes in the tradition of the French Enlightenment ideal of equality enforced by law (as opposed to the Protestant Enlightenment ideal of equality under the law, or isonomy). In this flavor, transhumanism seemingly has an emancipatory character akin to abolitionism (the fight against slavery in the nineteenth century) or utopian feminist emancipation, the theory that the two sexes should become equal in every respect. Proponents of this variant of the creed believe that all human beings could be altered using transhumanistic technology to achieve equality of outcomes.

We will see that none of these hopes can ever be even remotely fulfilled.

The second sect of transhumanists hopes to use transhumanism as a technical means of power in the spirit of *Brave New World*, which describes the engineering of human classes with planned properties in artificial wombs. Implanted sensors or molecular effectors (for example, delivering pulsated drug dosages into the circulation) are believed by transhumanists, along with genetic engineering, to afford physical control and manipulation of the masses, to direct their will and to leave most human beings superfluous.

Yuval Harari believes that Artificial Intelligence will make most humans obsolete; according to him, only a small élite of superhumans will be needed in the future. He also thinks that technology can be used to direct and manage the will of the masses by means of brain-chip-interfaces.

While technology can be used to manipulate the masses culturally, it cannot be used to control them physically (other than by promoting chronic mass intoxication and addiction, which is not a new phenomenon), nor to render them obsolete as a workforce. Also related to this intention is the idea of using the transhumanist narrative to exert cultural power via fear of the future, as has been done with Climate Change Fear Hype and Covid Fear Hype. This is by far the biggest effect that the transhumanist narrative has had so far, but it will lose its hold once its preposterousness and anti-scientific character become obvious and once its cultural precondition, the current collective Western spasm of Fear Hype, has dissipated.

Why Transhumanism Hype Is Wrong

Transhumanism is seriously mistaken because it aims to apply scientific methods to systems that cannot be modeled using mathematical physics, chemistry, or biology in the way transhumanists imagine. Let's look at the main plans cherished by transhumanists.

GENETIC MANIPULATION OF HUMANS

Eugenics is a nineteenth-century ideology which evolved as it became clear that most human properties are inherited. At first, the idea was to improve the human population using social pressure and euthanasia, artificially selecting the reduction of genetic disorders and thus breeding humans with superior qualities. The idea was very powerful in the first half of the twentieth century. Among well-known proponents were H.G. Wells, Bertrand Russell, and George Bernard Shaw, and other early members of the Fabian Society.

This ideology lost its popularity among intellectuals after it became clear how terribly these ideas had borne fruit in Nazi Germany and the Soviet Union. However, as we can see from Biden's executive directive quoted above, the idea is now very popular again among Western elites who believe that this time we'll get it right. Sure.

The goals of modern transhumanist eugenicists are: genetic programming of higher intelligence and other desirable traits, curing inherited monogenetic, polygenetic and acquired complex diseases such as cancer or schizophrenia, 'curing' or preventing aging to achieve longevity, and even genetic sex reprogramming or the de novo engineering of life. All of this is unscientific nonsense.

To begin with, we have no safe method of altering the human germline. In animals used as research models, we do this by genetically altering embryos to get the genetic change into the procreative cells of the reproduction system (sperms and eggs) to make the change inheritable. But there's no way to do this which would guarantee that no undesired effects occur. The CRISPR/Cas system, a bacterial system to fend off bacteriophages, viruses infecting bacteria, was established in the 2010s to be used in mammalian cells. It is now utilized to perform advanced genetic engineering in mice, but it cannot deliver safe genetic alteration of germline cells; it causes chromosomal damage in multiple ways at high frequency (Alanis-Lobato 2021).

More importantly, even if we develop safe and effective tools for genetic engineering, we cannot genetically reprogram our mind-body continuum because we are unable to model how the phenotypical (visible and inner) properties which we would like to alter are caused by our genetic material. This comprises our genome and the non-genetic cellular material we inherit from the blastocyst and which govern our embryonic and fetal development. We can causally understand diseases in which the function of one gene is hampered or missing, called a Mendelian inheritance pattern. Today, thanks to intense and brilliant research over the past fifty years, for many Mendelian diseases, we can say which gene is affected. This is called genetic disease etiology.

But in many cases we still don't know the pathogenesis, which is the mechanism by which the lack of function of a gene product leads to the damage we observe in the patients. Our knowledge of cell biology is limited; the cell is a very complex system which we only partially understand. And we understand even less how cells interact within the functional organ tissue (the parenchymal cells). Though there are models of organ tissues, these can give us only a partial understanding of the situation in a living body. At the level of interaction of the various local and systemic organs in our body, we understand very little.

Looking at complex polygenetic diseases such as schizophrenia or diseases with hereditary and environmental co-causation such as essential arterial hypertension (elevated blood pressure), many forms of dementia, and cancer, we have no real understanding of the genetic causation beyond so-called genetic risk factors. But we cannot create models of the causality of such diseases, let alone their pathogenesis. And it is unlikely that we will ever obtain such knowledge, because humans are incapable of creating comprehensive models of complex dynamical systems. I explain this more fully in Chapter 1.

We now know that even body height has an omnigenic inheritance pattern, which means that we need to take into account a huge proportion of the genetic material and its variance we see in human populations to statically explain something as simple as differences in individual height (Boyle 2017). Intelligence and other desirable properties of the human mind certainly also have omnigenic inheritance patterns; we have no idea how they come about. Even if we had safe technologies to manipulate embryos we would not know which genetic sequence to change to enhance intelligence because we do not have causal models of how intelligence is genetically encoded.

To illustrate this a bit more, let's look at cancer, dementia, longevity, and sex reprogramming.

Cancer and dementia are both complex disease groups with a multitude of individual diseases in each of them. For some cancers, we know the etiology, for example we know that asbestos can cause pleural mesothelioma, a fatal and incurable cancer of the lining of the lungs. We also know that generalized atherosclerosis, the clogging of arterial blood vessels, can cause vascular dementia. For both diseases, however, we do not know the pathogenesis—exactly how the pathological changes come about in the course of the disease. Both diseases are fatal and incurable; once vascular dementia becomes clinically visible, the treatment cannot even delay the progression very much.

For most cancers and dementias, we don't know either cause or pathogenesis very well. Certainly not well enough to design causally effective treatments. These diseases, such as Parkinson's Dementia or colon cancer, are not one single disease each (what physicians call a nosological entity), but merely bundles of pathological features which occur when the disease process becomes clinically visible. This visible bundle is almost certainly caused by many disease processes which differ in the affected individuals at the molecular level and merely have a common final symptomatic path. We call what becomes visible as this path evolves the *disease entity*, but in reality we have multiple diseases leading to the bundle of pathological properties we call a disease entity.

So we do not treat the causes at all; what we treat are the symptoms which occur once the various different disease processes are so advanced that they create a common picture. The same is true for schizophrenia and many other diseases, including auto-immune diseases.

On the other hand, in medicine, there are many examples of technologies that successfully alter properties of the body, such as surgery, implants, or many highly effective pharmacological treatments, such as antibiotics or narcotics which are indispensable for surgery. But they can only address partial systems and are unable to model and manipulate the complex system of the mind-body continuum as a whole.

Longevity has been a dream of mankind forever. Now transhumanists tell us we can achieve it using nanotechnology, gene therapy, and new types of drugs. In Klaus Schwab's book *The Fourth Industrial Revolution*, we read that soon we will have nanomachines "that can drill through the body and kill cancer cells in seconds." Transhumanists also believe that such machines could manipulate somatic genomes within cells, an absurd idea showing that they have no idea of how the genome is tightly packaged inside the cell nucleus.

Aside from the fact that we don't yet know how to build such tiny engines, which we might possibly learn to do one day, it's not clear how these machines would move inside the body. In the vascular system, there is tremendous turbulence which would knock such a tiny device around hopelessly, so that it would be impossible to navigate. And in the intercellular space, the space between the cells in organs, the environment is so viscous that, according to the well-corroborated Scallop Theorem, no swimming object can achieve a net displacement, no matter what type of propulsion it uses.

Klaus Schwab and the other confabulating nanomachine fans have never thought this through. Furthermore, biological processes are chemical in nature, mechanical functions like the action of the muscles result from chemical interactions happening at the molecular level. The idea of interfering with chemical events mechanically is not really practicable.

What are the important cellular property bundles (syndromes) of aging? *Vascular decline* is a process due to which the lining of the blood vessels become rougher, sclerotic, and eventually clotted which leads to impaired or disrupted transport of oxygen and other compounds transported by the blood to the functional tissue resulting in tissue decline and cell death.

Aging also means a *spontaneous loss* of functional cells due to the essential limitation of the cells' life expectancy, which is genetically encoded, for example via telomeres. The process is called apoptosis. This leads to a decline of the body's functionality and senility with a natural decline in physical and mental performance.

The reduction of the functionality of the *immune system* leads to multiple secondary effects, most notably cancer, which is always a failure of the immune system to detect and eliminate newly emerging tumor cells which form every day. But the reduction of immune system functionality that comes with age also enables natural death by harmless infections like SARS-CoV-2 or the rhinovirus with which the healthy younger body can deal easily. Biologically, these aging processes are necessary to remove individuals from the population who have served their purpose to reproduce and oversee the raising of the next generation. They die and are transformed into biomass nutrients for cavengers specialized in using dead bodies as energy source.

Sexual reproduction, aging, and death of previous generations all tend to optimize population variance and the chances of species survival. In nature, survival and reproduction cannot afford to feed old individuals at the expense of the group. Humans do this to some extent, but nature limits this activity quite tightly.

Neither vascular decline, nor the spontaneous loss of cells due to apoptosis, nor a decline of the immune system can be altered in any way. Neither do we know which parts of the genome we would have to change, because we do not understand the processes well enough to do this, nor can we intervene with drugs for the same reason: We don't really know what's going on, we don't know which aspects of the cell physiology to alter. And given the complexity of the system, it's likely that we will never know.

Sex reprogramming is another idea of transhumanists. They believe that in the future, it will not only be possible to perform surgery and hormone therapies to alter the outer appearance to match the self-assigned gender, but also to truly change the biology of all somatic cells so that they really change to the opposite sex. This would mean that we could alter the many hundreds of billions of sex chromosomes (X or Y) of the cells of our body and regrow organs many years after the end of embryonic development during which the morphology and function of the sexual organs is physiologically developed. We do not know much about the cellular and molecular details of these processes, especially the highly complex cell interactions within the developing tissues since we lack the model systems to obtain such insight. We do know that somatic gene therapy even at the level of a single gene is tremendously hard and only possible under very special conditions. It's forever impossible to change entire sex chromosomes and to create new organs within a body after birth. The idea is truly insane.

The ultimate dream of transhumanists is to become like God by engineering life from inanimate matter, which in their Hyped pronouncements they call 'artificial life'. Some of them dream that using such technologies we'll be able to make better life forms than those which exist today. Even the creation from inanimate matter of the most primitive animate organisms has not been achieved to date. We have only been able to take living bacteria and replace their natural genomes with fully synthetic genomes. This is a fascinating achievement, but has nothing to do with artificial life.

In organisms, life is the ability to make energy-conveying molecules (ATP and a few others) from inanimate matter, sunlight, and carbon dioxide, or dead bio-matter and oxygen (animals). The theory of the origins of the molecules of life from inanimate matter is patchy and, according to leading chemists, amounts to nothing more than pseudo-science. We have no idea what the first molecules of life were, how they got assembled, and how life emerged from them (Tour 2020). We certainly don't have the slightest idea how to make life from non-living matter. This is never likely to change, given the vast complexity of even single-cell organisms.

Cyborgism, Thought Reading, Digital Immortality

Other fantasies of transhumanism are as naive and absurd as its eugenic expectations. The central nervous system is connected to the rest of the body via afferent systems bringing in sensory signals from the surrounding world and proprioception of our own body (such as pain). Our body can move via efferent systems, mainly nerves and muscles, which allow us to act in the world.

Why can't we improve these systems? Let's begin with the sensory part. We cannot build interfaces to our sensory apparatus, because the models of the neuronal systems we have are far too superficial and partial in nature. One problem is that we don't even understand in detail how the different types of energy reaching our various sensory cells are translated into neuronal signals. While this shortcoming in our knowledge could possibly be remedied, we won't be able to achieve more than harnessing the afferent neurons that are already present in the nervous system. In other words, we can't add new sensory modalities.

For example, we cannot add a modality to perceive radioactivity. Instead, we must use sound or visual effects to convey to our brains that we are measuring a given level of radioactive decay. Today, this is usually done with a Geiger counter that gives clicks proportional to the decay level, or shows it on analogue or digital scales. One could, as in a sci-fi movie, also visualize radioactivity levels via augmented reality spectacles tinting the environment in shades of red in proportion to the radiation. Why can't we do any better? Because the sensory unit from the peripheral sensory cells to the end points in our central neuronal processing form a hard-wired, closed biological system that we cannot change. Therefore we can't add neuronal subsystems to our nervous system, with the specialist task of processing radioactivity, to add a 'Geiger sense' to our heads. The brain is a highly evolved and tightly regulated complex system to which we can't add anything without harming it.

A flick through a modern textbook of neuroscience is highly instructive in this context: it contains almost no mathematical models, and thus the severe limitation of what can be engineered is certain. We can only engineer if we have mathematical models that allow us to calculate the characteristics of a technology. True, engineering is also a heuristic science; but its process of discovery is always based on scientific models.

Now to motor-enhancement. Though we can build prostheses that can be connected in a rough-and-ready manner to motor nerves (and also to the cortex with sensors implanted under the skull), we won't be able to model the sensorimotor circuits that drive our conscious and unconscious motions at a level sufficient to build a 'cyborg'. Nor is such a project necessary, as we already have interfaces with which we can direct high-precision instruments such as quantum sensors or huge machines like the Large Hadron Collider and the International Space Station.

That's not to say that further technical progress will not happen, but our ability to change humans is restricted by the complexity of the mind-body continuum, the most complicated individual complex system there is. The same applies to human thought and mind. Transhumanist slogans to the effect that we will soon be able to 'read thoughts using quantum sensors and AI' are ludicrous. They merely show that figures producing this empty talk do not have the slightest idea about that whereof they speak. They are merely asserting what is technically known as 'BS', or bad science.

This is because even when we become able to measure some of the signals occurring during the physiological process that we experience as propositional cognition (thinking in sentences) with higher temporal and spatial resolution than today—which we certainly will shortly be able to do—we still won't be able to understand how the hundred billion neurons of the brain (and the additional glial cells that support them, ten-to-fifty-fold more numerous) encode propositional thoughts. That is a process in which the cells involved use hundreds of thousands of different molecules each. The same is true for nuanced emotions, acoustic, olfactory, or visual memories, and all the other rich modes of inner experience with which we are endowed.

Furthermore, transhumanist dreams of *digital immortality* are just fanciful nonsense. Suggestions by transhumanists that we could upload our identity to a computer are ill-informed and ill-conceived. The mind-body continuum is a unity. We cannot separate our identity from this unity, if the body ceases to live, there is no mind anymore (whether a soul remains is a matter of religion). After a century of furious philosophizing and research on the subject, we still don't understand the processes that we experience as consciousness and inner experience. Certainly, they are bound to the functioning of the continuum of body and mind, as is our memory and our identity. It is impossible to model the processes which constitute the mind to an extent that would allow us to emulate these processes in a Turing machine. It would even be impossible if we could model them much better than today, because logic systems (computers) can never fully replicate complex systems—they can only partially mimic their behavior at a very general level.

Transhumanists like Harari who extrapolate from the technology that is available today to predict achievements of transhumanist technology do not appreciate how the insights of physics were translated into technology over the last three centuries. Transhumanists fail to grasp the limits of physics and engineering. They have no idea of biology and the limitations of science. In other words, their predictions reveal that they do not understand science at all. That is why these visions should not scare us: they are all mere fantasies. Transhumanism is nothing but neo-Lysenkoism, ideological pseudoscience. However, there is a dangerous aspect of transhumanism, just as there was a massive danger in the eugenic ideology of the Nazis and Stalin.

The Hazards and Failure of Transhumanism

As long as transhumanism was just an ideology detached from reality, it did not warrant too much attention. The first fundamental application that the transhumanist ideology could relate to was the surgical and hormonal change of the outer appearance of patients with transsexual personality disorder who have a normal sex chromosome karyotype (XX or XY chromosome pairs; I leave out the very rare cases of sex chromosomal abnormality for the sake of simplicity). Of course, these successful interventions do not change the fundamental biology of the treated person; but with the introduction of these methods erroneously called 'sex reassignment surgery' (erroneously, because the intervention does not change the sex, only the appearance) since the 1960s, early transhumanists were flushed with the hope that more might be possible.

As I explain in Chapter 14, today's widespread employment of gonadotropin-releasing hormone modulators ('puberty blockers') to stop the onset of adolescence, and the performance of surgery on underage children with a normal sex chromosomal karyotype (without a long period of clinical observation to establish the diagnosis of a transsexual personality disorder, which might possibly represent a valid indication for such treatments), demonstrates the dangers and the nihilism of the transhumanist ideology. The damage inflicted on children is grievous in the extreme, and once the cultural hysteria that brings about such surgical activism is over, Western societies will reel under the weight of coming to terms legally and culturally with this collective crime against humanity. Of course, some of the parents who subjected their underage children to such horrendous treatments will not want to accept that their deeds were evil, and will fight for a positive perception of what they did, but they won't have a leg to stand on.

Another example of the danger of transhumanism is the so-called Covid 'vaccination' program, which led to a catastrophic outcome, still worsening at the time of writing. The willingness to perform this medical atrocity, the worst in human history, was clearly impelled by transhumanism, with its stated intent to genetically modify those who were 'vaccinated' to prevent them from catching a virus harmful only to patients at the end of their natural life. Politicians and health executives who support these programs subscribe to a transhumanist agenda. This is evident from recent government publications across the Western world.

The executive order on biotechnology issued by the Biden Administration on 12th September 2022 states:

> We need to develop genetic engineering technologies and techniques to be able to write circuitry for cells and pre-dictably program biology in the same way in which we write software and program computers; unlock the power of bio-logical data, including through computing tools and artificial intelligence; and advance the science of scale-up production while reducing the obstacles for commercialization so that innovative technologies and products can reach markets faster.

To view biological systems as deterministic electric circuits that can be programmed like a computer is highly charac-teristic of transhumanism. This quotation exemplifies all the characteristic traits of the transhumanist ideology. Trying out such anti-rational methods on human beings is dangerous and criminal.

Pursuing the transhumanist program, in January 2023, US lawmakers have changed the legal basis for the approval of drugs for human testing. Congress passed a law enabling pharmaceutical companies to obtain permis-sion from the FDA to start drug testing on humans, with-out prior animal testing. The idea is that all tests which were previously done on animals can now be done using 2D and 3D cell-culture models to obtain enough evidence that a drug is effective and safe. This is an illusion, as such systems are very remote from entire organisms and cannot replace them as biological models to predict the effects of drugs on the human body.

In theory, pharmaceutical companies could now legally proceed against regulators who insist on animal testing and skip animal toxicology and pharmacokinetics testing in ani-mals, if courts would enforce the new law. This is highly unlikely, but if this were put into practice, we would imme-diately see a massive increase in deaths and maiming in clinical trials. Animal testing is a vital precautionary step in drug development, and the fact that the US govern-ment removes this requirement shows how delusional the transhumanists are and what an enormous influence they have gained on US politics.

Transhumanism will fail when the functional élite, the roughly ten to fifteen percent carrying out the management of society (the "outer party") on behalf of the tiny class of rulers (the "inner party" in *Nineteen Eighty-Four*), start to understand to what extent they themselves have been physically damaged by ineffective 'therapies' that do nothing but harm. Transhumanism is bound to fail because its goals can't be achieved—they are technically infeasible, and will not pass the reality test. The Covid vaccination campaign clearly illustrates this, but it could turn out that far more harm will be done before the failure becomes apparent to a major proportion of the population.

The Cultural Roots of Transhumanism

Transhumanism has several major cultural sources. Here are the most important ones:

- **self-actualization, an idea originally developed in the Italian Renaissance which was further elaborated and popularized by Johann Gottfried Herder but which has since degenerated into an atrophied form of hedonistic consumerism;**

- **emancipation in the sense of the French Enlightenment;**

- **Cartesianism and neo-positivism;**

- **postmodern anti-rationalism;**

- **and eugenics.**

Self-Actualization

The idea of self-actualization was originally developed by Pico de la Mirandola, Petrarch, and other thinkers of the Italian Renaissance. It was a program for cultural élites to realize the full potential of their personality and arose with the discovery of the modern individual. The individual was thought to be primarily related to himself and was tasked with maximizing his own culture, knowledge, and pleasure.

In the eighteenth century, the German Protestant theologian Herder reformulated the concept as a philosophy for the masses, but in accordance with Christianity. Self-actualization was meant to happen in the context of the 'liberty of a Christian' (a doctrine as old as the New Testament) who is simultaneously "a freeman unto himself, but a bondsman unto all" (Martin Luther). In the nineteenth century, when the followers of Hegel separated the modern individual from God, one of them, Max Stirner, enunciated a radical agenda of self-actualization by declaring that each man is his own god, possessing his own uniqueness and tasked with unfolding it.

The Western bourgeoisie developed a romantic manifesto of self-actualization during the nineteenth century, which became a broad social movement of the upper classes. However, its subjectivist tendency quickly became apparent. Heidegger, one of the fathers of contemporary anti-rationalism, saw this movement as a form of "subjectivism, including the most dangerous kind, which is hidden in the cult of the personality." He also saw a link to globalism (which he called 'planetarism') and said that 'planetarian imperialism' (by which he meant US-led globalization commencing in the 1930s) would culminate in an "oblivion of being [*Seinsvergessenheit*] embedded in subjectivism."

In like vein, Heidegger calls this Western subjectivism the 'rule of Man', an elegant pun in the original German. Hard to translate, this coinage means the rule of a standardized, soulless type of post-human. After all, a trans-anything is on the way to leaving humanity behind altogether and therefore becoming 'post'-humanity. Michel Foucault—who, like his main sources, Bataille, Marx, and Heidegger, is rarely a source of valid insight—adequately characterized this cultural mega-trend as the "the Californian self-cult," and later Charles Taylor called it "pseudo-authenticity" in his *Ethics of Authenticity*, a book on this very topic.

All of these thinkers realized that this pseudo-self-actualization is a form of consumerism in which the realization of the potential of the person is trivialized to a certain selection of goods and services churned out by the mega-machine (Lewis Mumford). In transhumanism, the idea of self-actualization attains a peak. Transhumanists affirm that we can completely reshape our entire bodily and mental existence to maximize the potential of our personality. The trans woman Martine Rothblatt, who not coincidentally resides in California, is the consummate embodiment of this ideology.

Emancipation

Emancipation is an idea originating in the French Enlightenment and containing a factor that the Protestant Enlightenment (Britain, the Netherlands, the German-speaking countries, and Scandinavia) does not comprise. The main ideas of the Protestant Enlightenment are the dignity of the individual, the individual's freedom and rights, and the sanctity of design of the bourgeois society built on these ideas, namely a state respecting and protecting the rule of law and enabling democratic participation.

In the French tradition, however, there is the notion of creating a secular paradise on Earth, described explicitly by Étienne-Gabriel Morelly in his *Code de la Nature* (1755), the first communist manifesto. Morelly proposed the creation of the state that confiscates everything and distributes goods and services to achieve perfect equality and social justice. His ideas influenced Rousseau, who distinguished the vulgar volonté de tous (the will of everyman, a bottom-up democratic participation in Scottish Enlightenment terms) from the ostensibly noble volonté générale (the universal will), to be discerned and implemented by an élitist oligarch group supervising and directing society to achieve a higher level of civilization.

The idea of emancipation, according to which humans need to be liberated from oppressive power structures of society by breaking with traditional rules, was very potent in the French Revolution, and later on in feminism, as well as in anti-racist movements. It has, of course, a fully justified core that is clearly visible in abolitionism (the expensive nineteenth-century campaign led by France and Britain to end slavery) but tends to become dangerous if the liberation it seeks is combined with the intention of planning a new and better society with new social norms from scratch, as the French revolutionary Babeuf described it. It did not take long for Burke and Hegel to realize this and point out that societies can only be stable if social norms evolve spontaneously, and that it is impossible to plan and implement new social norms.

In transhumanism, there is the idea that technical manipulation of human nature can free us from the burden of our physical existence and make us immortal. It is a secularized eschatology aiming at the total absence of constraints imposed on us by nature or society, a natural system which results from human nature by the interaction of individuals in large groups). The slipping of the bonds of nature is part of the self-actualization aspect of transhumanism, but the creed also contains an aspect of social emancipation based on technology. This view is thoroughly detached from any realistic perspective on anthropology.

The latest non-transhuman emancipatory promise based on technology was propagated in the 1990s: it was the idea of the free Internet, which was supposed to be shared by mankind and to enable new models of participation. Today, the Internet has instead become a tool of commercial data collection and exploitation, mass surveillance, propaganda, and political exclusion, trammeled knowledge, and censorship.

Cartesianism and Neo-Positivism

Cartesianism—the philosophy of Descartes summed up in the deductivist maxim 'I think, therefore I am'—has many aspects, but the one we are concerned with here is the view that humans can systematically describe, understand, and manipulate the world using mathematics and the sciences based on mathematics. For Descartes, the entire world is a mechanism that can be modeled mathematically to enable its delineation and manipulation. Major Cartesians were Joseph-Louis Lagrange, Julien de La Mettrie, and Pierre-Simon Laplace.

Lagrange was a mathematical genius who invented a very elegant mathematical expression of Newton's laws. Like the British physicists Boyle and Hooke, Lagrange believed that the laws of physics were "written by God into the book of nature" and merely await our discovery, which is the task of science. La Mettrie, a contemporary of

Lagrange, was an extreme materialist who saw the human being as a machine. Laplace, who lived a generation later, believed that if we could measure all physical magnitudes of the world, we could write down a gigantic system of differential equations, plug the measurement values into it, and calculate the future: an idea later dubbed the 'Laplacian demon'.

Scientists with a higher power of judgement than the French scientific utopians, like Adam Smith and Immanuel Kant, saw that this was impossible, and it became apparent in the course of the nineteenth century that classical physics (mechanics plus electromagnetism) was running into problems that could not be resolved in the universal framework originally defined by Newton, Leibniz, and Euler.

Many philosophers apprehended early on that we are unable to model and manipulate nature in the way the Cartesians longed for. Giambattista Vico may well have been the first, but others—from Johann Gottfried Herder to Max Scheler, who solemnly pronounced Cartesianism dead—followed in his wake.

When, with the development of quantum mechanics, it became evident that the mathematical models of particles making up matter lead to merely stochastic models of reality, many physicists abandoned Cartesianism as well. The theory of complex systems which emerged from thermodynamics made it obvious to every physicist that the models we have are superb for predicting the behavior of highly restricted systems and for engineering technology based on them, but that we cannot model complex systems using mathematics.

Though Cartesianism is dead from the point of view of philosophy and mathematical physics, it is still a major driving force of our culture, as is evident from the fact that so many engineers, entrepreneurs, biologists, representatives of the humanities and politicians believe in it. They are hoodwinked by Cartesianism because they do not understand physics and because they are bedazzled by the great success of physics and its applications over the last two centuries.

Closely related to Cartesianism is neo-positivism. It is the heir to positivism, an ideology which was fully formulated by Auguste Comte, who coined the term. The basic idea of positivism is that all true propositions which constitute scientific knowledge have to be based on empirical data that can be verified using independent observations or experiments. It is founded on the English tradition of empiricism going back to Aristotle and Bacon (*Novum Organum*), Locke, and then the Scottish Enlightenment; above all, David Hume. No sources of science other than experience and its verification are allowed; there is therefore no religious, metaphysical or a priori knowledge. Therefore, positivists cannot explain the existence of the number π, and thus they obviously have a problem.

Positivism is strongly linked with the idea of the teleological (end-state), necessary progress of mankind, a secular (post-Christian) eschatology. Comte believed that there was a necessary movement towards a science-based global culture that would enable mankind to surpass its current dismal state. He founded the secular-positivist 'religion of humanity' (*église positiviste*) for 'positivist societies' to fulfil the cohesive function once held by collective worship.

Though positivism was dismissed as an ideology by Scheler, the Vienna Circle in the 1920s revived its ideas in the new form of logical positivism. The movement failed philosophically, but the ideas of positivism are still alive in transhumanism and its teleological ideas. A core feature of both Cartesianism and positivism, conspicuous in transhumanism, is the alleged technical feasibility of effecting a change in human nature employing mathematical models.

Eugenics

The ideas of eugenics go back to Arthur de Gobineau, the theoretician of the master race, and Herbert Spencer, coiner of the term 'survival of the fittest'. Eugenics became a political movement in the 1920s in the United States and Britain. Its core idea is that the genomes of the individuals of a population (the totality of their genetic material) should be improved to yield a higher genetic quality of individual and a better overall genetic quality of the population. It was inspired by the success of animal and plant breeding in agriculture, first genetically explained by Mendel and then systematically applied to improve the properties of agricultural life forms.

But because even basic human traits such as body height have an omnigenomic inheritance pattern (the whole genome encodes the trait), and since nothing is known about the genetic causation of higher qualities such as intelligence or emotional stability, eugenic strivings can't succeed, even theoretically. Any attempts to implement eugenic programs, such as those pursued by the Nazis in the 1940s, are deeply anti-human and evil. Nevertheless, today's powerful and growing transhumanist ideology is full of dreams of improving mankind using genetic manipulation.

Postmodernist Anti-Rationalism

Transhumanism also has a deeply anti-rational aspect. Postmodern thinkers like Jacques Derrida, Michel Foucault, and Judith Butler reject the idea that there even is reliable knowledge of the world. For them, human language is an expression of power; all propositions have to be interpreted from a power perspective. The will to surmount biological sex by replacing it with 'gender', to overcome racism by pronouncing that races don't exist, to transgress traditional cultural identities and social norms by declaring that they are merely oppressive structures— all are hallmarks of postmodernist anti-rationalism. The emancipatory arm of transhumanism is inspired by these ideas.

Food Hype

Mens sana in corpore sano (A healthy mind needs a healthy body).

—JUVENAL, *Satire X*

Food Hype has bombarded us since the 1970s when Peter Singer published his book *Animal Liberation,* preaching veganism.

Vegetarianism as an ideology was invented in the nineteenth century, but veganism was rather new when Singer wrote his book. It took thirty years for the ideas of that book to become familiar in popular diet and nutrition. Meanwhile, Western consumerism and hedonism produced multiple Food Hypes, such as the macrobiotic diet, slow food diet, vitamin-rich diet, low-carb diet, carnivore diet, and the recent success of veganism, especially among those born after 1985.

Some of these nutritional ideologies have created Hype waves, and it is easy to see why. Many people think of eating habits as one of the most easily changeable behavioral patterns— though it turns out to be harder than it looks. Humans strive to improve their well-being, and diets are rather easy to follow, especially those not linked to caloric intake reduction. And overweight, even obesity, has become a mass phenomenon in affluent Western societies, while many individuals, for various reasons, wish they could be slimmer.

Diets: How to Navigate and Apply Them

There are three types of diets: Caloric intake reduction diets, medical diets to treat metabolic diseases such as monogenetic defects, and fashion diets. The second type can be life-saving, as in phenylketonuria, an inherited metabolic disease in which patients lack a functional copy of the phenylalanine hydroxylase protein. But these are not Hype diets. Caloric intake and fashion diets, however, are often the subjects of Hype.

Caloric intake diets work by a reduction of the caloric food supply below the energy consumption level, which leads to a weight reduction. These diets very often lead to over-eating after the diet with a rebound to the weight level before the diet was undertaken, which is called yo-yo dieting. The only way to avoid this is to change the fundamental eating behavior to a food intake level that corresponds to the energy needs of the body. Usually, increased exercise alone, which leads to an increment of the required energy, does not reduce weight because it is often compensated for by eating more. To permanently lose weight, exercise needs to be combined with reduced calorie intake. But exercise may help to improve perception of the body and its needs, and can therefore be a useful component of a weight-loss strategy.

In general, weight loss should proceed slowly since rapid loss is often correlated with malnutrition, for example when no-fat or low-fat diets are used. Fats contain fat-soluble vitamins that cannot be obtained in sufficient amounts from fat-reduced or fat-free food, so a dangerous hypovitaminosis can result. And we already saw that rapid weight loss often leads to rebound. But which caloric intake reduction diet to choose?

Many diets don't lead to long-term caloric intake reduction, therefore, the success rates of diets is rather low. Those willing to lose weight often look for trendy diets, which are usually expensive to follow since they require investment into some types of dietary foods. If they follow the diet and then experience a yo-yo effect, they merely enrich the vendors of the diet and its recommended foods. Are there any caloric intake reduction diets that avoid this effect more than others? Probably not, the key is to reduce intake of all food types proportionally in the long term. Rapid weight loss ought to be avoided; shedding weight should be gradual, which requires patience and discipline.

Ultra-Processed Foods

Nevertheless, there is a new finding in dietary research, established over the last fifteen years, that's highly relevant to understanding the overweight epidemic in Western countries. The food industry has developed *ultra processed foods*. These are synthetic food types such as chocolate spread or cereal-based snacks. The Nova food classification system developed by Carlos Monteiro and co-workers defines these as follows:

> Industrially manufactured food products made up of several ingredients (formulations) including sugar, oils, fats and salt (generally in combination and in higher amounts than in processed foods) and food substances of no or rare culinary use (such as high-fructose corn syrup, hydrogenated oils, modified starches and protein isolates). . . . Processes enabling the manufacture of ultra-processed foods include industrial techniques such as extrusion, moulding and pre-frying; application of additives including those whose function is to make the final product palatable or hyperpalatable such as flavours, colourants, non-sugar sweeteners and emulsifiers. . . . Ultra-processed foods are operationally distinguishable from processed foods by the presence of food substances of no culinary use . . . or of additives with cosmetic functions . . . in their list of ingredients. (Martinez et al.)

These ultra-processed foods now make up to seventy percent of caloric intake in some social strata, especially low-income groups. It has been shown that, together with many other individual and socio-economic factors, high intake of ultra-processed food can contribute to the development of food addiction, leading to obesity and super-obesity with a body-mass index of over 40.

These foods are cheap and have a long shelf-life so that they can be used by destitute individuals and families lacking refrigeration. Their consumption is higher among the poor than in the middle-class and elites. Often, they don't provide a sufficient sense of satiation, so that they are over-consumed. From the manufacturer's perspective, ultra-processed foods are highly profitable and attractive since their contribution to food addiction increases the likelihood of customer satisfaction and chronic over-consumption.

Individuals who develop eating disorders as children and adolescents have a low likelihood of overcoming food addiction. Currently ten to fifteen percent of US minors have fatty liver disease, an indicator of widespread obesity among the masses which has no historical precedent (historically, fatty liver disease was a rare consequence of obesity later in life). They become patients and get chronic prescriptions for pharmacological interventions which don't cure their conditions but merely manage surrogate parameters (such as blood cholesterol levels) without improving their health outcomes. Furthermore, these drugs have serious side effects.

For example, semaglutide (trade name Ozempic) is a glucagon-like peptide-1 receptor agonist, a drug that was initially developed for the treatment of diabetes Type II (usually a consequence of obesity). But semaglutide in the form of monthly injections gained government approval as a permanent lifelong treatment for over-weight.

It works by inducing a feeling of satiation or fullness, which reduces the body weight of its consumers by about fifteen percent. It certainly has substantial side-effects such as acute pancreatitis, angioedema, anaphylactic reactions, renal failure, and cancer. Its annual sales are now above fourteen billion dollars a year globally. The evidence shows that the modest weight reduction induced by semaglutide does not improve health outcomes (morbidity or life expectancy) in the obese. The spending is in vain, resulting in an illusory benefit, while the actual impact of the treatment is nothing but harm.

As this depressing example shows, obesity is profitable for both the food and pharmaceutical industry for the entire lifetime of the food-addicted patients. The success of hazardous ultra-processed foods and the uncritical consumption of toxic prescription weight-loss medicines shows that our mass culture has forgotten the nat-ural way to live and interact with nature. Billions of Western (and now Asian) citizens are food-addicted and try in vain to compen-sate for their mental illness by using toxic drugs that in fact don't improve their health.

Fashion Diets and How to Eat

Fashion diets are those diets which do not aim for weight reduc-tion or the treatment of a medical condition, but which express an attitude towards life. Important examples of these are vege-tarianism, veganism, the macrobiotic diet, or a currently less fashionable form of esoteric vegetarianism with small supple-ments of fish. There's also the carnivore diet, which consists of eating only meat.

None of these has yet been shown to yield any health benefit. On the contrary, some of them are harmful. For example, vegan-ism is dangerous since a vegan diet is unable to provide enough of some essential nutrients, notably Vitamin B12. Without adding

supplements, long-term vegans suffer from anemia as well as neural damage which can lead to peripheral neuropathy and organic
psychoses. Parents who feed their children a vegan diet with no
supplements are occasionally prosecuted when the children suffer
harm or die.

Why are the fashion diets not producing the effects their
designers and proponents claim? Because humans are omnivores,
animals which eat all types of food: vegetables, mushrooms, fruit,
fish, meat, and even insects. During evolution, our body adapted
to be able to eat all these types of food, but also to rely on them.

Other animals can synthesize vitamins we cannot, for example
cattle can synthesize vitamin B12. We lost this ability not only for
the vitamins, but also for the eight essential amino acids we can't
synthesize. We are therefore dependent on eating organisms that
make nutrients we can't produce in our own bodies. Diets which
do not take this into account lead to deficiencies in vitamins or
essential amino acids. The least harmful fashion diet is the carnivore diet, if it is combined with fruit to provide vitamins, because
this combination contains all essential nutrients and the dietary
fiber required for proper digestion.

Why are fashion diets so popular given this situation? Eating is
necessary for life, it leads to multiple vegetative reactions of the
body and is an act of deep emotional importance. Because eating
is central to our lives and is done several times a day, diets are popular since it seems intuitive that they can change our life or health.
And diet certainly can. But what is the best diet?

How to eat. This is easy to answer. It is better to eat several small
meals a day than two or three big meals. It is risky to eat more than
one warm meal a day, because people tend to overeat warm food.
You should avoid processed and ultra-processed foods, which yield
a disproportionately low sense of satiation. You should eat rather
slowly so that satiation can develop while eating. You should sense
when you're 'full', and consciously resist eating beyond that. You
should rarely eat sweet desserts and candy.

You should also get sufficient physical exercise—at least three
to four hours of intense physical training a week during which the
pulse frequency should be over 120 and the blood pressure should
be high—since a healthy body has a better sense of satiation so that
regular physical activity contributes to balanced energy intake.
Weight fluctuations are normal and should be tolerated, but significant weight gains should be compensated by a light form of diet
to slowly reduce weight again.

Weight reduction should never be fast because this always leads to rebounds. During diets, the urge to eat needs to be consciously controlled, even if the energy intake is merely reduced to 95 percent of the energy consumption. Overall, each act of eating should be conscious and slow. A balanced omnivore diet with vegetables, starch sources, animal protein and fruit is the diet that corresponds to our evolutionary situation. Food containing toxic chemicals, such as hormones, remnants of fertilizers and pesticides or microplastic should be avoided.

And that's all there is to healthy eating. It is indeed a form of living that most Western citizens have forgotten about. Fashion diets and ultra-processed foods are a form of cultural uprooting, of loss of the cultural tradition that evolved because it is beneficial to those who practice it. Our Hyped life is destroying these traditions and replacing them with new social neo-norms that are geared towards optimal rent extraction in the domains of food and medical products, and also in many other areas where we're driven to over-consume for the benefit of those who own large enterprises forming an oligopoly.

New Types of Food Production

Food Hype is now generated in behalf of new, unconventional methods of food production, processing, distribution, and preparation: neo-food. Organizations such as the WEF and the United Nations, but also many other PR-intensive lobby groups are aggressively advocating more radical changes in the food-value chain, such as radical genetic engineering of plants and livestock, soil microbiome manipulation, vertical indoor farming, lab-grown cultured food, insects as sources of proteins, synthetic and so-called functional foods, 3D food printing, or non-thermal preparation.

Indoor Farming

Indoor or vertical farming refers to the idea of cultivating plants in closed or semi-closed buildings by stacking the horizontally arranged plants on top of each other. They are cultivated using artificial nutrients, lighting, and also carbon-dioxide-enriched gas mixtures. They can be grown using hydroponics, which means that the plants root in artificial solid substrates (such as stone wool or phenolic foam) instead of soil, that are optimized to take up and deliver nutrients. They can also be grown employing aeroponics, which is the use of scaffolds engulfed in artificial mist. For some of these ideas, there are already precursors, such as the Dutch agriculture sector using closed environments to increase carbon-dioxide concentrations as plant fertilizer.

Proponents of these ideas believe that the controlled environment of vertical farming would be free of most pests and pathogens, independent of the weather and climate, and with algorithmically optimized delivery of water, light, and nutrients. Certainly, indoor farming can keep off insects and animals that reduce the harvestable amounts. Currently, the market share of vertical farming is tiny, and this approach to farming is mostly used to grow products such as berries, lettuce, or tomatoes.

Many plants cannot be grown under indoor conditions. Furthermore, it requires a dedicated infrastructure, is very energy-intensive, and also prone to new types of infections, for example via the irrigation system. *There is no need for indoor farming.*

3D Food Printing

3D food printing is the process of extruding liquefied or semi-solid edible food precursor material through a nozzle which moves in all spatial directions to build up food products of arbitrary shapes layer by layer. It is a form of ultra-processed food. After printing, the product is usually baked, fried, or dried. The technology is advertised as a way to utilize low-value parts of food production, for example fruits or vegetables close to their expiration date or lower quality by-products of meat and fish processing. It could also be used to make insects, worms and other alternative protein sources more attractive by giving them positive shapes and colors. 3D food printing is already in use for potato products such as chips and fries and also for pasta or fruit processing. There are many questions around the safety of these food products (allergens, poor structure, low quality of ingredients) and customer acceptance is higher in the lower social strata which now consume more than fifty percent of calorie intake in the form of ultra-processed foods. In the upper strata acceptance is rather low given the overall trend to so-called organic and natural food.

There is no need for 3D food printing using artificial semi-liquid food precursor materials.

Neopesticides

Crop yields and quality are reduced by pests such as insects, fungi, weeds, and bacteria. Traditionally, all of them have been suppressed by chemical pesticides, also used in combination with genetic modification (GM) of plants to make them resistant against herbicides. The best known is Glyphosate, which is used as a herbicide on GM plants that are resistant to it, so that the crops can tolerate a rather high dose of the herbicide, while the weeds cannot. In Europe where GM plants are banned, Glyphosate is used before seeding the plants to clean out the weeds.

All herbicides and pesticides, however, lead, by natural selection, to resistance in the organisms they are directed against. Furthermore, many pesticides are toxic for the environment and also harmful for humans, as they may get into the food chain. Agribusiness and its providers are constantly developing new pesticides: fungicides, insecticides, nematicides (against worms), and herbicides, many of which are, like Glyphosate, supposed to be used with GM plants resistant to them. All of them can be seen as elaborations on the pesticide strategies established over the last thirty years.

And now there is a new trend, so-called biopesticides. These comprise microbial pesticides (living pesticides), biochemical compounds, biological macromolecules as well as GM plants, which are discussed in a later section. Among the macro-molecules, the most interesting is RNA interference (RNAi). The core of this technology consists of small RNAs that can bind to the messenger RNA of a specific gene and disrupt the function of the protein it encodes in insects or other pests. The gene is temporarily inactivated and no protein can be made of it. Monsanto, for example, is developing RNAi directed against genes that convey Glyphosate-resistance. The aim is to spray GM crops to disrupt the Glyphosate resistance which the weeds have acquired. The agri-giant is also developing RNAi molecules to specifically kill certain insect species which cause a lot of damage to crops.

The safety for humans of the various pesticides is very hard to assess. There are several sources of safety concerns. One is acute intoxication of humans exposed to high concentrations (farmers, people living in farming areas). Such effects can usually be ruled out in pharmacological experiments. But there are also chronic effects of residues of pesticides accumulating in the food chain via the processing of the plants, livestock consuming products which contain these residues, or fish ingesting them through the water.

Such chronic intoxication can cause allergies or chronic diseases such as auto-immune disorders, damage to the nervous system, or cancer. And pesticides reduce the species variation in the areas in which they are applied because the organisms they suppress are themselves parts of biological food chains. Therefore, they also repress the populations of predators of the organisms they kill. And they also kill organisms which do not harm crops intended for human consumption. These effects can be additive or multiplicative.

From an evolutionary perspective, the use of all types of pesticides always leads to the emergence of resistance because pesticides create selection pressure for species resistant to them and thus select for resistant mutants. The pharmacological opportunities for effective pesticides that do not harm the environment or humans are limited. As with antibiotics for human ingestion, it will become harder and harder to develop effective compounds with low toxicity. RNA interference faces a similar problem, as targeted species will evolve compensation mechanisms.

Eating Insects?

Protein intake via meat is regarded as inefficient because livestock needs to consume twenty times the amount of calories during the animal's lifetime for each calorie of consumed meat that can be obtained from it. Furthermore, acolytes of the climate creed blame livestock for greenhouse gas emissions. The world's herds of livestock occupy a remarkable proportion of land directly or via the farming land dedicated to producing their food; in total it amounts to eighty percent of the arable land, according to the Food and Agriculture Organization. The animals also consume large amounts of fresh water, though it is unclear whether land occupation and water consumption are problematic.

Nevertheless, these consequences are marshaled to promote the idea that we need to embrace new protein sources for human consumption. Such new sources are insects, jellyfish, micro-organisms (for example micro-algae), and edible macro-algae. The idea of having to eat insects has aroused disgust in Western populations. Such food will certainly be rejected here. It is culturally hard to imagine that Western populations will eat entire insects in the way they are served, for example, in rural China and other parts of East Asia, where certain bugs such as bamboo insects, ants, termites, locusts, bees, wasp larvae, or silkworm pupae are served fried or in other preparations, even *Ophiocordyceps sinnesis*, the caterpillar fungus, are consumed as food.

Nevertheless, the proteins and other nutrients obtained from insects and the other organisms mentioned above will certainly be used as ingredients for processed food.

As long as the extraction of these nutrients avoids harmful substances, this is certainly a possibility, but it isn't yet clear to what extent these protein sources are environmentally more beneficial than livestock. While insects have a much better feed-to-food conversion ratio than livestock, grow faster, can be packed more densely in space and need less water, it's not clear what the net effects of large-scale insect production would be. Their production would have to occur indoors and require energy to heat, cool, and illuminate the factories, so insects farmed at industrial scale would have higher per-unit energy requirements than under currently studied conditions, and, as with large-scale raising of bees, their farmers would have to deal with hygienic farming conditions and infectious diseases affecting the farmed insects. We do not know anything about those farming details, and neither do we have experience with the downstream processing, transport, and storage conditions of edible insects and the products made from them.

Our knowledge of allergens and toxic contents of insects is limited. These may come not only from the insects themselves, but also from organisms infecting them (such as insect-pathogenic fungi or micro-organisms) or from man-made chemical compounds deployed to the environment ending up in the insect-based food chain.

Another alternative protein source is the in vitro production of proteins using cultivated myocytes (muscle cells) to create lab-grown muscle fibers that can be harvested and compressed into artificial meat. This process is highly energy- and material-consuming and has no future. There is the possibility to produce proteins and other nutrients using large-scale cultures of genetically modified bacteria and yeast, to be used as food supplements or ingredients after purification from the producing cells. But these are niche products and their energy efficiency is below conventional production conditions.

Taken together, alternative protein sources are probably over-hyped. Like vertical farming, 3D-food printing, neopesticides, the set-up and maintenance required for the farming and production of new protein sources is very capital-intensive and cannot be undertaken by small autonomous business units.

Genetically Engineered Micro-organisms, Plants, and Animals

Genetic engineering of animals was made possible using transgenic genome manipulation technology in the 1970s, and the first transgenic mouse able to pass artificial genetic modifications to its offspring was created in 1981. The first genetically modified plant was created in 1982, a tobacco plant resistant to antibiotics.

These more than forty-year-old *transgenic* technologies operated by random integration of genetic material into the genome of the receiving organism. This is a serious disadvantage, as random insertion can lead to undesired effects of the manipulation. In the 1980s, Oliver Smithies and Mario Capecchi developed the technology of *site-directed mutagenesis* using homologous recombination in mouse embryonic stem cells, which led to a revolution of genetic engineering in mammals (mostly mice). It became possible to modify or disrupt the function of a genetic sequence, in many cases a genomic locus encoding for a gene, in the mouse embryo, and to breed the resulting mice using classical Mendelian genetics to create animals in which both copies (alleles) of the gene are changed in the intended manner. This technology revolutionized functional genetic research in biology and allowed targeted altering of genetically encoded traits.

But the technology has a disadvantage: it requires the cultivation and injection of embryonic stem cells into early embryos (blastocysts), which was mainly established in mice, and it leaves traces of the genetic manipulation in the genome of the engineered organism.

The invention of *genome editing* with systems such as CRISPR/Cas during the 2010s has enabled site-directed mutagenesis for all species and does not leave traces in the genomic sequences other than the intended alterations. CRISPR/Cas or similar gene editing technologies such as Zinc-finger nucleases or transcription activator-like effector nucleases work by cutting the genome and inserting the desired piece of DNA or modifying a nucleotide at a specific site. However, it very often leads to serious chromosomal side effects in the manipulated organisms, a point to which we will get back later when discussing risks.

A very ingenious application of genome editing are *gene drives*. This technology utilizes genome editing to enforce the genetic propagation of a change to one allele to both alleles in all generations, that is to say the total inheritance of a change to all offspring.

Normally, only half of the genes of an organism are transmitted. In insects, for example, the genome is diploid, every gene has two copies. If two insects mate, one of which has one altered copy, only a quarter of the offspring will have the altered copy as well. Therefore, the efficient spreading of a genetic alteration requires both parent organisms to have at least one copy of the changed gene. Gene drives can enforce the full propagation of a gene in the offspring even if the original organism has only one copy. Unlike in classical inheritance, even in the case of the mating of such offspring with unaltered (wild-type) partners, the change can be rapidly spread into the entire population.

This is done by inserting a gene drive mutagenesis system into a specific genetic locus in one allele of the germ line cells of the initially modified organism. Germ line cells are the cells involved in genetic reproduction. When these cells divide, the gene drive eliminates the non-altered allele and changes it to become like the modified allele. Upon reproduction, this also happens in all offspring organisms. In this way, a gene drive can spread across the population and eliminate the wild-type gene over time. However, the system is not perfect, because the genome editing systems create genomic side effects.

Potential of These Technologies for Food Production

Genetically modified (GM) *bacteria* and *yeast* can be used to synthesize pharmaceuticals or certain proteins that can be used as food additives. GM yeast is used to synthesise cannabinoids, opioids, but also cocoa-butter compounds and animal (milk) proteins. GM micro-organisms can also be used to upgrade low-value by-products of the agri-food industry as input for fermentation processes. In this way, molasses from sugar production or pulp from starch production can be re-used.

Genetic engineering of *plants* to obtain higher-yielding or more robust food-producing organisms has been practiced for decades now. For some species, the global adoption of genetically modified (GM) crops is very high: Globally 80 percent in cotton, 74 percent in soybean and 33 percent in maize. In Europe, however, only Spain and Portugal grow some GM crops, the rest of the continent does not. GM plants can be engineered to have enhanced pest and drought resistance, enhanced nutritional content, and less allergens or toxic compounds. Novel plant traits include pest resistance, drought tolerance, reduced environmental impact (though this is doubtful), extended growing season, or higher production efficiency. Also, there are efforts to create plants able to tolerate poor growing environments such as areas of high salinity, or plants specifically designed to deliver a bio-remedial function, breaking down toxic compounds and taking up heavy metal contamination to purify polluted soil. These plants can then be harvested and the pollutants can be dealt with in concentrated form.

In *animals*, genetic engineering can be used to allow the manipulation of traits or the transfer of beneficial genes between breeds and animal lines, as well as transferring genes across the species barrier, which is of course impossible with traditional selective breeding. As with plants, GM animals have the potential to enhance product properties such as faster growth or higher muscle mass and quality, such as nutritional content, tissue composition, properties and content. GM animals could also be engineered to display increased disease and pest resistance.

Though many prototypes have been engineered over recent decades, only one GM animal species made it into production, the so-called AquAdvantage salmon, a traditional transgenic animal which achieves slaughtering ripeness within eighteen instead of thirty-six months thanks to GM-enhanced growth hormone production. Its prototype was available in the late 1980s, but it took twenty-five years to obtain marketing authorization in Canada, where a few tonnes of this salmon were sold in the mid-2010s. The FDA approved the salmon in 2021. No other GM animals have been put into the human food chain so far.

What about *gene drives*? These can be used in all organisms to rapidly alter an entire population to a predetermined genetic state. For agricultural plants and animals, it's possible to obtain GM populations via breeding of heterozygous organisms (in which there is only one copy of the altered gene). Therefore, there is no need to use gene drives to accelerate the genetic propagation of an allele in a population created under controlled conditions for plant seeding or animal farming. However, there are *plans to eradicate harmful insect species* such as mosquitoes transmitting malaria, using gene drives. They could also be used against the parasite itself.

The first aim would work by inserting a gene drive carrying a gene that is genetically transmitted but reduces reproduction rate in homozygous animals. This way, it would be possible to delete entire species. The second approach works by inserting genes into vector species (animals which transmit diseases) that lead to the expression of proteins that can kill the infectious agent. For example, the group of A. James of UC Irvine recently reported the creation of two gene-drive mosquito strains expressing effector genes coding for antibodies which target malaria (*Plasmodium falciparum*) ookinetes and sporozoites (reproductive cells) in the African malaria mosquitoes *Anopheles gambiae* and *Anopheles coluzzii*. In the laboratory, these showed a massive reduction (ninety percent or more) of malaria infection levels in the mosquitoes.

Another idea is to eliminate invasive species by introducing species-decimating gene drive mutations into the population. New Zealand, consisting of islands and therefore protected against an uncontrolled spreading of genetically modified mammals beyond its borders, is considering this for mammals. The Predator Free 2050 program aims to eliminate eight invasive mammalian predator species (including rats, short-tailed weasels, and possums) by 2050 using gene drives.

In all these genetic engineering approaches, the upper boundary is our understanding of the relationship between genotype and phenotype, between inheritance and physiological traits.

Risks

What are the risks of transgenic plants, animals and the usage of gene drives?

In all genetic engineering technologies there are two fundamental risks, each with further sub-risks:

1. **environmental consequences for ecological systems of interdependent organisms:**
   —undesired side effects of the engineering on the genome of the genetically modified organism (GMO).
   —mutations to the engineered trait giving rise to unexpected phenotypes.
   —an uncontrolled distribution of the GMO into the natural environment.
   —a flow of the engineered genetic trait into related or other species.

2. **harm to humans:**
   —harm to organisms in the food chain of the GMO via toxic effects, leading to direct or indirect effects on humans.
   —direct harm of the GMO to humans.

In GM crops and animals, the main concerns are around risks to human consumers, whereby GMO might be toxic for human consumption via allergies or other toxic effects, for example toxic side-effects from proteins expressed from the gene added to the GMO's genome. Gross food safety problems with GMOs for human consumption can often be ruled out quite easily, but some risk, especially for allergies or auto-immune disorders, can only be ruled out by observing many consumers over longer time periods. Some NGOs may also alter the human intestinal microbiome, but that is a problem with many drugs (such as antibiotics) as well.

The risk of a loss of control over the genetic engineering is especially serious with so called genome editing, because the CRISPR/Cas systems frequently lead to massive chromosomal side effects by which entire chromosomes get disrupted or huge chromosomal parts get lost. When used to perform single-nucleotide editing to induce point-mutations in proteins, the system often performs unintended bystander edits of other nucleotides. Genome editing with CRISPR/Cas has been reported to lead to up to 30 percent of chromosomal aberrations (Papathanasiou 2021). Unintended point mutations and chromosal aberrations can lead to malformations, cancer, and other diseases. They are very damaging to the organism and the environment it is put into and this makes it impossible in practice to use the system in mammals.

The second, enivronmental concern is more complex.

First, the mechanisms listed under 'environmental consequences' above may lead to biodiversity risks. 'Resistant genes that are derived from herbicides, insects, diseases, or stress may produce dominant populations or malignant weeds, causing the changes of structure and breaking the dynamic balance, of the original population' (Short et al, 2021). In the same risk category, we find selective pressure of pesticide genes that promote the resistance of pests and change the host range of pests. We already see this arms race of GMO and pests clearly today, and it will get worse.

Secondly, 'risks on the ecologies of soil would affect the microbial community, insects and mollusks' (He, 2020).

Thirdly, the flow of genes is risky and may lead to hybrid plants in which exogenous genes hybridize with nontarget plants thus producing new pathogens.

Fourth, toxin-producing GMO may lead to pollution of air, soil, and water.

Finally, GMO can change ecosystems by disrupting food chains and natural equilibria, as it happens when invasive species lacking natural enemies are brought across oceans or other natural barriers.

These concerns are hugely amplified when GMOs contain gene drives to enhance the distribution of the genomic modification in the population. Because gene drives are designed to exponentially insert themselves into the genome of an entire population, they rapidly increase all the risks described above so that these can materialize in just a few generations after the release of the GMO into the wild. For instance, if gene drives are used to exterminate species hoping to remove mosquitos, intermediary hosts for a protozoan parasite (malaria), other species which nowadays play a minor role as disease vectors, could rapidly fill the niche left by the extermination of the original host.

Why Food Hype?

All these ideas are propagated as Hope Hypes. We've seen that it's unlikely that they improve human impact on the natural environment, so that the main arguments in favor of these innovations can mostly be dismissed.

What is their economic rationale?

The main innovations to agriculture were the Liebig fertilizer (and its many improvements since), the mechanization of agriculture, the improvement of crops via breeding and genetic engineering and the development of pesticides. Fertilization and small-scale mechanization were still affordable to small and medium sized farmers who produced their seeds from their own crops. But since the 1930s, farmers have become more and more dependent on *optimized hybrid seeds* which are genetically optimized but—unlike traditional crop seeds—cannot be used to obtain new seeds in the next generation. Nowadays, most farmers cannot produce their own seeds from their crops, but have to buy new seeds every year: They've become dependent on Agribusiness, which is dominated by a small group of gigantic corporations and their major owners. Not only do farmers buy their GM-seeds every year, but these are often optimized to work with specific pesticides which are bought together with the seeds as a package from one vendor such as Bayer-Monsanto.

Furthermore, the capital intensity of farming has increased via the advances in mechanization. While the main drivers of agricultural progress have massively increased the reliability, quality and safety of food production, *small farmers have been under pressure from their suppliers and their buyers*: their supply is dominated by a few oligopolistic vendors with considerable pricing power. But they also face an oligopsonistic demand structure—only a few large buyers, mostly huge supermarket chains, buy their products—which tends to lower the prices at which the farmers can sell. *This constellation together with the increased capital intensity of farming has driven many small farms out of business and led to a concentration of agricultural production.* In Germany, the number of farms has declined by seventy-five percent from 904,000 in 1975 to 256,000 farms in 2022, while the size of the remaining farms and their output has steadily increased.

The food innovations described in this chapter are highly capital-intensive. Those which will be realized will lead to a further increase in the industrialization of food production. Their utilization will increase the value creation in the food chain, which allows the suppliers to extract more profits from food production and distribution. This trend will accelerate the global concentration of the sector in more and more oligopolistic organizations in supply of materials to farmers, farming, food processing, and distribution.

5

Medical Hype

The Vaccine should be tested on politicians first. If they
survive, the Vaccine is safe, and if they don't, then the country
is safe.

—MONIKA WISNIEWSKA, 2025

Over the last few years, Fear Hype of a respiratory virus,
SARS-CoV-2, and Hope Hype for 'vaccinations' have had
spectacular effects on our culture and society.

Never before have we experienced a simultaneous global
mass panic, and never before have societies with fundamentally different social structures reacted in such a uniform
manner. It was a Hype of unprecedented strength and
breadth that has led us into the biggest crisis of modern science. It also caused the biggest crisis of human rights and civil
liberties in the West since World War II.

We saw videos of people dropping dead in the streets. We
saw health care professionals wearing hazmat suits more usually employed when dealing with the deadly Ebola or
Marburg virus, which cause hemorrhagic fever and kill
more than seventy percent of the infected. We saw police
and paramilitary units enforcing lockdowns in China. We
saw military trucks transporting dead bodies to cremation
sites in Italy. We saw quarantine stations set up in Manhat-
tan's Central Park. We saw ICUs jam-packrd with people
on respirators. We saw empty streets and empty skies as
even air transport was reduced to a minimum during the
lockdowns. Billions of people were scared almost to death
in an unprecedented Fear Hype.

Societies that used to call themselves 'free' and 'open' and traditionally describe themselves as operating under the rule of law and enabling democratic participation, locked down entire populations following totalitarian patterns which previously were only known from Communist tyrannies like North Korea.

By previously accepted standards, there was no 'pandemic'. *But didn't we all lose friends or relatives to the pandemic or at least know of its victims from hearsay?* Weren't we told that the virus killed millions around the globe? It turns out that that the overwhelming majority of the 'Covid victims' did not die from Covid, but

- **were test-positive but had no Covid disease and died from another cause, such as stroke or heart attack, or**

- **died from unnecessary and dangerous medical procedures such as sedative drugs, virostatics drugs, and intubation, or**

- **died from the effects of 'vaccination'.**

The calculations shown to us were wrong or fraudulent; they were certainly not based on scientific epidemiology.

The deadliness of a virus is determined using the infection fatality rate (IFR), the proportion of infected patients that dies from the infection. It is calculated by determining how many of a population that undergo seroconversion die of the infection. Seroconversion means that somebody who did not have antibodies against a virus develops antibodies because he got infected and his immune system reacted. Dying of SARS-CoV-2 infection means to die of viral pneumonia, which must be diagnosed using a chest x-ray showing a specific pattern of pulmonary shadowing.

Using these criteria, comparatively few people died of SARS-CoV-2 infection in 2020 and 2021. The virus had an IFR well below that of the influenza strains of the last global wave in winter 2017–18 (influenza A H1N1pdm09/strain B Yamagata). What we saw was a normal wave of a mild respiratory virus with a lethality in the range of a rhinovirus. A pandemic is an infectious disease affecting the entire human population and killing infected patients of all ages proportionally to the population's age distribution, like diphtheria, bubonic plague, or cholera. We experienced nothing like this, but instead just a normal respiratory virus infection wave from which a very few old and frail or massively immunocompromised patients (1–2 in a thousand infected, on average) died, as a natural cause of death. The so-called 'pandemic' was a pseudo-pandemic.

When SARS-CoV-2 started to spread around the world, eighty percent of the population already had a solid cross-immunity against the virus based on previous infections with genetically similar related Coronaviridae such as OC43, HKU1 and SARS-CoV-1. Based on the low IFR, this existing cross-immunity against SARS-CoV-2 and the age pattern of those who died from a viral pneumonia, we can safely state that from the beginning of 2020 to March 2022, not more than 100 to 200 thousand patients died of SARS-CoV-2 in the US, with an average age of well over eighty. This is the contribution of a respiratory virus family to the normal proportion of death due to viral pneumonia which we expect. SARS-CoV-2 is a *natural cause of death*, nothing more.

As we'll see, the measures taken against the virus were nonsensical and unnecessary, they only harmed the population, none of them was epidemiologically useful or had a medical indication. *There never was a serious threat at all due to SARS-CoV-2.* What happened? How did the Fear Hype and the Hope Hype unfold to yield such a colossal degree of damage? To understand this, we need to look at the emergence of modern mass society, and its medical systems. We also need to look at how we perceive death in modern societies before coming back to Covid and other problems of modern medicine.

The Modern Welfare State and Its Medical System

Modern mass societies have existed since the 1880s, when water supply, sewer systems, and electricity were installed in Western cities. As they evolved, these societies introduced the welfare state to provide pension schemes and health insurance for the masses. Soon, the politicians and magistrates became concerned with public health and discovered that hygiene, sanitation, balanced nutrition, avoidance of addiction, and physical exercise can support individual health and raise the health standard of the entire population.

In 1855, Rudolph Virchow suggested that all diseases are malfunctions of the cells of the body, and he turned out to be right. He had discovered the theory of cellular pathology. A bit later, during the last quarter of the nineteenth century, Robert Koch, Louis Pasteur, and other physicians and scientists discovered micro-organisms, first bacteria, then protozoa like malaria, and then viruses. They started to study and model the role of these micro-organisms in infectious diseases that spread via contagion. They understood that these micro-organisms infect the body and its cells.

Edward Jenner had invented the principle of vaccination eighty years earlier in Gloucestershire, England, but Pasteur discovered how and why vaccination could be effective. Simultaneously, chemistry enabled the birth of modern pharmacology, which led to a methodical treatment of diseases. The theory of bodily 'humors' disappeared; modern medicine was born.

It was a huge success story, and a gigantic industry concerned with health preservation and recovery was built—the healthcare industry with the ambulatory and the hospital sectors run by physicians, and the array of institutions and businesses supporting them and producing the goods that they used and prescribed: pharmaceuticals, medicinal products, medical devices, diagnostic products and services, paramedical professions. In parallel, health insurance for everyone and a set of public sector institutions regulating and supervising this industry were established. The public sector also provided health education and socialization. Today, healthcare spending amounts to 12–20 percent of GDP in Western countries.

Modern man sees himself as a medical subject, but is also treated as a medical object. As subject, he is concerned with his own health and well-being and knows which behaviors are healthy and which are unhealthy. This doesn't mean that most people live a healthy life, but most have some idea what a healthy lifestyle is. As subjects, people demand healthcare for many situations within the primary scope of medicine, when they suffer from acute or chronic diseases or undergo primary prevention measures such as vaccinations or tumor screening.

They also use the medical sector for lifestyle purposes. For example, a significant portion of psychoactive drug prescriptions can be subsumed under this category: they are not prescribed to cure or alleviate psychoses or other serious mental illnesses, but to allow their consumers an easier life. Lifestyle medicine also comprises interventional convenience medicine such as medically unnecessary Cesareans, or abortion as a replacement for contraception, or many cosmetic interventions.

On the other hand, the health institutions treat almost every citizen as an object from birth to death. Most of us are born in hospitals, and many die in retirement homes or hospitals. Certificates are produced on both occasions. The private and public medical institutions produce a lengthy data trail about each of us during our lives, and the massive Western bureaucracy that evolved since its inception in the eleventh century thoroughly records and stores medical facts about us in electronic form.

Death in Our Culture

Along with the emergence of modern mass societies, philosophers, sociologists, theologians, and other thinkers began to reflect on how the consciousness of individuals changes under the conditions of anonymous, urbanized societies. They soon realized that one of the most important changes was a new attitude towards aging, dying, and death. With it came a new view of health care, medicine, and medical technology.

What does death mean to us? Max Scheler analyzed the certitude of our own death which he sees as an absolute intuition of humans. We are aware that the totality of our life is limited by death. Our life is a process in which we accumulate more experience, but also have the certainty that we can experience less and less in the future as our remaining lifetime gets shorter. The reduction of possible experience makes us aware that life is limited and that our lives continually move toward what Scheler called a natural death, unless we happen to die an unnatural death by accident, disease, or violence.

Yet modern urbanized societies are consciously focused on life, youth, and beauty. All of these ideals are closely related to modern consumerism and materialism as sources of sense-making, individuation, and a feeling of participation, community, and belonging. The underlying ideal, in the words of Michel Foucault, is the "Californian cult of the self," the hedonistic ideal of maximizing our pleasure in a life of individual choices. Our culture is deeply materialistic and hedonistic, geared towards obtaining the highest possible amount of pleasure from life. When mass culture focuses on death, it is usually violent, unnatural death as presented in thrillers and action movies. This emphasis expresses the unease we have with respect to natural death, while it reveals the ongoing human need to acknowledge the reality of death, which remains a universal human concern.

But within this ideal, age and the virtues related to age—such as wisdom, temperance, moderation—are seen as unattractive. Decay, disease, and dying of a natural death are removed from people's attention; the idea of age-caused, natural death disappears from our consciousness. Despite the continuous increase in the relative proportion of the elderly in the indigenous population, the old are placed at the periphery of society and do not figure much in the mainstream contents of our culture: While in pre-industrial societies, the elderly grew old and died within their families, today they are herded away from families or communities, into special residence and care homes.

Our culture wants to focus on getting the maximum from our lives, which is understandable given that the idea of life beyond death is now only accepted by a dwindling minority. We don't want to think about aging, senescence, decrepitude, and senility. The refusal to face up to death leads to a view of death which Jean Baudrillard describes as follows:

> Natural death is that death which comes under the jurisdiction of science, and which is destined to be wiped out by science . . . Death is inhuman, irrational, senseless, like

nature when it is not domesticated. The only good death is
a conquered death.

Today's cultural view of medicine is rooted in this refusal
to pay serious attention to the inevitability of death. Due
to the rejection of senescence and death in our culture,
there is a strong focus on health and the maintenance of
full functionality in all domains of life. Our culture's
rejection of the beyond and the idea of the eternal life of
the soul has left individuals with this life as their only
option. This rejection and the hedonistic materialism of
our culture are the necessary conditions for our Medical
Hype, but they are not sufficient. Pleasure-seeking drives
a very high expectation, a Hope Hype, that medicine can
maintain health and cure diseases.

What are the sufficient conditions?

In his book *Medical Nemesis*, Ivan Illich pointed out that
the medical system of Western societies is dysfunctional.
Within the system, we get continual medical overtreatment, which often does more harm than good, as Illich
showed with good empirical evidence. As we shall see, this
has not improved since Illich wrote; rather, it has gotten
worse. Illich explained that under full insurance coverage
of medical procedures, there is both an incentive to over-
consume medical care on the side of the patients and to
offer too much on the side of the health care professionals
and the industries assisting their work. The affordability of
high-tech medicine for the masses and technical progress
in pharmacology, surgery, and appliance engineering provides the sufficient conditions for medical technocracy.

Medical Technocracy

Technocracy is a form of rule in which the political will is
not formed using the principle of popular participation,
but is based on the opinions of technical experts, which
may or may not be based on scientific knowledge. This
means that decisions are not made by a bottom-up
process of political opinion formation in which institutions
that reach into communities such as churches or trade
unions transport the political will from the basis of society
to the political centers, or in which laws are informed by

social norms that evolve spontaneously, but instead that laws and executive decisions are made or ultimately decided by experts. Very often, these experts decide in the interest of a minority that holds the power over society. Of course, no society is a pure technocracy, but technocratic societies tend to exclude the vast majority of the population from the formation of the political will.

In the medical domain, this is certainly the case in Western societies. Centralized institutions define the choices for health care which are funded by insurance systems. Individual physicians usually make the standardized therapeutic choices; they generally tend to adhere to centrally determined guidelines. And patients rarely deviate significantly from their GPs' advice; though there are, of course, groups of refuseniks who tend to avoid the established health care system altogether.

In pharmacotherapy, influential technocratic regulators such as the Food and Drug Administration (FDA) in the USA, the European Medicines Agency (EMA) in the EU or the Medicines and Healthcare products Regulatory Agency (MHRA) in the UK make choices that are followed by smaller regulators, payors, and health care professionals all over the world.

At the global level, the World Health Organization (WHO) is a key technocratic organization impacting the way health care is planned and delivered all over the planet. It played a major role in the pseudo-pandemic: It declared the pseudo-pandemic and was a major international driver of the spread of Fear Hype and Hope Hype around the pseudo-vaccines. It is technocratic in the full sense of the word: 1. Its staff is made up of experts. 2. Its decisions are completely detached from the bottom-up formation of political will; instead it attempts to make and enforce decisions top-down. 3. Its funding is to a large extent provided by huge private foundations which have been set up to promote the agenda of a small, extremely wealthy minority.

How is health understood by this medical technocracy? The WHO sees health as "a state of complete physical, mental, and social well-being and not merely the absence of disease or infirmity" (WHO 'Constitution'). This definition is obviously absurd. No human being is ever in a state of total well-being; human nature prevents this. This has two causes. First, even those humans who have no acute or chronic disease suffer from mood undulations or small inconveniences like the famous 'sand in the eye' or a sudden light headache.

Secondly, and more importantly, humans are driven. This means that we always tend to want "more, better, faster, and more often" (Friedrich Nietzsche). Plants and animals are also driven in the sense that their behavior is geared towards survival and reproduction, both of which are fueled by the energy flow through the organism's body. But an animal is satisfied and rests for a period once it digests or has had sex, while in principle, the human thirst for experience and the accumulation of goods is not satisfiable. In a certain sub-population of humans, this leads to an unlimited will for power, because power allows an individual to realize more possibilities at the expense of others, now and in the future. This is the foundation of the power structures we find in all human societies. But the human drivenness is so strong that it also generates addiction, a state which can only artificially be induced in animals.

Because of human drivenness, humans are rarely satisfied and in a state of complete well-being: Very often, we all believe we could have more than we currently have.

So the WHO's health definition is obviously wrong. But then, why was it formulated in this way? Because those in whose interest the WHO acts want to drive up the demand for health care and also justify medical interventions into human life. With a definition of health as a state that even a normal human being can never achieve, even over a single day, the WHO sets the bar for health so high that the threshold for medical interventions to improve this type of 'health' becomes very low. And indeed, we see that in high-income countries like those organized in the OECD, the consumption of pharmaceutical products is gigantic. The OECD reports that in 2019, in the US, per-capita spending was close to $1,400 per annum, followed by Germany, Canada, and Japan with $935, $811 and $803 (calculated from the local currencies using the purchasing power parity method), respectively. Global sales of pharmaceutical products amounted to $1,480 billion in 2022, roughly 50 percent of which was generated in the US and

Canada, 24 percent in the EU, 9 percent in China, and 6 percent in Japan: High-value pharma consumption is a privilege of the rich countries and the amount of drugs consumed is proportional to age.

As we will see later, at least two thirds of this consumption has no positive effect on health or is even toxic. Roughly one third of the consumed volume has a real benefit. The WHO contributes to the acceptance of this over-prescription, which enables the pharmaceutical industry to extract a rent from the consumers at the expense of their health.

The WHO, which is supposed to be an institution concerned with the health of the human race, is now concerned with maximizing the use of interventional medicine independently of its benefit to the population. It has also been transformed into an institution propagating and participating in the biomedical control of the population, as we shall see.

The Covid Hype

The history of Covid is, like most Hype stories covered in this book, a story of Fear and Hope. Fear is usually created first, then hope is promised by the private-public partnership which brings us the pretense of a solution to our fears.

FEAR HYPE

It was expensive to create the biggest Fear Hype in the history of mankind around a pathogen that never had an infection fatality (lethality) rate over 2 per mill in the population aged over eighty, and a negligible lethality for the under-seventies. As we have seen, the reports of millions of Covid deaths were unwarranted. Furthermore, as in-depth analyses of hospital bed occupancy have shown, there was never a shortage in hospital beds.

In Germany and the UK, the number of beds was even massively reduced during the Covid years. The virus was never as harmful as an average influenza virus strain. SARS-CoV-2 is merely one of many viruses which can cause a natural death at the end of a long life. What did it take to create this absurd Hype around a virus with a lethality similar to the common-cold-causing rhinovirus?

We don't know for sure, but governments spent a lot. For example, the UK government spent more than 180 million pounds sterling on Covid communication in 2020, which does not include the British Broadcasting Corporation and other public broadcasting service costs, and private companies invested much more. It's reasonable to estimate that the spending for communication, PR, and news focused on spreading fear amounted to up to a third of total media revenues in 2020. Under this assumption, in Germany, for example, roughly four billion euros were spent from March to the end of 2020 for COVID communication.

This means that every week, roughly a hundred million euros were spent to instill Fear into the population. But not only were newspapers and broadcasting stations key to propagating the Fear. Swiftly, academic institutions were transformed into propaganda machines to produce evidence of the 'mortal danger' of this comparatively harmless pathogen. Public money was poured into so-called Covid research, which was tasked to produce the results required to support the panic. Entire scientific fields were rapidly transformed into domains of anti-science, producing absurd nonsense. This nonsense was then taken up by the mass media to support the colossal Fear Hype.

As an example, take the preposterous models produced by the epidemiologist Neil Ferguson at Imperial College London. He drastically overestimated the infection fatality rate of SARS-CoV-2 and the expected deaths that would be caused in the UK by the 'pandemic'. These are excellent examples of a specific type of government-compliant, technocratic anti-science. His assumptions were wrong, his methods were inadequate, his numbers and conclusions were unscientific, as was quickly shown by honest epidemiologists like John Ioannidis. But thousands of scientists queued to obtain vast amounts of Covid research funding and joined the choir of anti-scientific Lysenkoism led by figures like Ferguson, Christian Drosten, and Anthony Fauci.

The Covid Fear Hype was also picked up by the Woke movement. Woke activists, politicians and bureaucrats wanted to realize the biologically absurd goal of 'zero Covid', the extermination of the virus, which is impossible with a virus transmitted via respiration. The entire movement was an example of neo-Lysenkoism.

Lysenkoism is a form of anti-scientific frenzy in which scientists produce anti-rational, pseudo-scientific contents which are aligned with and meant to support government policies. Lysenkoism was named after the mad biologist Trofim Denisovich Lysenko who propagated an anti-Mendelian theory of heredity with the support of the Soviet dictators, Josef Stalin and Nikita Khrushchev. Under Lysenkoism, dissident voices were ridiculed, demonized, or silenced.

Something very similar happened in the Western world beginning in March 2020. Prominent critics of Covid-Lysenkoism such as John Ioannidis, Sucharit Bhakdi, Robert W. Malone, or Luc Montagnier, courageous men, who were scientifically right from the start, have been massively attacked by Lysenkoists and are still vilified as 'Covid-19 misinformation' agents, discredited as 'Covid deniers', 'disinformation spreaders', and 'Covidiots'; some of them, like Bhakdi, are prosecuted under the pretense of penal law in several Western countries.

However, their views about the true nature and relative harmlessness of SARS-CoV-2, the total medical uselessness and harmfulness of the non-pharmacological measures against the virus and their insights into the toxicity of the somatic gene-therapeutical injections misleadingly dubbed 'vaccines' were all scientifically confirmed in the course of 2021, and continue to be verified with an ever-increasing accumulation of evidence. Their views form the starting point for the future reconstruction and rehabilitation of virology, epidemiology, and vaccine research, as well as intensive care medicine and applied infectiology, all of which are currently in the deepest crisis since their inception in the nineteenth century.

All medical disciplines which were involved in building this web of pseudo-scientific untruths have been discredited and deeply damaged by the anti-rational, Lysenkoist wave that is still going on, and it will be a very hard task to restore trust in medicine as a science once the population realizes what has happened since 2020.

Not only were experts who recognized the truth about the virus and the counter-measures discredited. In collaboration with the state, social media such as Twitter, Facebook, and Youtube systematically suspended or deleted user accounts or put them under reach reduction ('shadow banning') if users made true statements about the topic. In Orwellian manner, these true statements were called 'misinformation', the false statements about the danger of the virus or the efficacy and safety of the pseudo-vaccines were called 'authoritative information'. Protests were made illegal and protesters were violently prosecuted by the executive. At the peak of the collective hype, frail old ladies peacefully protesting were beaten up in Australia and in Germany, where such pictures raised bitter memories of the darkest times we once went through.

Based on the Fear Hype initiated in March 2020, non-pharmacological measures were introduced to deepen the fear and spread panic: lockdowns, mask wearing, social distancing, constant testing, and absurd, harmful therapeutic protocols for Covid inpatients.

The lockdowns did nothing but harm the economy and damage the physical and mental health of the population. They could not stop the natural spread of the virus, which continued via supermarkets and public transport and rapidly caught up to its predetermined, inescapable biological course so that we had herd immunity by summer 2020, long before the 'vaccination' campaign started. Politicians and magistrates forced people to wear masks that have no effect at all on reducing the load of viral particles inside buildings with public access such as supermarkets, schools, or business offices. Masks and 'social distancing' protocols did not prevent contagion and themselves caused enormous damage to people's lives and health.

Access to many private and public institutions was linked to obtaining antigen or PCR-tests that made no medical sense at all. There are 7–8 viral families (influenza, rhinoviridae, Cox-sackie viridae, Corona viridae, paramyxoviridae, adenoviridae, mastadenoviridae, and reoviri-dae) which comprise at least a hundred viral species causing respiratory tract infections in humans that are as dangerous as or more dangerous than SARS-CoV-2. We do not mass test for these either, because they are a natural part of our lives and not especially dangerous. Neither is SARS-CoV-2. The tests were technically flawed and solely performed to maintain the anti-scientific myth of a deadly plague-like pandemic using meaningless numbers.

For virologists, biochemists, and other medical professions with the standard knowledge of immunology and experience in working with viruses in laboratories and in the clinical setting, it was absolutely clear that none of the measures were even meant to be effective against the spread of SARS-CoV-2. Their purpose was different—to spread and maintain Fear. Along with the constant media reports featuring overcrowded ICUs and millions of Covid deaths, the experience of repeated lockdowns and permanent compulsory mask wearing in public kept the Fear alive. The masks also allowed individuals to demonstrate their agreement to and compliance with the esoteric, ridiculous public narrative. The majority of the population were convinced that there was indeed a dangerous virus justifying the insane behavior of the politicians and administrators.

The testing requirements provided the Covid 'incidence' numbers that were reported on the mass media every day. However, these were no incidence numbers at all, because the incidence of a disease is defined differently.

The treatment protocols for inpatients advising early sedation, intubation, and artificial ventilation of SARS-CoV-2 positive patients were deeply flawed and massively contributed to iatrogenic deaths inflating the so-called Covid death toll ('iatrogenic', an increasingly useful word, means death or injury due to medical intervention). Only a tiny fraction of the patients who were hospitalized should have been in hospital at all, and only a few of these would have benefited from ventilation. The measures were medically wrong, their purpose almost seems to have been to create iatrogenic deaths to drive up the Fear. But the Fear had no basis in reality. The in-patient statistics show that the hospitals were never overcrowded. In Germany, we had 10 percent fewer ICU patients in 2021 than 2020, and 15 percent fewer in 2022 than 2020. There was no excess mortality at all in 2020.

Then, as the Fear Hype was at its peak, the global North and parts of the South established a mass 'vaccination'

Sidebar: Incidence and 'Testing'

In epidemiology, incidence is the number of newly diseased persons per 100,000 inhabitants in a certain time interval. To obtain this number for contagious diseases, we have to determine the rate of the seroconversion of a representative sample of the population. This means that we must measure how many people switch from having no antibodies against a pathogen to having antibodies in the time interval in question. But this was not done, because it would have shown that by June 2020, 80 percent of the global population had cross-reacting antibodies or T-cell-receptors against SARS-CoV-2, and that humoral and cellular herd immunity had been achieved.

Instead, point-wise prevalences (number of patients divided by total population size during a given interval) of the presence of virus particles in the upper respiratory tract were measured with a test of poor specificity. This means that due to the flawed PCR protocol that was used, the test produced many false-positive results.

So, the test was unspecific and led to false-positive results. But even if the test had been highly specific, it still would have been inadequate to establish an infection. An infection is the presence of a pathogen with symptoms. But the vast majority of persons with a positive test had no symptoms and were not contagious. Nevertheless they were forced to 'quarantine' at home, a medically useless measure used solely to ramp up Fear and control the population.

---

program that lured and forced entire populations into 'vaccination' using propaganda and a large range of coercive 'mandates' linking the nucleic acid injections to access to locations, shops, the workplace, or travel.

The 'Vaccine' Hope Hype

When the campaign began, 80 percent or more of the thoroughly manipulated and fearful Western populations were queueing to get the 'vaccines' first, there was 'vaccination envy' among those who had to wait longer than others to get their 'jab'. The propaganda pushing the injections was dense and overwhelming and used all media and modalities of psychological mass manipulation. The 'vaccines' were praised like a God-given miracle of science; criminal entrepreneurs and companies who knew perfectly well that the substances they were producing were of low manufacturing quality, ineffective against the SARS-CoV-2 infection and dangerously unsafe, obtained public praise and medals.

But the 'vaccines' have no effect on the epidemiology of the virus and are *five to ten thousand times* more toxic than a real vaccine. In many Western countries, some professions were forced to take the poison to keep their jobs: soldiers, policemen, physicians, nurses and other health-care professionals. Twelve billion doses of the poison have been injected into billions of humans. Quantitatively, it was the most successful Hype campaign ever. So far, it has crippled at least 25 to 50 million 'vaccinated' and killed at least 5 to 10 million. The program has not saved a single life. Let's understand why.

NO INDICATION

In medicine, an indication means that there is an evidence-based rationale to use a drug for a disease, a syndrome, or a symptom. For example, aspirin has an indication for headache in the absence of conditions that make its use dangerous or prohibit it for other reasons, which is called a contra-indication. Small children, for example, have a contra-indication for aspirin because they can develop the dangerous Reye Syndrome when taking it.

The nucleic acids injected to vaccinate against SARS-CoV-2 have no indication and are not medicinal products.

Despite the clear and well-established facts, the 'vaccines' were developed, cutting out at least five years of development time, and brought to the market with unprecedented haste. Prior to thalidomide, there was almost no controlled clinical development. Thalidomide changed all that—until Covid (and AIDS, as we shall see below). The evidence presented to the regulators showed that the mRNA 'vaccines' have no prophylactic effect and are toxic. Based on pre-clinical results, the regulators should not even have approved the trials. Furthermore, it was clear that the production quality was, and still is, insufficient to meet the current Good Manufacturing Practice (cGMP) guidelines which were normally considered necessary to obtain marketing authorization.

Sidebar: Why the "Vaccines" Are Not Medicinal

1. By summer 2020, there was global herd immunity against the virus. The first 'wave' of SARS-CoV-2 infections occurred between the fall of 2019, when the virus began to circulate in Wuhan, China, and April 2020. By April 2020, the point-prevalences of the virus measured by the antigen and PCR tests declined globally, the end of the 'first wave' was declared. This wave was caused by the so-called a-variant of the virus, also called Wuhan-variant, and its immediate genetic descendants.

Why did the prevalences decline? Because the virus could not spread any more in human populations: Herd immunity was achieved. A virus spreads as long as infected individuals can infect others, or more precisely, as long as an infected individual infects more than one other individual (> 1) on average. When most individuals the infected persons encounter are immune because they were previously infected, the number of newly infected per infected individual drops below 1 and the prevalence declines. This happened in April 2020, the achievement of 'herd immunity'.

2. We are unable to create effective vaccines against viruses causing infections of the upper respiratory tract (influenza and flu-like syndromes). Since the 1960s, all attempts to effectively vaccinate humans against these viruses have failed. For influenza, this is a shame, since its IFR can be up to 0.4 percent and its most aggressive strains can kill the young, though not at high incidence. The reasons for this failure seem to be that these viruses show a rapid shift in their antigenic profile, making vaccines obsolete before they are even applied, and futhermore the route of administration is unphysiological and does not elicit the immunological response required to create immunity by vaccinating as we know it from measles or tetanus.

3. An important reason for the failure of flu vaccinations is that those who die of flu have an immune insufficiency. Since a vaccination requires an intact immune system, this group cannot benefit from it. In other words, we cannot avoid or circumvent natural death from respiratory viruses.

4. The Covid virus has an IFR similar to the rhinovirus. It is completely harmless for the healthy normal population, and it is a natural cause of death affecting the frail elderly and the immunocompromised. There is no 'long Covid' beyond the very low incidence (one in 10 to 20 thousand infected) of similar rare syndromes, such as pericarditis or myocarditis which are also caused by other flu-like infections of the upper respiratory tract. Therefore, there is no need to vaccinate.

Toxicity

It was clear even before development started that the 'vaccines' would lack efficacy and be poisonous, for the following reasons:

1. **Pre-clinical data had shown in 2012 that mice vaccinated against SARS-CoV-1 with three different vaccines showed pulmonary immunopathology (lung auto-immune disease) when infected with the virus after vaccination. The authors concluded that the vaccination principles were not fit for this purpose.**

2. **As had already been shown shown in 2014, the spike protein as a vaccination antigen leads to antibody-dependent enhancement (ADE), a vaccine-induced aggravation (Vaccine-Associated Enhanced Disease, VAEH) of the natural disease progression.**

3. **The trials to establish a vaccine against SARS-CoV-1 had to be stopped because the antigen (the spike protein) was toxic and led to cases of death among the vaccinated trial participants.**

All of this was known to those who selected the spike protein of SARS-CoV-2 as the vaccination principle for the development of the somatic gene-therapeutical 'vaccine', although it is more than ninety percent homologous (molecularly similar) to the toxic SARS-Cov-1 spike protein.

In the first two months of 2021, it became evident from the CDC's Vaccine Adverse Event Reporting System (VAERS) database that in the three months after December 2020, there were more cases of vaccine-related injury and death in the database than in the total period from the establishment of the system in the late 1960s. Operation Warp Speed to vaccinate the entire US population in record time had been started in November 2020. By the end of the first quarter of 2021, thousands of suspected death cases linked to the 'vaccines' had been reported. It should have been considered necessary to stop the program immediately. But that was not done.

Why are these drugs so toxic? First of all, we must understand how they work. Both types of nucleic acids based 'vaccines' introduce nucleic acids into the cells of the vaccinated which leads to an expression of the SARS-CoV-2 spike protein by the human cells. The cells get temporarily genetically modified: This is a somatic gene therapy.

——— Sidebar: A Somatic Gene Therapy ———

The modified RNA (modRNA) 'vaccines' made by Moderna and Biontech/Pfizer are transfected into the cells by lipid nanoparticles which serve as vector. The modRNA contains an altered nucleoside (RNA component) that makes the modRNA so stable that it can persist in cells for months instead of 20–30 minutes like natural mRNA. After the injection, the lipid nanoparticles distribute throughout the organism and transfect cells. Once the cells are transfected, they start to produce viral spike protein which is encoded by the modRNA. They then express this protein or fragments of it on their surface. The immune system identifies these cells as infected and destroys them.

With the cDNA-based 'vaccines' made by Johnson and Johnson, AstraZeneca and others, the mechanism is different, the transfection vector is a genetically modified chimpanzee-adenovirus (ChAdY25). After the transfection, the gene driven by a promoter encoding the spike protein on the viral cDNA forces the transfected cells to transcribe mRNA, which in turn is translated to spike-protein. Again, the cells expressing the protein get killed once there is immunity (in the absence of natural immunity, after the first injection).

This approach violates the well-established *dose-effect relationship* at the heart of modern pharmacology because the effect varies by several orders of magnitude depending on the quality of the batch, the mode of injection (intramuscular or intravenous), and various parameters of the patient's condition. This is another reason why this 'vaccination' platform should never have been approved. A major core principle of pharmacology was abandoned.

Based on this mechanism of action, there are several causes of the toxicity of these somatic gene therapies.

1. Each dose of the 'vaccine' leads to the genetic alteration of endothelial (inner blood vessel wall) and parenchymal (functional) organ cells. The cells are forced to make the spike protein and transport it or fragments of it to their membrane, which is the part of the cell which delimits it from its environment. Once antibodies against the SARS-CoV-2 spike protein are present in the body-either through natural immunity or 'vaccination'—the presence of the spike protein on the cell membrane leads to the

destruction of the cells by cellular immunity. This causes damage and scars in organs: myocarditits, cerebral infarction, destruction of brain neurons, liver, kidney, joints (leading to temporary arthritis and permanent, disabling osteoarthritis), and other organ damages. This effect of the 'vaccines' can be observed in at least one of every five hundred vaccinated cases and is the main cause of 'long Covid', which is mainly a 'vaccination'-induced disease.

2. Chronic autoimmune diseases. These are diseases in which the immune system destroys the cells of its own body. It can be caused by antigen-independent, T-cell induced autoimmunity or via spike-protein cross-autoimmunity. The first effect is based on an overstimulation of the T-cells, which form the cellular immunity of the immune system. This can occur with repeated applications of the 'vaccines'. The second effect is based on molecular similarity of structures of the spike protein and structures of the body. At least one out of ten thousand of the 'vaccinated' develop such a syndrome. Examples are neurological syndromes such as the Guillain-Barré-Syndrome, Bell's Palsy, or Multiple Sclerosis.

3. Chronic vaccine acquired immune deficiency syn-drome (VAIDS), technically called vaccine-associated enhanced viral disease (VAEH), is a condition in which the vaccinated have a much weaker immunity than healthy individuals and leads to strongly increased susceptibility to infectious diseases and to an increased risk of developing cancer. The 'vaccinated' are also much more likely to be infected with SARS-CoV-2 because the 'vaccines' elicit non-neutralizing IgG4 antibodies. These are antibodies which prevent the binding and neutralization of the virus or cells expressing the spike protein. VAEH explains why countries with high 'vaccination' rates have higher sick leave rates than before the campaign. It is likely that 0.5 to 1 percent of the 'vaccinated' suffer from this syndrome.

4. Direct organ-toxicity of the spike-antigen leading to various kinds of organ damage. Rather rare.

5. Toxicity of the nanoparticle lipid shell (not contributing to the overall toxicity very much).

6. Acute anaphylactic shock as an allergic reaction to extracellular modRNA (modified RNA) administered via the injection of broken lipid nanoparticles (rare, less than one in ten thousand).

Many of the toxic effects of the gene therapies were anticipated by experts. The Pfizer files analyzed by Naomi Wolf and her co-workers have shown that Pfizer knew very early on that their 'vaccine', BNT162b is dangerous, toxic, and useless. And they reported it to the regulators, who chose to ignore it. We see again that the campaign has not improved public health, but massively damaged it.

Lack of Benefit

Not only were the 'vaccines' toxic, they also had no curative or preventive effect. How can we know this?

To show that a pharmaceutical product has a beneficial effect, its effect needs to be compared between a group of treated patients and a control group. The control group is either treated with a placebo or the standard of care. To obtain robust, representative, statistically significant, and meaningful results with minimal bias, the trial needs to be randomized, prospective, and double-blinded.

For the clinical trials conducted to obtain a marketing authorization for the 'vaccines' by Pfizer, Moderna, Astra-Zeneca, and other manufacturers, most of these principles were ignored to make sure that the trials showed the desired effect. *They were among the most biased major trials ever published* and would never have been accepted for scientific publication if the peer-review system, which is supposed to guarantee high quality, were doing what it is supposed to do. The trials themselves should never have been approved because the design flaws were visible.

Given the multiple flaws of the trial design, the FDA should never have allowed Pfizer to conduct them, and Pfizer should never have given a marketing authorization based on their results. The FDA and EMA also saw the toxicity of the 'vaccines' in the first weeks of 2021.

The 'vaccines' had no clinically relevant effect in preventing the infection with SARS-CoV-2 and no benefit for the patient's health, but instead had a purely damaging, toxic effect. We can safely say that those who designed these trials knew how to bias outcomes extremely well. The multitude of retrospective studies performed once the vaccines were marketed could not show any benefits either; they were even more biased than the trial analyzed above.

───── **Sidebar: Flaws of the Pfizer Trials** ─────

1. The inclusion criteria were not designed to generate a trial population for which the vaccines would have been useful: the elderly and the immunocompromised, the only groups for which SARS-CoV-2 is dangerous. But the average age of the trial population was much too low and their health status was much too good. This was not the population that would derive any benefit from 'vaccination'. It was chosen because the elderly do in general benefit much less from vaccinations since their immune system is weaker.

2. Persons that had a past positive SARS-CoV-2 test or antibodies against the virus were excluded from the trial to make sure that the 'vaccines' were tested on non-immune patients. If the patients with existing immunity had been included (like 80 percent of the population at the time of the trial, which started in August 2020), it would have been impossible to show any effect. This patient selection was highly biased and scientifically inadmissible because it deliberately avoided taking into account the herd immunity situation that was found in the population when the trials were conducted.

3. The trials only analyzed flu-like mild or moderate symptoms for SARS-CoV-2 positive cases over a period of twelve weeks after the 'vaccination'. But the reason to vaccinate was the fear of hospitalization or death from the infection over a long period (at least six to twelve months under the assumption that the vaccination has to be repeated once a year as with influenza). The trial did not show any effects for these outcomes for such a period. Therefore, it did not show anything of clinical relevance.

The results even for this clinically irrelevant outcome were so weak that this procedure removed the last bits of relevance. To reduce mild to moderate flu symptoms, which are clinically irrelevant and a normal part of human life, for one single vaccinated person, one has to vaccinate 120 persons. This is called 'number needed to prevent' (NNP). This corresponds to a relative risk reduction that is clinically and epidemiologically completely irrelevant. In measles, we have to vaccinate one person to get total sterility against the infectious agent. The NNP is 1. *This is what we want, and not an NNP of 120 for mild symptoms in the young and healthy.*

4. Furthermore, the outcome of interest would have to be flu-like symptoms independently of SARS-CoV-2 detection which would have measured whether the 'vaccinated' were less sick than the unvaccinated. Even if the 'vaccine' were not toxic, such an effect is unlikely, as there are a hundred other pathogens with a clinical profile similar to SARS-CoV-2.

That's why the outcome was designed to include the test for this pathogen—otherwise the extremely small effect would have been drowned out.

5. The blinding was discontinued four months into the trial, subsequently, almost every participant of the control group was 'vaccinated' as well. The control group was in effect removed. Evidently the intent was to conceal the outcome inferiority of the 'vaccinated' against the control group which became apparent soon after the roll-out of the 'vaccines'.

6.The blinding was incomplete; the patients knew whether they had been given the vaccine. This creates a bias against the reporting of adverse events.

7. The safety data for the trial were fraudulent; in the Pfizer files which were published after 2022, it became apparent that serious adverse events including cases of death in the 'vaccinated' group had been hidden.

With the exception of the last point, all of this was clear when the paper describing the 'pivotal trial' for market authorization was submitted to the New England Journal of Medicine. The dossier was submitted to the FDA and the EMA in 2020, long before the trial was conclusive.

Quality

Aside from the clinical aspect, the production quality of the 'vaccines' was so poor that they could never have been approved if the GMP standards had been enforced by the regulators.

This is especially true for the modRNA vaccines. They were contaminated by plasmid DNA used to produce the modRNA in genetically engineered bacteria. While this is not harmful, as the DNA gets rapidly degraded by cytosolic DNAses (enzymes within the cells that recognize DNA outside the cell nucleus and destroy it to prevent the DNA from causing harm) if it gets into the cells, it does show that the production process was sloppy.

More worryingly, a big proportion of the nanoparticles were not intact upon injection—either because the particles had decomposed along the logistic chain or because they were not assembled correctly. It is estimated that only 15 to 20 percent of the batches were dominantly composed of intact nanoparticles. In the other batches, the proportion of intact nanopartcicles was lower.

Upon injection of damaged particles, these particles do not enter cells or the blood circulation but get destroyed by the innate immune system which recognizes naked mRNA in the extracellular space. This can lead to allergic reactions and has caused a small fraction of the vaccine-induced deaths via anaphylactic shock, a strong allergic reaction. For the 'vaccinated', it is good that only a rather small fraction of the batches contained mainly intact lipid nanoparticles, because otherwise the damage of the campaign would have been much higher. Nevertheless, the competent authorities should not have approved a drug of such poor production quality.

The Devastating Outcome

The 'vaccination' program killed millions globally including children and fetuses, and chronically harmed tens of millions, while it did not save a single life.

We know with high certainty that the excess mortality calculated for Germany in the years 2021–2022 by Kuhbandner and Reitzner, 100,000 deaths, must be attributed overwhelmingly to the vaccination campaign. Germany has roughly fifty million 'vaccinated', one hundredth of the globally vaccinated population. This sample size is largely sufficient to allow extrapolation to the global population. Therefore, we must have roughly ten million deaths globally.

In addition, we have evidence that at least 0.5 to 1 percent (but probably 3–4 percent) of the 'vaccinated' become chronically ill. This means that globally, we have twenty-five to fifty million chronically ill, many of whom will in due course die a premature death due to the 'vaccination'. And yet the 'vaccines' are still used globally; their marketing authorizations have not been withdrawn in most countries. Furthermore, pipelines of biopharmaceuticals are full of nucleic-acid-based somatic gene therapies that have been approved by regulators for clinical development. It may well be that the antigens (protein fragments) encoded by the nucleic acids for the new vaccines may not be toxic in themselves as is the SARS-CoV-2 spike protein. But if they are immunogenic at all, they will have the same general toxic effects as the Covid 'vaccines' described above because they will trigger destruction of the endothelium and cells of the parenchymata.

Along with the vaccination campaign, states rolled out analogous and digital vaccination certificates that were used to control access to institutions, shops, cultural and entertainment events, education and means of travel. We have to be aware of the fact that many of those who planned this coercion directed against fundamental human rights knew that the 'vaccines' were toxic and were ineffective against Covid.

Planned or Spontaneous?

Rulers plan; they always have. They plan infrastructure such as bridges, roads, canals, prisons, the education system, the military and many other systems. They then use tax revenues or borrow to realize the plan. The Covid pseudo-pandemic seems to have been carefully planned and executed with the goal of rolling out a mass-'vaccination' program globally and thus enrolling the populations into a digital biomedical certificate scheme. It is likely that the virus was genetically engineered, as is evident from its sequence, which contains DNA-motifs that cannot be explained by natural evolution from related Corona-viruses. The goal was probably to increase the virus's infection rate, but not its lethality.

It first appeared in Wuhan in fall 2019 during the seventh CISM Military World Games. SARS-CoV-2 'vaccines' to 'prevent infection' were developed well before and probably patented with the aim of unleashing a planned pseudo-pandemic on the public, creating panic via countermeasures, and then appearing to dispel the panic via the 'vaccination' program. We also know that international institutions had performed pandemic planning games for at least one decade.

Without insight into highly confidential documents which we will not get access to for some time, we cannot know why they wanted this. But there are two main possibilities.

First, the funding for health care provided by national and international institutions and promoted by the WHO and many NGOs does not primarily address the real causes of mass diseases: famine, malnutrition, tuberculosis, malaria and other infectious diseases that kill hundreds of millions in the Global South. Instead, it advertises vaccination against viruses. These vaccines are patent-protected and must be administered repeatedly. And while the vaccine-generated sales increment for the entire pharmaceutical industry during the Covid period was moderate, it would be significant if such vaccination campaigns were to be rolled out regularly.

The big pandemics of the past were caused by bacteria and by protozoa such as malaria. In rich countries they have been largely overcome, through sanitation, hygiene, and antibiotics. The WHO's pandemic preparedness program does not address bacterial diseases, it addresses diseases for which we have no effective treatment and for which no treatment is needed. The aim seems to be solely the creation of a huge revenue stream derived from 'vaccination' at the expense of the treated who get poisoned if nucleic-acids based 'vaccines' are used.

Secondly, it seems that we have witnessed an attempt to introduce a new digital biosecurity token, the digital 'vaccine' certificate, which allows states to control their populations' behavior and movements, accustomizing people to regular medical intrusions into their bodies.

In 1787, the English philosopher Jeremy Bentham proposed a 'panopticon' for the control of people in institutions such as prisons, hospitals, or factories which involves control over their perception, behavior, and bodies. The biosecurity certificate coupled with regular genetic interventions into the human body can be seen as a realization of this idea. The planners would like to turn our entire society into a panopticon. This explains why Russia, India, and China rapidly developed their own SARS-CoV-2 'vaccines': They wanted to be able to control the biomedical intervention coupled to the digital certificate themselves and not depend on Western products for this new instrument of state control.

The scheme of the WHO and other elite-driven institutions, of forcing everyone to accept the regular application of a somatic gene pharmaceutical product that has no benefit and causes vast and terrible harm, is fundamentally directed against the Christian-humanist idea of the autonomy and dignity of the individual. Once such a scheme is in place and operating, those enrolled into it lose control over their fate. They are no longer autonomous individuals, but modern slaves.

The pseudo-pandemic was a planned attempt to drive us into this form of biosecurity-control of our lives and to take away our civil liberties. Such a huge operation cannot evolve spontaneously. *There is strong evidence that the pseudo-pandemic was planned.* Only historians in future generations with access to all sources will be able to establish whether this is true and to say exactly who planned what, how and when.

While it's easy to spontaneously speak the truth, it's hard to systematically lie against overwhelming evidence. The evidence that SARS-CoV-2, even if it were engineered in laboratories, is a normal viral pathogen causing an upper respiratory tract infection, also known as the common cold, was overwhelming. Therefore, the entire Covid story was a system of blatant untruths. It required careful planning, funding, and execution to create, roll out, and maintain such a gigantic scam. The WHO's ongoing efforts to create an "International Treaty on Pandemic Prevention, Preparedness and Response" shows that the plan to introduce this new instrument of rule is still pursued by the global elites who fund and run the WHO.

HIV Hype

At the beginning of the 1980s, in a subgroup of homosexual patients suffering from a syndrome initially called 'Gay Related Immune Deficiency' and a bit later 'Acquired Immune Deficiency Syndrome' (AIDS), the French virologist and Nobel laureate Luc Montagnier discovered a virus that the CDC called 'Human Immune Deficiency Virus' (HIV).

The subgroup was characterized by very high promiscuity and drug abuse. Rapidly, the hypothesis was established that the HI-virus (scientific names: HIV-1 and HIV-2) causes AIDS as a pathogen in the sense defined by Robert Koch.

Based on this idea, a massive Fear Hype was created in the 1980s, huge public PR and education campaigns were launched, children from the age of thirteen had special HIV prevention lessons and a tangible mass Fear of HIV arose. Then, a Hope Hype was created as antiviral drugs to treat HIV infections were conceived and rapidly developed. Subsequently, they were prescribed billions of times and have been swallowed by millions of HIV-positive individuals over the last four decades. Only very few stubborn refuseniks among the HIV-positive in the Northern hemisphere refused to take them, and strangely, many of those did not develop AIDS.

Nevertheless, etiology, pathogenesis, diagnostic and therapy of HIV and AIDS have been regarded as firmly established medical knowledge since the 1980s. But according to an argumentative minority of scientists who criticize the HIV/AIDS hypothesis, this hypothesis is pseudoscientific and false. To many, this can only seem absurd at first blush, due to the firmly established majority view.

According to the mainstream view, HIV is a retrovirus transmitted via blood and is the pathogen causing AIDS. The latter is a syndrome with many symptoms and sub-syndromes. Its main characteristic is a deficiency of cellular immunity leading to infections with opportunistic pathogens that a healthy organism can always defeat. Furthermore, almost all forms of AIDS lead to dementia. A subgroup of patients also suffers from special forms of cancer, the Kaposi-sarcoma and lymphomas. The immune deficiency leads to death in the final stage of AIDS. Over the last forty years, four groups have been affected by AIDS:

1. **male homosexuals with a very high degree of promiscuity and intensive usage of psychoactive substances (50 to 65 percent of the HIV-positive patients in the USA and Europe),**

2. **drug-addicted persons with intravenous (i.v.) use of opioids or cocaine (30–50 percent of the above patient population.),**

3. **blood transfusion patients (1 percent) and children of HIV-infected mothers (1 percent), as well as**

4. **black Africans from regions with chronic mass famine—almost all pharmacologically untreated AIDS patients in Africa are severely malnourished.**

Heterosexual AIDS patients without intravenous drug abuse or viral transmission via blood transfusion or birth are and have practically always been absent in the USA and Europe; they play no epidemiological role.

The scientific consensus maintains the view that right after contagion via blood contact the HI-virus infects CD4-T-helper cells belonging to the cellular immune system. Thereafter, the immune system kills most of the infected cells and the virus disappears from the circulation, the patient becomes HIV-positive. *This means that the patient has IgG antibodies against the HI-virus.* The theory then states that the virus stays latent in CD4-cells and starts replicating again after a latency period of approximately ten years. This, the theory affirms, would lead to destruction of cellular immunity with the AIDS syndrome. And indeed the non-African AIDS patients show a CD4-cell-depletion upon the onset of AIDS which seems to explain the characteristics of the syndrome.

The Arguments of the Critics

What are the arguments of the critics who dispite all of this and are vilified as AIDS deniers by the mainstream media? They are also sometimes described as mentally ill by their colleagues (Kalichman 2014), a Lysenkoist procedure which we otherwise know from totalitarian societies like the Soviet Union and the German Democratic Republic.

The HIV-AIDS theory doesn't fulfil the modern version of the Koch postulates about the causation of infectious diseases by transmissible pathogens. A twenty-year-old scientific review by Duesberg, Koehnlein, and Rasnick that is scientifically still valid summarizes the arguments of the minority critics against the establishment view as follows:

1. The clinical syndromes of the various groups mentioned above differ so much that it seems wrong to classify all of them under one disease (scientifically speaking, one nosological) entity, AIDS.

    Only homosexuals develop the Kaposi sarcoma and lymphomas, while the other non-African groups share only the non-neoplastic (non-cancer) symptoms with the homosexual patients. The African patients only show a fraction of the AIDS symptoms, namely weight loss, tuberculosis and some other infectious diseases. Looking at the full epidemiological picture, we have not one nosological entity, but three: (1) a syndrome of highly promiscuous homosexuals and i.v. drug abusers; (2) a syndrome of the African famine population; and (3) a syndrome of the blood transfusion and gestation (children of AIDS patients) victims.

Thus HIV, unlike all other pathogens that function according to Koch's postulates, does not lead to one specific nosological entity.

2. After an acute infection which leads to a viremia (viruses in the bloodstream), the HI-virus is absent from the blood of an HIV-positive patient. This is even true for patients in the final stage of AIDS. During no phase of the disease after the initial infection is it possible to physically identify the virus in the blood. *Absurdly, the diagnostic criterion for HIV is the demonstration of immunity against the virus, and not the presence of the virus.*

3. There are multiple HIV-positive healthy humans who never develop AIDS. And conversely, many patients with AIDS-like syndromes lack anti-HIV antibodies. Together with the previous point (absence of virus), this is in direct contradiction to the first Koch postulate stating that the pathogen must always be associated with the disease and may not be found in healthy organisms.

4. The textbook theory that the virus destroys T-helper-cells of type CD4 (CD4-cells) has so far not been shown. In the acute phase, the vast majority of mucosal cells (skin that lines various cavities in the body) are depleted because T-killer cells destroy them as a part of the physiological immune reaction against HIV-infected cells. But the cell populations recover soon thereafter. During the full stage of AIDS, only one of 500 T-cells in the serum is HIV-infected. *The T-cell depletion observed in these patients must thus have another cause.*

5. There is no other known virus that can act as a pathogen after the formation of full immunity. In chronic hepatitis B, for example, there is no elimination of viral antigens in the liver, and thus no full immunity. Against HIV, all infected patients form full immunity. But AIDS only starts ten years after the initial infection. Yet the virus is only biologically active during the acute infection before full immunity is formed. Therefore, the hypothesis that HIV causes AIDS despite full immunity is not plausible. *So*

far, no convincing pathological mechanism supporting this mainstream hypothesis has been proposed.

6. Despite more than forty years of effort, there is no clinically effective vaccine against AIDS. Though it might be possible to create an efficient vaccine against HIV, this would have no clinical effect if HIV does not cause AIDS. Due to the epidemiologic properties of HIV as an opportunistic retrovirus, it would not be possible to prove the efficacy of a vaccine, because an infection cannot be generated for ethical reasons and the vaccinated and non-vaccinated would show no differences in their clinical outcomes (ceteris paribus—all variables being equal).

7. The epidemiologic properties of AIDS make it unlikely to be a disease caused by viral infection.

Looking at the full picture described by Duesberg, HIV is but an opportunistic retrovirus; he calls it a "passenger virus" which causes a robust immunity during the acute infection. It does not cause AIDS, but is replicated in the final stage of diseases which have a different causation—like Pneumocystis carinii, an opportunistic fungus which replicates in the lung of patients in the final stages of AIDS, but does not cause it.

Duesberg's view has one weakness: *It does not explain why at the beginning of the AIDS syndrome in HIV-positive individuals the viral load measured by quantitative PCR increases as the T-cells get depleted.* Isn't that a proof of the mainstream theory? What's going on here?

First, while the depletion in T-cells is explained by the virus-mediated destruction of these cells in the early stage, in later stages only one in five hundred peripheral lymphocytes contains the virus. Nevertheless, there is much more HIV-nucleic acid (viral RNA) in the blood in the initial stage than during the latency phase. The antiviral therapy is determined based on the measurement of this viral RNA. *But nobody knows where in the body these nucleic acids are synthesized.* It's certain that the virus must replicate more during the AIDS-phase than during the latency phase. But this does not happen in the blood. Newer hypotheses state that the replications occurs on the mucosae, but that cannot explain AIDS. It is much more plausible that HIV is replicated

Epidemiological Evidence Against the HIV/AIDS Theory

1. The clinical picture of AIDS is heterogeneous. The incidence of AIDS among HIV-positive subjects is 1 percent. This roughly corresponds to the general population mortality and is too low for a lethal viral disease.

2. The transmission likelihood upon unprotected sexual intercourse is under 1 per mil. Because in 2020, only one in a thousand Germans was HIV-positive, the likelihood of being infected upon such intercourse with a stranger sampled at random is lower than 1 in a million. Since 1985, the likelihood has always been in this order of magnitude. The number of HIV-positive persons in the USA has been constantly about 1 million since the late 1980s. There has never been a relevant population of HIV-positive prostitutes without i.v.-drug consumption. In contrast to Ebola or other viral diseases transmitted via the blood and body fluids, there have been no cases of infections of health care professionals caring for these patients. *After the acute phase, HIV-positive individuals are not contagious.* This explains the very low infection rate in heterosexuals. HIV neither causes an infection rate nor an infection dynamic that is characteristic of the epidemiology of contagious diseases. There is no general HIV epidemic or pandemic, but only a limited epidemic of highly promiscuous homosexuals and i.v. drug abusers

3. AIDS shows the temporary epidemiologic profile of a chemically induced disease such as lung cancer induced by smoking or the pleura mesothelioma caused by asbestos. Once the damaging chemical agent is reduced, the prevalence of the disease drops. We observe the same pattern with AIDS. Because the virostatics used for HIV treatment today are much less toxic (though as unnecessary) than the highly toxic azidothymidine (AZT) used in the 1980s, we have fewer AIDS casualties today among the treated patients than we had back then. But we still have treatment victims because the antivirals we give the HIV positive patients are still toxic. But it takes them much longer to kill a patient than it took AZT.

opportunistically at the end of the disease, because the immune system fails for another reason.

The AIDS-Pharma Victims

So Duesberg and other opponents of the HIV-AIDS hypothesis explain the AIDS syndrome by a chronic chemical damage to the immune system: in homosexuals and i.v. drug abusing prostitutes via the usage of psychoactive substances, in black Africans via chronic malnutrition, in HIV-positives treated with antivirals by the very drugs used to treat them. This means that non-treated HIV-positive individuals with a healthy lifestyle would never develop AIDS, *and that the treated acquire the syndrome from the treatment and not from the virus.*

Thus, the HIV-therapies are pharmacologically nonsensical, because there is no viral replication in clinically normal HIV-positive individuals who are deemed eligible for treatment with these drugs. Whereas during a streptococcal sepsis, for example, an adequate antibiotic can suppress the replication of the bacteria in the blood and the organs, there is no viral replication in healthy HIV-positive individuals that could be treated. The HIV-virus is a retrovirus which is hardly active. If it gets activated in CD4 cells, these are rapidly destroyed and replaced by new cells. The AIDS-syndromes we see are caused by chemical intoxication of or malnutrition damage to the immune system, the virus only starts replicating at the end of the process because of an immune deficiency caused by another agent, not itself.

Looking at this evidence from a distance, which is the task of scientists according to Max Weber, Duesberg's theory seems much more plausible than the HIV/AIDS hypothesis. It explains the epidemiology of both HIV and AIDS, both of which do not show the epidemiologic progression pattern of a classical pathogen in a classical epidemic. Duesberg and colleagues defined very clearly how clinical trials could easily refute the HIV/AIDS hypothesis in an ethically indisputable manner. Such trials would also validate the chemical origins of AIDS. But such trials are not conducted.

The entire HIV diagnostic and therapy schema is based on interpreting the immunity against HIV as a diagnostic criterion for an HIV infection, followed by a toxic therapy for symptom-free, healthy individuals.

Who are the victims? The weak members of our society: homosexuals with very high promiscuity living under precarious conditions, i.v. drug addicts or children of HIV-positive mothers, most of them i.v. drug-abusing prostitutes. Billions are made by giving these individuals a 'therapy' which slowly poisons them until they develop AIDS.

In the spirit of Hope Hype, this inhumane procedure is morally praised. Everyone knows the *red loop*, the symbol of solidarity with the AIDS victims. *But its real meaning is a pledge of allegiance to the poisoning of weak members of society for the benefit of the pharmaceutical industry.* The costs are paid by the contributors to the health insurance systems, the general working population.

Scientists like Duesberg, Kary Mullis, or Luc Montaignier, who have pointed out the inner inconsistency of the HIV/AIDS hypothesis, have been excluded from the scientific discourse and demonized as 'HIV/AIDS denialists'. This is the new Lysenkoism that was initiated in the mid-1980s, when Anthony Fauci pushed Duesberg and those sharing his views out of science funding and means of publication, as Kennedy reports in his book about Fauci.

While HIV never affected more than a minority, because the virus does not lead to an epidemic, with SARS-CoV-2, Fauci, Drosten, and many other anti-rational pseudo-scientists have now established a pseudo-scientific, Lysenkoist narrative to regularly 'treat' the entire population with toxic drugs. This is not medicine or public health, this is mass control and exploitation, willingly accepting harm to millions.

De-Hyping Medicine?

As Ravetz and Illic demonstrated in the early 1970s, science and medicine have become part of a politico-economic complex that has changed their motivations and methods. The main driver of scientific progress in physics, mathematics, biology, engineering, medicine, and the other sciences from the middle of the seventeenth century to the 1920s, was the adequate modeling of reality, to discover knowledge and technical applications based on it. This was also in the interest of those who financed science, most of this period the European princes and, from the nineteenth century onwards, also the bourgeoisie and their institutions. But this began to change with the emergence of eugenics after the end of the nineteenth century. The twentieth century witnessed the increasing employment of science in the interests of huge corporations and their owners. During the last hundred years, the sciences became more like the humanities—which never did produce knowledge in the way that the positive sciences and mathematics did, but always tended to produce combinations of evidence and ideology in the interest of the rulers.

It is in this context that we need to understand the pseudoscience around SARS-CoV-2. This anti-science did not come out of the blue. It is part of a long tradition in biology and medicine going back to nineteenth-century phrenology, racial theory, and eugenics. But while most of the output of medical research until the early 1980s contributed to progress in pharmacology, surgery, and clinical medicine, a paradigm change occurred in cancer therapy after the 1960s and in the treatment of infectious diseases after the 1980s.

Medical Hype prevents rational treatment and leads to damaging overtreatment in core medical disciplines. Very often, patients are given treatments which are unnecessary or harmful. With SARS-CoV-2 and HIV, we have analyzed the most important examples of pseudo-medical narratives of our time. During the pseudo-pandemic, we saw that, with very few exceptions, the entire medical establishment was demoralized and accustomed itself to prescribing or delivering therapies that are not medicines, but toxins.

We must de-Hype medicine, but as in 1517, when Luther asked for a reform of the Church, parts of the medical-industrial complex will oppose a reform, because they were involved in the crimes we have been witnessing.

6

Quantum Hype

If you think you understand quantum mechanics, then you don't.

—RICHARD FEYNMAN

Quantum Hype is mostly Hope Hype with only a small Fear Hype element in it. What's this Hype about?

The promises made by physicists and lay journalists are colossal. Quantum Hype is focused on engineering maanchines that employ principles of quantum physics in their functionality. Well-known examples are the laser and NMR (nuclear magnetic resonance) machines used to visualize structures of material, for example in medical imaging (MRI, magnetic resonance imaging).

The main fields for quantum devices are research and development in quantum sensors, quantum communication, quantum simulators, and quantum computers. Most of the Hype we currently experience deals with quantum computers and quantum communication.

We're promised that quantum computers and simulators will revolutionize artificial intelligence, batteries, fertilization, cybersecurity, drug development, electronic materials discovery, financial modeling, solar capture, traffic optimization, weather forecasting and climate modeling.

What do these topics have in common? They're linked to other Hype stories (such as AI or climate change), or they deal with topics that are currently in vogue. But more importantly, they have in common that most of them are actually unrelated to quantum engineering.

The Hype gets even more extravagant. In his new book, Michio Kaku, a theoretical physicist known for his series of popular science books, predicts that by 2050, quantum devices will have cured cancer, enabled nuclear fusion, and turned space trips to the Moon into mass tourism. He also writes about quantum computers solving questions such as the origin of life, climate change, curing aging, and other Hype topics without revealing *how* quantum computers will pull off these neat little tricks. In other words, Kaku presents quantum computing in the way medieval alchemists talked about the Holy Grail or nineteenth-century medical charlatans presented their panacea, the medicine supposed to heal everything, usually a kind of juice they were selling to settlers from their wagons.

The more recent promises for the combination of quantum computing and communication made by public science founding institutions are also vastly inflated. The EU's 'Quantum Flagship' tells us that a 'Quantum Web' will have the following properties:

> Quantum computers, simulators and sensors interconnected via quantum networks distributing information and quantum resources such as coherence and entanglement. On the corresponding timescale—which is in fact longer than ten years—the performance increase resulting from Quantum Technologies will yield unprecedented computing power, guarantee data privacy and communication security, and provide ultra-high precision synchronization and measurements for a range of applications available to everyone locally and in the cloud. (www.qt.eu, 2023)

This type of Hope Hype is in line with today's exaggerated and unrealistic expectations towards science. So far, this is pure Hope Hype, but there's also a small dollop of Fear Hype: The so-called 'quantum arms race' with China. For example, the MIT Review told its readers in 2019 that the West is in a race against China to develop quantum-based defense systems such as the 'quantum radar' that is supposed to detect 'stealth' airplanes protected from conventional radar detection. There is a competition here, but so far this arms race is far away from any real warfare applications. With many such ideas, it's unclear whether they can ever be feasible at all.

Certainly, the US race with Russia and China in conventional warfare should concern policy makers much more: The West has fallen behind Russia in the domains of air defense and hypersonic guided missile technology, and this shows on the battlefield. Fear Hype, as in other fields, is used to drum up anxiety among policy makers or investors in order to get public funding or venture capital investments into quantum startups. In the domain of quantum engineering, there isn't much substance to the Hype claims.

There is still a lot to gain from quantum physics applications in engineering. But it is a slow and demanding process. As I will prove to you, almost all of the Hype lacks substance and is truly unwarranted.

Consequences of the Hype

Currently, Quantum Hype is leading to massive private and public spending on the various ideas for quantum devices. A proportion of the investments into quantum sensors will pay off because the technology has been proven and can realistically be developed. Given the current Hype, the overall return on investment into quantum technology might not be that high, but once the Hype cools off, investments will be more careful and realistic, so that a reasonable equilibrium of investment and return may evolve.

However, the massive Hype around quantum computers and large-scale quantum communication is driving investments which are not likely to pay off at all. This may lead to a collective realization that the goals cannot be achieved, and subsequently to a bursting of the quantum bubble. When this will occur is hard to predict, but overheated fields that do not deliver on the promises made by their protagonists have regularly crashed in history.

Historians will look back and explain what was going on. But let's try to understand the causes of the Quantum Hype from today's perspective.

Reasons for the Hype in Our Scientific Culture

Since its inception, quantum mechanics and its later refinements, such as quantum electrodynamics, group theory, and quantum field theory have always been surrounded by a nimbus of awe and admiration. This is due to the strange properties of quantum particles, such as the wave-particle dualism, or the paradoxes of quantum mechanics, such as entanglement or non-locality, which have puzzled and fascinated physicists and laymen alike. There are two reason for this.

1. **The experimental observations and mathematical models we develop based on the quantum phenomena contradict our classical common-sense view of the world. What we experience in our daily lives seems intuitively incompatible with the quantum models of nature. This makes them fascinating and creates special expectations.**

2. **Among scientists and even more so the lay public, there is a huge over-estimation of our ability to rationally understand nature and manipulate it using technology, an outlook that can be summarized as 'scientism'.**

Modern Physics and the Natural World

Arnold Gehlen describes man as an instinct-deficient animal. This means that to cope with our environment and to guide our behavior, we need our cognitive capabilities and, above all, socialization and the culture resulting from it. Socialization is the process of learning the behavioral patterns that dominate the community socializing the individual.

The foundational capability enabling socialization is intersubjectivity, the innate ability of humans to understand the intentions of the other human with whom they communicate. Socialization leads to the acquisition of behavioral patterns and social norms, and later on to theories that enable individuals to interpret the world and react appropriately to it.

As described by the anthropologist Robin Horton, human beings use two distinct methods of cognitive coping with the natural and social environment: Primary and secondary theory. Primary theory enables us to cope with the basic needs of survival and reproduction in the horizon of reality given to us by experience of our complex environment. Primary theory is the foundation of the planning of survival by making sure we have access to edible food, drinkable water, shelter, and clothing. It also prevents us from putting ourselves into dangerous or threatening situations.

Horton argues that primary theory is shared by all cultures and comprises the fundamental patterns of individual and social human behavior. The anthropologist and human ethologist (behavior specialist) Eibl-Eibesfeldt draws a similar picture of fundamental human behavioral patterns observed in primitive and modern societies alike. He identified these patterns by careful observation and comparison of human behavior in various geographically unrelated primitive cultures. Primary theory roughly corresponds to what is called the common-sense view of the world, but it is more stable: Common sense is less directly linked to survival than primary theory and therefore changes during the evolution of cultures. It is also influenced by and linked to secondary theory.

Secondary theory is the theory that humans use to explain what they observe and experience, such as storm and thunder, the motions of the planets, the daily, monthly and annual rhythms of nature, and the existence of the world. It is highly culture-specific. In primitive cultures, we observe totemism and other mystic religions in which the acts of deities are used to explain nature and society. In the most primitive cultures, the deities are embodied in animals or inanimate entities, such as trees, water sources, lakes, or stones.

In the first urbanized cultures, gods are still the major content of secondary theory, but they are now imagined in a transcendent beyond. At this point, Hellenistic culture started to develop rational scientific enquiry as a new method to obtain a secondary theory. The next step is the development of monotheism, in which humans related only to one God, the creator of the world and conceived in the image of the faithful. This relationship with God provides the faithful with a satisfying explanation of the world and their lives. Such a view is coupled with the promise of eternal life after death and many other dogmatic teachings which provide an interpretation of the experienced world.

As the evolution of science progresses, the technically most advanced cultures with the highest level of social differentiation and individualization give up God as the main content of secondary theory altogether and use science to explain the world and develop secular humanities to interpret it.

Classical physics is tightly connected to primary theory: Most of the systems and system elements it considers can be experienced with the raw senses or visualized easily, such as electro-magnetism. Magnitudes such as mass, velocity, acceleration, or force occur in the three-dimensional space we experience in linear time. Its mathematical models can be formulated in a very abstract and intellectually demanding manner (such as the Lagrangian or Hamiltonian mathematical description of classical physics), but they can be imagined in the way we experience our environment with our senses.

However, modern physics, which began to emerge around 1900, is incompatible with our natural experience of the world. Its models are created using differential geometry and functional analysis, which are both advanced mathematical topics for graduate student. The entities used in these models cannot be imagined with our natural understanding of the experienced world, but only through mathematical abstract thinking. For example, we don't understand and can't imagine the magnitudes we measure in quantum physics. Our models describe something we can't imagine. *We merely form mathematical analogies of what we measure.* Physicist themselves can only think in terms of the mathematics of the phenomena they measure with complicated machines. Quantum phenomena such as entanglement, non-locality of effects, or superposition are incompatible with the way we experience the world with our senses.

But because the mathematical models of quantum physics allow accurate predictions, they have enabled many new technologies described in this chapter, including the atomic clock, the MRI, magnetic field detectors or the laser. This and the mysteriousness of quantum mechanics have led the general public to expect huge further advances from quantum science in the near future. This expectation is, as we have seen, unwarranted.

Scientism

For Descartes, the world consists of matter and brains that create knowledge from the observable matter by processing reality and giving it a mathematical order. In England, this view merged with empiricism, the idea that only sensory experience can lead to knowledge. In the nineteenth century, it further evolved into positivism. It then radicalized as scientism, which remains the dominant view among scientists and the lay public—only science can give us an understanding of the world. As Williams (2014) summarizes, scientism has several other characteristics:

- **The world is structured in such a way that only positive knowledge has validity, and that can be obtained from and about every aspect of the world.**

- **A certain scientific method, inductivism, is the exclusive path to positive knowledge.**

- **The methods of physics are appropriate to all domains of the world and can be used by all sciences, including the humanities, a position first articulated by Auguste Comte, the father of positivism. He called sociology 'social physics' and planned to formulate it using mathematical equations.**

- **The world is structured the way the methods of physics assume it to be.**

- **There is no transcendence, no a priori entities (essence) or relations between them (essential structures), no metaphysics: Metaphysics is just physics.**

- **The role of science is to explain the world in a way that enables interventions into it that improve it for humans.**

- **All problems we encounter are of a mechanical nature and can be resolved by intervening in the causal relationships by which the world is governed.**

The most important argument against this position is, first, that scientism itself is based on a specific metaphysical view of the world, namely that it is made of matter and that all the events taking place in it are caused by the interactions of particles. This view, *empirical materialism*, competes with two other fundamental metaphysical frameworks: *idealism*, which states that the world we experience in our consciousness is a product of the human mind, and *skepticism*, which rejects the idea of knowledge altogether.

From a metaphysical perspective, none of these positions has eidetic (truth-level) superiority to the other, because they all need axioms that cannot be grounded any further. Which one is used is a matter of choice, and the dominating choice that depends on the culture of a society. We cannot know which view is really true. Modern science is convincing due to the technology it enables, but that does not make its metaphysical assumptions true.

Further, scientism can be criticized because its rejection of metaphysics removes our ability to interpret the world and creates an inadequate view of human beings by negating their essence. It is therefore morally damaging and cannot provide a foundation for a flourishing life.

Even within physics, this view has many inconsistencies, the worst being that we do not, to the major discontent of physicists, know which type of particle mediates gravitation. The standard theory of matter, the quantum field theory, has many more issues (see Freeborn et al. 2022).

These arguments are certainly correct, but the most important argument is the following: Even if we assume that the materialist view of the world is correct and consistent, the assumption that all systems of nature can be modeled, which means: described or explained, mathematically, is plainly and obviously wrong. From thermodynamics and statistical mechanics, which was discovered by Ludwig Boltzmann, we know that we can only mathematically model certain types of systems with multiple particles. They're called logic systems and I have said something more about them in Chapter 1.

We have already seen that all mathematical models treat all systems as logic systems. If a natural system, like the solar system seen as a gravitational system, can be modeled adequately as a logic system, the model will be of very high explanatory and predictive quality. But if a complex system that deviates significantly from a logic system is mathematically modeled, information is lost and the model has a low descriptive and explanatory value.

For example, the weather system is highly complex. Therefore, weather models only have local and short-term predictive value. Overall, only a small fraction of animate and inanimate natural systems can be seen as logic systems without losing too much information about them. Examples are the solar system and many other mechanical systems, including biological systems such as human anatomical subsystems.

Thus, we can only model a tiny fraction of natural systems, or small parts of them, as logic systems, because most systems are too complex to allow high-quality mathematical models of their totality. Scientism, however, asserts that empirical observation leading to induction, which is the formulation of laws based on observation using mathematics, can be extended to the entire universe. That, however, is wrong. *This is the main reason why scientism is wrong even if we swallow the materialist view of the world.*

We have seen that a misinterpretation of the role and function of science is at the heart of scientism. But the problem goes further, we are witnessing an erosion of science in the West.

The Problems with Quantum Computers

Right from the get-go we need to understand that so far, there is no physical universal quantum computer of the type that David Deutsch defined in 1985. No quantum computer can factor 15 into its two prime factors 3 and 5, and neither can any quantum device calculate 3 x 5 = 15 or 3+5 = 8. There are, as we shall see, quantum annealers, but these are not universal computing machines (Turing machines) like the classical digital computers we have. So far, quantum computers are a purely hypothetical idea, and any proposition to build them so far, should be preceded by Rolf Landauer's words from 1996:

> This scheme, like all other schemes for quantum computation, relies on speculative technology, or does not in its current form take into account all possible sources of noise, unreliability and manufacturing error, and probably will not work.

To understand why Quantum Computer Hype is unwarranted, we need to understand how quantum computers are supposed to work. But before that, let's mention some important theoretical results about them:

1. **The only advantage of quantum computers over classical computers would be the potential speeding up of the computations. The set of problems that can be computed with a quantum computer is the same as that of a conventional computer. The Church-Turing-thesis which delimits what a machine can compute is also valid for quantum computers.**

2. **For every calculation where a quantum computer would be faster than a classical computer, the classical computer can calculate the same task in more time. There can be no 'quantum hypercomputation' allowing us to compute algorithms that are not computable on a classical computer.**

3. **Due to the way quantum computers are designed, the scope of problems for which they can provide relevant speeding up is small. For many algorithms, including the computations required for statistical learning (so called artificial intelligence), it is clear that the theoretical acceleration would be eaten up by the hardware requirements for error correction (see below) so that there is no net gain.**

Computers as Modeling Tools

Quantum computers would not fundamentally change what we can compute. Unlike technical systems we can build, most systems in animate and inanimate nature cannot be mathematically modeled holistically; this limits what we can compute. As we see in several other chapters of this book, this limitation of science is poorly understood today and not taken into account when making up Hype stories.

We've seen that computers are merely tools to run mathematical models of the world (or of pure mathematics), which are called algorithms. This creates essential limitations. First, only a fraction of all possible mathematical algorithms are computable and can run on a computer (a universal Turing machine). Secondly, the mathematical models we can run on Turing machines map the systems we wish to model to logic systems.

In the context of quantum computing, the consequence is that when we model a natural, complex system by mapping it to a logic system model, we lose some of the richness of the real system in the mapping process. This limits the model's ability to explain what's going on in the system and also our ability to make predictions using the model. The quantum computer does not enable us to compute any more models than the classical computer can. In theory, and under certain circumstances, the quantum computer can do it faster. Let's look at some examples.

A good example of a natural system that can be modeled as a logic system is the solar system as a system of gravitation. Historically, it was the first natural system modeled with mathematics, and it drove Newton and Leibniz to invent calculus. The model is very exact, it can calculate the orbits of the planets, eclipses of the moon and the sun and many more celestial phenomena. But some of the details of the motions of the planets get lost in the model. For example, the Earth does not orbit the Sun on a perfect ellipse, but it slightly wobbles on its trajectory due to the gravitation from the Earth's neighboring planets, Venus and Mars.

Nevertheless, the logic system approximation of the natural complex system is very good in this case. We can build an orrery (a mechanical model of the solar system) that tracks the movements of the planets really well, and we can create excellent computer simulations of the system. Such models which can emulate the entire behavior of natural systems are called synoptic.

But most other natural systems are very complex and do not allow synoptic models. For example, it is not possible to obtain a synoptic model of a living organism; if we could do that, we could make living organisms out of dead matter. Our models of the function of living cells and the molecules that they are made of are only very partial. These organisms are systematically beyond our modeling capabilities, and they have all the properties of complex systems that prevent synoptic mathematical modeling.

Quantum computers will not change this in any way, because they can only run the same algorithms that classical computers can. Therefore, it is nonsensical to say that quantum computers can improve climate models, cure cancer, understand the origins of life, solve climate change, or cure aging. All of these problems are complex-system problems which we understand only to a very partial extent. *That has nothing to do with the computational speed of computers, but with the essential limitation of our ability to model complex systems.*

Quantum computers will make no difference at all to this, and we shall soon see that the range of problems for which they can potentially be applied to beat classical computers on the basis of speed is quite narrow.

Quantum Computing Speedups

There are two types of quantum computing speedups: polynomial and exponential. A *polynomial speedup* means that the computation time of a classical computer is accelerated by a polynomial operator, for example if the classical computer takes N computation steps, the quantum computer would only need $\sqrt{N}$ steps. For example, this would be $\sqrt{2^{20}} = 1,024$ instead of $2^{20} = 1,048,576$ steps, a factor of 1,024. *Exponential acceleration* means that when a classical computer takes 2^N computation steps, the quantum computer would only need N, for example 20 steps instead of 2^{20} (over a million) steps, which is a factor of 50,000, which would be very impressive.

A classical computer works with registers, which are arrays of bits to which the computational operations are applied. Quantum computers would also have registers made of so-called qubits.

Because of the error-prone way in which a qubit works, for each logical unit in its processing register, an overhead of at least 1,000 to 100,000 physical qubits per logical qubit would be needed to correct the physical qubit error. This means that the polynomial acceleration will be eaten away in almost all cases by the necessity to use a large overhead of physical qubits.

It follows that only *exponential accelerations* are practically relevant for quantum computing. But it turns out that there are only a few algorithms for which such an acceleration can be obtained using quantum computers. Currently, mathematicians working on the problem of quantum computing think that the problems amenable to exponential quantum acceleration require a hidden special structure within the problems called Abelian group structure (after the great algebraist Abel). The most famous examples of this are the algorithms for finding the prime factors of an integer and the discrete logarithm problem, both theoretically solved by Shor (1994). It's still not known whether the discrete logarithm can be computed in polynomial time on a classical computer, in which case the exponential speedup by quantum computers would become irrelevant.

The factoring problem is highly relevant for cryptography. If the Shor algorithm could be realized on sufficiently big, fully fault-tolerant quantum computers (with at least a thousand logical qubits), that would revolutionize cryptography and make today's internet security obsolete. There are also more recent examples of exponential quantum speedups, such as the problem described by Yamakawa and Zhandry. But like the Shor algorithm its realization requires a big fault-tolerant quantum computer. Some specialists think that such a computer can never be built.

Some non-Abelian group structure problems might also allow exponential acceleration, but there has been very little progress in this field. A candidate is the graph isomorphism problem which is about determining whether two graph structures (nodes and connecting edges such as a circuit connecting elements) are structurally related in a special way.

But whenever we have less structure in the problems the algorithms are supposed to solve, we can only obtain polynomial speedups, and then the quantum computer provides no net acceleration.

Quantum Supremacy

For a certain class of problems, quantum supremacy, the ability of a quantum computer to solve a problem that a classical computer cannot solve in a feasible amount of time, has been demonstrated without fault-tolerant quantum computing. This is a type of sampling problem in which a non-fault tolerant quantum computer is used to create a random distribution. A classical computer needs much more time to do this. However, this is a rather primitive problem, because it merely shows that a quantum computer is better at generating a random distribution. More importantly, the main problem with quantum computers, the errors they generate, does not have to be taken into account in this setting. However, the errors have to be corrected in all other settings.

Quantum Computers and AI

One of the computational practical problems currently devouring the most resources is machine learning for so-called AI solutions. Quantum computers are still Hyped with regard to AI applications. Until 2018, it was thought that for some problems in machine learning, the quantum computer would be exponentially faster than the classical computer. But then it was discovered that with new algorithms, classical computers could solve the same problems in only polynomially slower time than quantum computers, thus removing the Hyped 'quantum advantage' again. Overall, there do not remain many domains in which quantum computers would be superior to classical computers.

How Quantum Computers Are Supposed to Work

A classical computer is made of registers, which are arrays of bits. Logic gates are the smallest units of the logic circuits that manipulate the bits to perform Boolean functions such as land (AND) or (OR). They can be put together in circuits that perform elementary calculations such as addition or data manipulation such as multiplexing (data selection and forwarding). Many such circuits form a microprocessor, which is the core component of universal digital computers. Such computers can compute any Turing-computable function.

At the beginning of the 1980s, Richard Feynman and Yuri Manin independently proposed the idea of quantum computers. Shortly thereafter, David Deutsch proposed a formal definition of the quantum computer as a universal Turing machine. Instead of bits, it was supposed to use qubits, which are thought of as the smallest register unit of a quantum computer. He defined a quantum computer as a set of N qubits forming a register enabling each of the following operations:

1. Each qubit can be prepared to be in a basic state $|0\rangle$, which is a quantum state we will discuss below.

2. Each qubit can be measured in a basis $\{|0\rangle, |1\rangle\}$.

3. A set of gates enabling universal computation can be applied to any register of a fixed size.

4. The qubits only change their state by the above operations, not spontaneously.

A quantum computation is supposed to apply a series of gate operations to the register, before a measurement is performed. The gain in computational efficiency is based on the superposition of states of the qubits and possibly on the entanglement of the qubits of the register. Superposition means that a non-measured qubit is not in one state, but its state is the combination of its two base states.

Entanglement means that the qubits contribute to the wave function with 2^N continuous parameters together. These two properties of the qubits and how they interact via entanglement enable the theoretical computational superiority of quantum computers.

Wave Function of Qubits and Entanglement

To use a quantum particle as a qubit, you need to choose a property of the particle which can be measured and modeled using two independent basis states, which are defined in a Hilbert space, a special mathematical coordinate system.

For example, if the spin, a quantum property of particles, of an electron is used to create a qubit, when we measure the spin, we can only have a value of +1/2 or -1/2 on any axis. We can now choose one axis arbitrarily, for example the z-axis, and define the two possible values of the spin as the quantum states $|0\rangle$ and $|1\rangle$. Then, the general (unmeasured) state of the electron is defined as a wave function, which is a combination of the two basis states, $\Psi = \alpha\,|0\rangle + \beta\,|1\rangle$, where the two complex numbers a and b are the so-called quantum amplitudes that satisfy the condition $|a|^2 + |b|^2 = 1$. This unmeasured state is also called *superposition* state.

This practically means that an unmeasured qubit does not have two possible values like a bit, which can only take on the values off (0) and on (1), but an infinite number of values. Therefore, a quantum register with N qubits has an infinite number of states described by 2^N complex parameters. In contrast, a classical system with two-state objects, like the classical computers, has 2^N discrete states. As Dyakonov points out, even a system of N classical analogue pointers, each like a needle mounted at the center of a sphere that can point at any direction on the sphere, has only $2N$ continuous parameters, two polar angles for each pointer—and not 2^N like the quantum register with N qubits.

Entanglement is a quantum property in which two or more particles share a quantum state. For example, using one high energy photon (a light particle), one can make two entangled photons of opposite spin. If one then separates the particles and measures the spin of one of them, the other will have the opposite spin even if it is far away from the measured photon. Entanglement can be used for various quantum engineering applications.

We know that to compute anything useful with a quantum computer, we need at least 1,000 qubits. Therefore, if we want to perform computations on such a register, we need to exactly control $2^{1,000}$ continuous parameters. In contrast, an analogue pointer based machine with 1,000 pointers would only require us to control 2,000 continuous parameters. *What is the relationship between a quantum computer and a classical computer?* At the classical limit, the quantum computer is not a classical computer, but an analogous computer, with 2,000 continuous parameters for 1,000 analogue bits (which can be imagined like rotating needles, but with different properties). Therefore, it is exponentially more difficult to control a quantum computer than a classical analogue computer. Is this feasible?

Errors in Quantum Computers

Qubits are not very stable. A system that is not actively manipulated tends to enter into a thermodynamic equilibrium with its environment. For example, a cup of tea cools down to room temperature if it is left on its own. This is called relaxation. The relaxation time is the characteristic time in which a system exponentially reaches its stationary state, which would be room temperature for the cup of tea. For the spin of electrons, the relaxation time is in the nanoseconds. Noise, fluctuations and imprecisions in the manipulations of the register with the quantum gates upset the stability of the quantum register, which is a quantum wave over N qubits. Furthermore, the measurements of the computation results can be erroneous. Therefore, it is accepted that a quantum computer can only be realized with error correction.

The idea used for such corrections is to encode a logical qubit by 1,000 to 100,000 physical qubits. So now, we would not need a thousand qubits for a useful quantum computer, but a million (10^6) to a billion (10^9). The mathematical threshold theorem states that under certain axiomatic assumptions, a quantum computer can be built that can bring the error rate below the decoherence, noise, and fluctuation rates so that the machine can compute as long as needed or store the state of a qubit (or the register) forever. Dyakonov summarises:

- **a register of qubits can be initiated to the state l0000 . . . 00⟩,**

- **the noise in the register, the gates and the measurements is not correlated in time and space,**

- **the gates have no undesired effects,**

- **there are no systematic errors in the operation of the gates, the measurement, or the preparation of the qubits,**

- **no intra-register interactions between the qubits,**

- **no leakage occurs, and**

- **all manipulations can be performed on the register in parallel.**

But in the physical world, continuous quantities cannot be manipulated or measured exactly, so that the above assumptions do not hold for analogue computers, a classical analogy of quantum computers. Only discrete quantities, like the bits in the register of a classical computer or its magnetic storage device, can be manipulated exactly. But it's not possible to set all the qubits in the register exactly to the base state $|0\rangle$? The wave function of a quantum computer with 1,000 qubits has at least $2^{1,000} = 100^{300}$, continuous parameters which change due to the operations performed on them. No one has ever conceived how one can protect a wave function with 100^{300} parameters from an evolution into an undesired state.

Now how exactly do we need to fulfil the assumptions of the threshold theorem so that we can indeed correct the quantum register? We do not know, but we know that we can neither set the qubits exactly to state $|0\rangle$ (all states contain mixtures where even if a is close to one, b is not null in the equation $\Psi = \alpha\,|0\rangle + \beta\,|1\rangle$) nor can we make a measurement exactly along one axis. Small errors in the initialization of the register or its manipulation via the quantum gates will lead to an exponential increase of the error with time, a property of dynamical systems described by the Lyapunov exponent. This parameter describes the exponential rate of separation of two trajectories infinitesimally close to each other at the beginning of time series. Furthermore, the error correction theory does not take into account that while measurements needed to perform quantum correction are done, the qubits continue to evolve, so that they will be in a different state when we try to apply the correction. The correction models assume discrete action times of the gates, but that would mean the gates operate infinitely fast.

Will There Ever Be a Fault-Tolerant Quantum Computer?

Given all these difficulties, quantum computation skeptics like Rober Alicki, Serge Haroche, J.-M. Raymond, Gerard t'Hooft, Sukash Kak, Gil Kalai, Rolf Landauer, Robert Laughlin, Leonid Levin, Stephen Wolfram and Mihkail Dyakonov argue that we will never have a fault-tolerant, practically useful universal quantum computer. In addition to the problems explained in the previous section, Dyakonov lists more. The qubits making up the quantum computer's register have energy which is subjected to magnetic fields, even if these are tiny. These fields lead to a spontaneous evolution of the state of each qubit. For example, if the qubit uses spin, this will precess over time in the plane perpendicular to the magnetic field like a spinning top that moves on a table. With N qubits, the system will show dynamics of the wave harmonics of the frequency. But because the field is not homogeneous and there will be electromagnetic interaction between the qubits, the system will show a chaotic wave function over time. Overall, a quantum computer is not a logic (linear) system. Not only does it consist of its (at least 1,000) qubits, but also of the gate-operation and measurement performing classical apparatus. In quantum computing theory, the gate operations and the measurements are strictly linear, which they are not in practice. Dyakonov concludes: *"Thus the whole machine is a huge and strongly non-linear construction which generally will exhibit instabilities and chaotic behavior."*

It's inconceivable how such a machine could be constructed and run in controlled fashion. So the Hype around quantum computing and the revolutions it is supposed to bring is unjustified. What about the other Hype stories we hear about quantum computing?

Quantum Annealing and Simulation

Quantum annealing is an application of quantum physics to solve certain optimization problems. A famous example for this is the traveling salesman problem in which a salesman must determine the best path to visiting various destinations in one trip. Such problems are called discrete combinatorial because they consist of many combinations of non-continuous elements, like the destinations of the salesman. They usually have many different suboptimal solutions called local minima. Quantum annealing works by slowly moving a quantum system from one register state into another, where the second state is supposed to encode the solution to a combinatorial problem (The technically interested reader should refer to Hauke et al. 2020, and the literature cited therein.)

The idea is to formulate the problem in a certain manner that allows it to be solved in such a way that an optimal energetic state in which the system settles corresponds to the solution of the system. This is possible because discrete combinatorial problems can be formulated as energy matrices, Hamiltonians, which are mathematical tables of numbers expressing the way a system changes its energy state over time. In other words, the problem is formulated in the form of a Hamiltonian. The quantum annealer can then be built and configured as a physical model of the Hamiltonian. During the annealing process, it settles into an energetic optimum that is a model of the solution and can be translated back into numbers expressing the solution to the original problem.

There is, and this very important, a way to calculate annealing to find energetic optima using annealing simulation on classical computers. *Have we already won anything using commercially available quantum annealing devices against the conventional approach?* Currently, it does not look like it. Why?

First of all, repeated experiments on quantum annealers show that they are very biased towards certain optima, the distribution of optima they produce is biased towards certain solutions. Classical simulation produces much less bias, and thus better solution distributions.

Secondly, so far, benchmark experiments measuring search performance have not shown a relevant acceleration of solution search using quantum annealers.

Quantum simulators are quantum devices designed to simulate quantum physical phenomena which are hard or impossible to compute effectively due to the number of particles involved in the system of interest—the famous Schrödinger equation can only be applied to systems with very few particles. They are of high scientific interest, but are still in their early infancy; nevertheless, they are likely to contribute to a better understanding of certain quantum phenomena, such as problems in low-temperature physics.

So while quantum annealer devices are promising for the (rather narrow) field of discrete combinatorial optimization and quantum simulators are relevant for special questions in physics, neither of them is the universal quantum computer that Deutsch has described nor are they currently outperforming simulations on classical computers. Certainly, they do not justify any Hype, but are typical examples of the tedious and thorny paths which scientists have to follow in order to advance science in a dedicated, often frustrating life-work full of discipline with rare rewards.

Quantum Sensing

According to Degen and co-workers, Quantum sensing "describes the use of a quantum system, quantum properties, or quantum phenomena to perform a measurement of a physical quantity". A well-known example of this technology is nuclear magnetic resonance. Quantum sensing encompasses the usage of quantum coherence to measure a physical quantity. This means that the particles used for quantum sensing are in a state of superposition, so that the actual state is a combination of the basic states. It is also defined as the "usage of quantum entanglement to improve the sensitivity or precision of a measurement, beyond what is possible classically."

Quantum sensors are devices using quantum sensing. The technology uses a quantum property of particles, called spin. A magnetic field is used to measure energy differences between spin-states of atoms via resonance frequencies. All of these conditions can be fulfilled. Indeed, quantum sensors are already used very successfully. Atomic vapors and SQUIDs (superconducting quantum interference devices) are already in routine usage. Currently, they are the most sensitive magnetic field detectors. Atomic clocks, which are also quantum sensors, have become the optimal tools for the generation of frequencies and the measurement of time.

Because quantum sensors do not need to maintain highly complex states involving at least 2^{1000} parameters like quantum computers, but are much simpler systems from an engineering perspective, progress in this area will continue and is highly likely to lead to both high-end and consumer-device applications. But progress here will be gradual and very often not directly visible to the general public. Quantum sensors are highly useful, but they certainly do not warrant any Hype.

Quantum Communication

Quantum communication is the idea of using the quantum properties of particles as a means of communication. In quantum communication, qubits would be sent over a network of communication nodes. Quantum communication uses quantum entanglement to propagate information. In theory, quantum communication is very safe because quantum encryption is almost unbreakable. In practice, quantum communication would be using a quantum network. Small experimental quantum networks exist. They consist of quantum nodes, quantum wires, and optical switches. Networks with practical value would also require quantum repeaters to enable communication over long distances. The nodes generate quantum light (photon) signals which are to be transmitted over the network. They also receive signals from other nodes. The wires are used to transport the photons encoding qubits can be made of optical fiber. Vacuum tubes could also be used in theory. In such a network, optical switches are needed to channel the qubits to their destination node.

So far, quantum networks are experimental and small since there are no quantum repeaters (they are so far only a theoretical idea) and it is not possible to transport qubits over long distance due to decoherence, which means that the qubits lose their superposition or entanglement properties. In the absence of quantum repeaters, quantum networks have no practical use since the distances they can cover before decoherence occurs are too short (in the hundreds of miles only).

Today's experimental quantum networks use light beamsplitters and photodetectors to send and receive qubits in the form of photons, and this suffices to prove that rudimentary quantum communication in the sense of sending information using quantum devices is possible. But to make the communication meaningful and practically useful, at least small quantum computers would have to be used as nodes. However, as we have seen, we have no reliable quantum computers nor are any in sight.

Because we do not yet have quantum repeaters, and because it is still unclear how we can realize useful quantum network nodes, quantum communication or a 'quantum internet' are still science fiction today. It's likely that for limited secure communication purpose, simple quantum networks will be realized. But again, we should not expect anything spectacular; it will be a very complicated and demanding long-term effort proceeding in tiny steps.

II

Culture Hype

7

Globalism Hype

> The historically visible signs of the essential completion of power are planetarism and idiocy. Planetarism means a relation of power to the entire Earth in such a way that this relation is not the result of an extension of national power, but the beginning of a peculiar world government.
>
> —MARTIN HEIDEGGER, *Geschichte des Seyns*

Most people have only a hazy notion of 'Globalism' and how it relates to 'globalization'. Yet many people have heard the prediction "You will own nothing and you will be happy" or the prophecy that the future of diet is that we will all be eating insects, without realizing that these are elements of the propaganda for Globalism.

Much of the Globalism Hype emanates from the World Economic Forum, which the media treat a though it were an official body whose pronouncements carry some authority, when it is in fact a purely private setup, a bunch of billionaires and politicians, who are not experts on anything but possess public name recognition, and its policies just reflect the half-baked ideas floating around in the minds of wealthy people with controlling personalities at fashionable cocktail parties. On the basis of historical experience, one thing we can be sure of about such ideas is that a few decades later, they will have been completely forgotten, or will have become the occasion for ridicule and merriment.

In the 1920s there was Henry Ford, a brilliantly successful entrepreneur who held a lot of questionable opinions about human life and politics. Most people tacitly understood that you can be a genius at making cars and a dunce when it comes to thinking about human society. Today we have Bill Gates, who as a businessman has benefited many, and correspondingly made a lot of money for himself. Today's Americans are more gullible than Americans in the 1920s when it comes to taking seriously the undisciplined ramblings of a very wealthy person.

Globalism claims that we have global problems that national states cannot solve and which need to be addressed by transnational institutions overriding political will formation at the nation-state level. In many ways, Globalism is a continuation of H.G. Wells's campaign for socialism and world government, which Wells called The Open Conspiracy. *Globalization* in the strict sense denotes a process which has been going on for many centuries and happens spontaneously without conscious promotion: the economic integration of the world by trade. But now Globalists often talk of 'globalization' as though it meant the promotion of Globalist political measures.

The global problems supposedly addressed by Globalism are mostly imaginary or greatly exaggerated Hype phenomena we have debunked in other chapters such as global warming or pandemics. The Globalist narrative also conveys that we have no choice but to accept the influx of huge amounts of migrants into our countries, either because we have damaged the migrants' countries so much that it is a matter of social justice to accept their influx, or because of the more businesslike mentality that we need migrants to solve our national demographic problem.

A hallmark of Globalist thinking is the appeal to a 'stakeholder' economy, in which governments compel businesses to represent various interest groups on their boards. Such measures not only threaten business efficiency but also favor the growth of corruption and influence-peddling on a colossal scale. (Yes, yes, we already have corruption and influence-peddling on a colossal scale, but that's no reason to add to it.)

Closely related to Globalism Hype is a Finance Hype around infinite growth and the wonderful opportunities of priceless start-up companies and the stock market. But though global capitalism has lifted billions out of poverty over the last generation, especially in India and China, it has also created dichotomous societies. In the West, the standard of living for ninety percent of the non-owner population has dropped over recent decades as salaries could not keep up with inflation and taxation. In China and India, the process of integrating bigger parts of the society into the economy has slowed down or reversed. Nevertheless, there is a Globalism Hype, and global as well as transnational institutions such as the United Nations and the World Economic Forum are still seen as the institutions to identify and solve all of mankind's problems.

What's at the root of this Globalism Hype and Finance Hype?

Where Marx Was Right, for Once

Let's look first at where, after many long years of paying attention, we have given up expecting to find any answers: Marxism. While Morelly's *Code of Nature* (1755) was probably the first full description of a socialist society, Marx and his collaborator Engels really put socialism in its modern form on the map. Their *Manifesto of the Communist Party* (1848) made a big impact on European intellectuals.

Marx's ideas provided the theory for the workers' movement which gained strength in the second half of the nineteenth century. The poverty of the workers he described ultimately led to the creation of the welfare state. Based on his ideas, failed attempts at socialist revolution occurred in France in 1870 and in Germany in 1919. And then, in Russia in 1917, the Bolsheviks, later to style themselves 'Communists', managed to capture and keep power.

Most of Marx's theories, like his theory of value creation by 'living labor' alone, were simply wrong or nonsensical, yet his theory did offer some valuable insights. He saw that capitalism, still in its infancy in 1848, would conquer the entire world and lead to oligopolies and monopolies. These predictions were certainly accurate, and the second prediction started to materialize in the US as early as the 1880s, due to the special historical and cultural situation in America, a land devoid of feudal nobility.

I'm not an opponent of free markets in which there is competition of many small competing units, the type of market described by Adam Smith, David Ricardo, and other classical and neoclassical economists. But, as we shall see, once an economy becomes oligopolistic and financialized, market forces merely work for the interests of its oligarchs, who come to own almost everything.

At the beginning of the twentieth century, Thorstein Veblen was one of the first non-Marxist economists to show how the concentration of wealth in the US since the 1880s had created an *absentee owner* class accumulating an ever larger share of private property via huge oligopolistic structures in commodities (such as oil, gas, and metals) and trade, agriculture, transportation and logistics and many other business domains. He also realized that this new ultra-rich class of oligarchs was using its economic and financial power to influence political decision-making. Veblen argued that the goal of the ultra-rich absentee owners was to ultimately dominate politics and to rule the country by controlling the seemingly publicly elected politicians and magistrates who were supposed to serve the common good of the republic.

Indeed, empirical data from the US show that the capitalization and profits of the top one hundred US listed companies as share of all companies have continuously increased from 1950 to 2010—creating dominant oligopolies. In the same period, capital's income share has doubled from 7 to 15 percent of national income. What Veblen calls differential accumulation, a process I will revisit later, has led to this concentration despite the fact that the number of US-listed firms increased by a factor of 20 between 1926 and 2009, while the number of employees per firm declined by a factor of five.

Monopolies and oligopolies, enabling their owners to obtain an invisible, hidden influence on government and public institutions, emerged everywhere in the capitalist world. Around 1900, by the turn of the century, they were influential in the UK, the US, Germany, France and some other advanced industrial nations, though in Europe, they competed more with the old agrarian elites, the nobility, than in the US, which had no hereditary nobility with any influence after the decolonization of 1776.

In the thirty years before World War I, Karl Marx's prediction that capitalism would become global began to materialize. More and more countries adopted the highly efficient capitalist system of production and distribution of goods based on competition and free markets. This led to intensified global trade, which expanded by leaps and bounds.

The period of the two world wars and the Great Depression in the wake of the 1929 crash reduced globalization again, but it picked up quickly after 1945. Today, we have global oligopolies dominating the primary, secondary, and tertiary sectors of the economy. Some professions, especially personal services, are hard to centralize and buy up. But more than half of global value creation in all sectors which allow absentee ownership, that is, management of the business without the presence of its owners, are now owned by a few hundred families via their investment funds in highly complex structures. We have an unprecedented concentration of wealth. How did we get here?

Wealth Concentration

From the 1880s to 1970, a concentration process which is natural to the capitalist economy took place. There are three main mechanisms of this concentration.

First of all, economies of scale which enable bigger companies to buy and produce more cheaply than smaller units.

Secondly, corporations with bigger balance sheets have easier access to loans and can scale up even faster, reinforcing the first effect.

And thirdly, once a certain market share is reached, it becomes possible to get oligopoly (a few producers) and oligopsony (a few buyers) rents. The former are obtained by enforcing higher prices for the goods in the absence of alternatives, while the latter result from bargaining power if a corporation (or a tightly co-ordinated group of corporations) is the only source of demand for a supplier.

A company can also act as a monopsony (sole exclusive buyer) towards its own workforce once regional dominance is achieved; unless workers are willing to move, they may have no alternative but to work for the sole buyer of their product. In some business domains, natural monopolies can also be achieved, for example by creating or using networks; Google, LinkedIn, and Facebook are contemporary examples.

The concentration of production capacities in fewer and fewer hands was further reinforced by fiat money and the partial reserve system (Piketty 2015). Fiat money is money that has no material foundation and can be created at will. A partial reserve system is a banking system in which banks only need to hold a tiny fraction of their balance sheet assets as real liquidity or liquid assets. The Austrian school of economics (see the books by Mises, Hayek, and Rothbard) has described in great detail how this system leads, by various mechanisms, to boom-and-bust-cycles and also to the redistribution of wealth to the owners of the banking system.

The traditional main mechanism in this scheme is the creation of fiat money ex nihilo (out of nothing) by the commercial banks. When banks give loans to customers, they increase the quantity of money and give themselves and the bank to which the money is transferred (for example, the bank of the car seller if the loan is used to buy a car) net interest flows which are not justified by economic value creation.

It works like this: The loan-providing bank takes a loan from the central bank (CB) of the amount it provides to its customer. This CB loan has a lower interest rate than the bank receives from the customer. Therefore, the loan-providing bank gets a net revenue flow from this difference. Now the customer wires the loaned money to a vendor from which he buys something. The bank of this vendor receives the loan-based payment and uses this payment to reduce its debt towards the central bank. Because it pays more interest to the central bank than it receives from the account savings of the customer receiving the money, it makes a net profit from the transaction as well upon the reduction of its debt and the augmentation of the receiver's balance. *So both banks make a profit from the difference between central bank and their loan or savings rates.*

Because in a partial reserve system, banks can create ten to twenty times more loans (currently twelve times more) than they have assets (reserves), their profits are much higher than the basic banking profitability of three to five percent that would result from lending money to customers which corresponds to the savings they have taken in that are earmarked for lending (this is the hundred-percent reserve scheme).

Furthermore, they're protected from bank runs via the central bank. This allows them to privatize profits, but to pass losses to the taxpayer, which happened on a mega scale in 2008. *In the end, in the fiat money with partial reserve system, banks always make more profits than the real economy, so that wealth gets automatically distributed from the real economy to the financial sector.* They privatize earnings, but are protected against losses in a crisis by the central bank.

Furthermore, central banks (CBs) can also increase the amount of money, and from the early 2000s to 2022 (before the CBs started to raise interest rates), they hugely dominated money creation; only a small proportion of the new money was created by commercial banks. This was a new effect; from 1970 to 2000 private banks dominated money creation. CB money is used to a large extent to buy government and corporate bonds, making the central banks owners of public and private debt. The payments to states and corporations flow into the monetary system, fueling inflation. This privileges owners of real assets because their prices increase faster than the prices of consumer goods. The real-asset owners can easily use what they own as collateral to borrow and speculate to increase their wealth. Therefore, inflation distributes wealth from the bottom to the top. But there is also another major effect of the CB-money creation: CBs become owners of public and private debt and can influence decision making in both states and big corporations. This is a major source of power if the CBs are privately owned, as is the Fed.

Taken together, the fiat money and the partial reserve system lead to the automated distribution of real wealth from participants in the real economy to the banking system and its owners. But the fiat money plus partial reserve system also enables *financialization of the economy*, in which the volume of financial transactions, loans, and derivatives is a multiple of the total value of the real economy. When this disproportionate relationship precipitates a credit crisis, debt deflation occurs. In debt deflation, so many debtors are unable to pay their loans that they have to sell property. The prices fall, and the oligopolistic owner class can buy an even larger share of the property. Often, this is followed by massive inflation or even monetary reform, but the oligarchic class loses less property titles than the average citizens, because it is invested in a diversified range of real goods that are not affected by the inflation or partially protected from seizure by the state occurring following monetary reform to refinance the state (which is what happened in Germany in 1949, for example).

The concentration process made corporations so dominant in their home markets that it became easier to expand globally than to grow domestically, which is why the global corporation emerged. Today, all sectors are dominated by such global corporations, some of which like the tech giants Google, Meta, Microsoft or the fossil fuel producers like Saudi Aramco, China Petroleum and Chemical Corp, Exxon Mobil, or Shell form staggering oligopolies.

In these areas, we no longer find competitive markets, but instead a new form of planned economy in which oligopolistic and oligopsonistic structures are used by the owners of large corporations (investment funds and other financial firms) to extract rents from everyone else. Antimonopoly regulation does not help the situation either. While it can disrupt monopolies from time to time, the owners of the resulting units remain the same; this was the case, for example, when the big oligopolies like Standard Oil were dismantled. The owners kept their property titles. Therefore, such regulation cannot prevent huge fortunes from forming. The owners find new ways to form oligopolistic structures, for example via investment funds such as Blackrock or Vanguard, which they control and which lead to very complex ownership structures.

As we will see at the end of this chapter, these global wealth conglomerates demand a global political power, they feel restricted by the nation states which they see as cost factors and obstacles to their economic performance. Oligo-polistic owner families go one step further and believe it is better to rule the world using a centralized approach than via competing national jurisdictions.

Hyper-Debt, Financialization, Deindustrialization, and the Great Taking

The economic system we have today has triggered three major trends that dominate the shape of Western economic systems: hyper-debt, financialization, and deindustrialization, which are all intertwined. Our financial system leads to ever increasing debt levels. This is because debt increases exponentially.

Sidebar: The Exponential Increase of Debt

Debt increases exponentially because the loan volume rises proportionally with the exponent of time:

$$C_n = C_0 \ (1 + p/100)^n,$$

where p is the annual interest rate ($0 < p \leq 1$), n is the number of years, C_n is the debt level after n years, C_0 is the loan at the beginning of the lending period. For example, debt doubles after a period of 24 years and an interest rate of 3 percent if the interest is not paid. While debt growth exponentially, the real economy does not. Indeed, since 1971, when the USD was detached from gold and became purely fiat, the average growth of the total loan volume was much higher than the growth of the real economy. When public debtors cannot service their loans, but borrow to pay interest rates and spend even more, public debt can be increased over a very long period before no one wants to lend the state money anymore. Long before this happens, the central bank (which is privately owned in the US) prints money to buy public debt (treasury bonds), which all major central banks have now been doing since 2008. This inflates the money supply and the prices of real assets, which distributes value from non-owners to real asset owners and fuels the dichotomization of society.

Increasing debt levels have many harmful effects on the production and distribution of goods. Some of the most important are the following.

First, heavily indebted companies without sufficient revenues to pay off the debt but continuing to get loan renewals, so called *zombie firms*, impede economic growth by binding labor and production resources to low-productivity processes. Also, such companies are not able to invest and increase productivity, and this leads to a low aggregate rate. If their proportion becomes too high, as it is now almost everywhere in the West and Japan, they also endanger the banking system since more and more of them cannot service their loans. This can lead to a banking crisis.

Secondly, increasing household debt reduces consumption and hampers economic growth. If it gets too high, as in the 2007–08 housing bubble, it can induce a banking crisis, which is what happened at the time.

Thirdly, highly indebted states overtax their population to service their debt. Higher and higher proportions of the GDP are used for debt servicing, and because high debt phases often coincide with poor economic growth and structural economic problems, states tend to overspend on the welfare system, which is consumption and not investment. This is indeed the case everywhere in the West and leads to a reinforcement of the economic slump by reducing incentives to work for employees and to invest for entrepreneurs, as the rising tax makes it less attractive to generate profits.

Lastly, exponential debt growth always leads to a financial crash, and such events are usually very damaging for the affected societies. They often lead to wars, revolutions, or famines.

While the debt has been piling up, the private lenders have become richer and richer. Non-hereditary owners from the middle class borrow to buy houses or other assets. This drives both asset prices and debt levels. The owner/creditor class receives interest payments from the debtors who often do not manage to pay off the mortgage during their lifetime. When their children inherit the house, it is often sold, and in a debt deflation as we see now in the housing market, it goes to the owner class. The overall debt level rises faster than the income of the debtors. Creditors accumulate more and more wealth.

Michael Hudson calls this a finance-insurance-real-estate (FIRE) rentier economy. It can arise once a broad industrial basis has been established. The preconditions are powerful oligopolies, privatization of public goods (railroads, roads, water and sewer systems, energy production) and services (telecom, postal service, banking, insurance, health) which are bought by the monopolies. In the US, the ninety-percent non-owners are forced or coerced into debtor status for education, housing, and even medium-term consumables (such as furniture or cars). Debtors pay most of their income to creditors and the insurance sector. Consumers get caught in a loan-interest/rent payment cycle, and cannot build up property. This removes spending volume and prices the national economy out of international competitiveness, contributing to the deindustrialization and stagnation we see everywhere in the West. The rentiers extract rent from real estate and monopolies. Mortgage debtors have to pay house insurance on top of mortgage interest, so that the rent extraction becomes risk-free for banks and insurance companies.

This process of wealth concentration and indebtedness leads to the oligarchs owning banks, insurance, real estate and real economy monopolies (industrial and agricultural). Via insurance funds and banks, they own a considerable share of the public debt, and once this amount exceeds sixty percent of GDP and becomes very hard to contain, they can control politicians via the necessary loan renewals. Rich families also influence public opinion, science, and politics via NGOs, donations, and pressure lobbying. In the US, where they directly fund the election campaigns of the politicians, they can demand whatever they want because the politicians completely depend on them.

This process is very far advanced in the European Union, where national parliaments mainly vote to pass EU-legislation designed by non-elected administrators (seventy to eighty percent of the laws passed each year). Another such example is the WHO pandemic treaty, which was designed to bypass national executive powers.

The oligarchs influence fiscal and overall economic regulation and international trade and economic diplomacy in their interest. They demand and obtain regulation and taxation policies favoring the corporations and monopsonies to the disadvantage of small producers.

A financialized economy in which the public goods are owned by plutocrats has the following major goals (Hudson 2022).

- **Extraction of 'rents' without any obligations and minimal risks.**

- **Differential price inflation resulting from adding the monopoly rent to the prices.**

- Tax and regulatory privileges to the financial sector, for example low fractional reserve levels or the obligation to hold public sector debt as collateral.

- Privatization of public goods to include them into the rent-extraction scheme, a process that is far advanced in the US and Europe.

- The shift of legislative power to non-elected bureaucrats.

- The use of transnational institutions such as the United Nations or the EU, which are not based on the sovereign, but on international contracts signed by the elites, to enforce policies in the interests of the plutocrats.

- Centralization of tax revenue and spending to well-controlled centers and away from local decision making.

- Establishment of privately owned (US) or influenced (EU) central banks to enable the automatic distribution of wealth from money users to the banking sector.

- Banking sector to create money inflating real-asset prices (housing and stock markets).

- Massive encouragement of hit-and-run investment patterns in which companies change owners as long as their valuation increases, often based only on Hype. Financial engineering to raise asset prices such as stock buy-back schemes.

Overall, this leads to a massively dichotomous society and the dire consequences I will now look at.

Productivity Slump and Deindustrialization

The productivity growth of financialized economies is low. Since 2008, we have had a barely positive productivity growth in the West. Why? Productivity growth is the result of innovation and the replacement of manual labor by machines. This was the main driver of economic growth and of increasing wealth for the masses between 1880 and 1970. Where does the productivity slump come from?

Neoclassical economics has no good explanation. In theory, companies should compete to cut costs so that they obtain competitive advantages and get more market share. This mechanism is not completely exhausted, but it is overlaid by other mechanisms (Hudson 2022). Financialization takes mass income away from consumption, as debtors have to pay rent, leases, interest, and insurance, which together make up sixty to eighty percent of their income, depending on their life situation and choices. This diminishes domestic demand, and this is a major reason for the export orientation of Japan and Germany after WW2. Export economies do tend to have higher productivity growth rates than countries with a trade-balance deficit such as the Mediterranean countries in Europe or the US.

But the phenomenon becomes much clearer when we consider, in the tradition of Veblen (Nitzan and Bichler 2009), how corporations can increase their capitalization. Capitalization is the accumulation of capital, which is always differential—if every capitalist capitalized at the same speed starting from the same absolute profits, there wouldn't be any differential accumulation, but there is, as we can see from the difference in companies' balance sheets.

How can such differential accumulation be achieved? Either through more revenue or more profits, both of which can be achieved internally or externally. External growth occurs via differential employment, which results from price-based or innovation-based competition. Inorganic growth is achieved via mergers and acquisitions, which require massive financialization. Dominant capitalists fear over-capacity because it lowers pricing power and can potentially increase real wages (at least during a boom)—so they prefer inorganic over organic growth since the latter can lead to over-capacity; organic growth also has cultural limits (which we see especially in African and other third-world countries). Simply put, they prefer to buy up other companies rather than improving their own competitiveness via rationalization and cost-cutting (which they also do, as far as they have to).

Inorganic growth preference leads to first vertical, then horizontal, then cross-border integration via mergers and acquisitions—it explains globalization. The traditional way of profit growth, via internal differential profits that arise from innovation (labor cost reduction, which is increased productivity), is needed to remain competitive, but not to differentiate from the perspective of large capital. The last mode of differential accumulation is *stagflation, which Veblen calls sabotage capitalism.* What is this?

The easiest way for large oligopolies to differentially accumulate capital is a production level below the theoretical possibilities. Big, truly dominating corporations deliberately produce less then they could to maintain a certain shortage of goods (Veblen 1924). This keeps prices up and wages low because the corporations do not maximize the demand for labor (which drives labor costs up). This strategy is only possible once an oligopoly is established. Furthermore, oligopolists use their market position to inflate prices by raising them before other market participants can. This gives them an inflation seniorage, because they receive more money for a unit of goods before the inflation they create ripples through the economy. This seniorage is used to purchase real assets.

The effects of differential price increases actively pursued by the oligopoly owners are twofold: first of all, in periods of inflation, the corporate earnings per share divided by the wage rate increases, which means that capital owners differentially profit from inflation. Second, inflation drives distribution of wealth from small to larger firms: large firms can differentially increase their prices (much more than small firms can) and thus get increasing profits faster. This is the result of active price increments by big firms, because if inflation was a process to which all market participants are subjected to the same extent, big corporations would not achieve a higher differential accumulation than small ones in proportion to the inflation rate.

Since large-scale oligopolies emerged at the end of the nineteenth century, the value of the US dollar has dropped by a factor of 300 due to almost constant inflation. Often this inflation was accompanied by stagnation (stagflation). When inflation is low and growth is strong, amalgamation sets in because this is the easiest way to achieve differential accumulation under these circumstances. *This is the result of the aggregated activities of oligopolistic huge corporations collectively engaged in sabotage capitalism.* Exceptions to this rule are industries in which the products can be destroyed immediately by use, such as pharmaceuticals and the defense sector: These industries try to maximize their output because it is immediately destroyed upon use and the demand is not limited by consumer purchasing power (but by the amount of taxation the state can obtain and the debt it can issue to pay for defense and health care).

The velocity of money circulation is an indicator of the economic efficacy of inflation. It is the ratio of the price-adjusted GDP and the amount of money. When the amount of money increases faster that the GDP, the velocity of money drops. This has constantly been the case since 1997, when it reached its post–World War II peak. The newly-created money increases faster than GDP, indicating slump and debt accumulation. The inflation has no effect on the real economy any more, falsifying another dogma of the neo-Keynesians, the Phillips Curve. The last long-term drop in the velocity of money occurred from 1918 to the end of the Great Depression (Webb 2023, p. 5); we are facing another now.

The deindustrialization we are seeing has yet another reason. Once differential accumulation via growth became less attractive in the 1970s, US owners recognized that the outsourcing of production to low-loan countries that are not financialized yet can increase profits. This drove the deindustrialization of the US and Europe and the outsourcing to India, China, and other Asian countries which now produce more than half of the industrial consumption of the West. At home, deindustrialization leads to an economic decline of the working class and the small and medium sized suppliers of the big corporations.

The overall result of oligopolistic global capitalism is globalization with stagnation and de-industrialization of the West and poor economic development of the countries controlled by its economic model.

The Great Taking

In his notorious book, *The Great Taking*, David Rogers Webb—a former trader whose thoughts have to be taken with a big pinch of salt—argues that the fifty-year inflation period we have gone through will end with a massive debt deflation, during which we will witness a "confiscation" of huge proportions of private property by the central banks and certain banks selected to survive the crisis. How is this supposed to work?

Webb may have spotted an interesting aspect. He draws an analogy between our time and the Great Depression. Before 1929, when the stock exchange crashed and the Great Depression began, there had been a period of inflation and increasing debt. This debt then sharply rose in its real value due to deflation: When the purchasing power of money increases, the load of debt becomes much higher since a unit of debt has a higher value.

The debt deflation spiral described by Irving Fisher starts when debtors default on their debt and have to sell their collateral such as real estate or machines. This creates an over-supply of the previously inflated asset classes, their prices fall, deflation ensues. This deflation causes more to default on their consumer loans, mortgages and business loans, which leads to further fire sales and falling prices. The value of bank assets then falls because a huge proportion of them are loans and because the value of the collateral falls. The banks have to write off these losses in their balance sheets and consequently their equity falls below the minimal relative capitalization limits. This leads to a surge in bank insolvencies, bank runs occur. Banks cannot fulfil their transactional function anymore. The credit market stalls, there is sharp reduction in lending and spending. Production drops, there is then a combined supply and demand shock, a contraction that is worse than a mere recession. This was what happened during the Great Depression.

In the course of these events, in 1933, the US Federal Government closed all banks; it was the Bank Holiday. A third of the banks (those with the worst balance sheets) never reopened, only those selected by the Fed were allowed to reopen. As Webb correctly relates,

> People with money in banks that were not allowed to reopen lost all of it. Their debts were not canceled, however; these were taken over by the banks selected by the Federal Reserve System. If these people could not make their debt payments—which was now likely, since they had lost their cash—they lost everything they had financed with any amount of debt, e.g. their house, their car, and their business. (p. 43)

The remaining banks took the entire collateral of the debtors, even if they had almost paid off the debt over decades, because the debt deflation had devalued the nominal prices of the collateral to a level below the open debt. For example, a mortgage that was paid off 80 percent could not be ended because selling the house would yield less than 20 percent of the total mortgage value. The collateral went to the owners of the banks.

In this situation, the Fed engineered an additional wealth concentration by keeping the issuance of new credit low. Though interest rates were low, they were still higher than zero, and the Fed did not engage in a modern quantitative easing scheme (buying bonds). This led to a prolonged contraction and deflation, forcing many small businesses to close and their owners to sell their property. Overall, the economy contracted by 35 percent. Webb concludes: "If that was a comprehensive program to assure there was no recovery, it worked quite well."

To prevent the emergence of a new independent banking system and to drive demand for bank credit, the government made private gold property illegal in May 1933. It was illegal for almost forty years until 1971, when gold lost its function in backing the US dollar. Gold had to be exchanged for banknotes, which rapidly lost their value when inflation set in again. Gold possession was criminalized, so that most citizens complied. This way, the state stripped its citizens of the only way to protect small amounts of wealth from confiscation as collateral.

Gold ownership was now an exclusive privilege of the state and the privately owned Fed. The confiscated gold was taken into the ownership of the Fed, which is a public institution owned by private individuals. In other words, *the plutocrats owning the Fed confiscated the gold posessed by all other private owners.* The overall effect was a distribution of wealth from the middle-class to the bank owners, millions of citizens were ruined and driven into the debtor class. Given the history of the Great Recession and the series of actions taking by the Central Bank and the government, it seems that there was an intent of the financial elites to transfer property from the middle of society to the top, in other words that the spontaneous evolution of society, though of course not planned, was used by the elites to achieve this redistribution and wealth concentration. This seems plausible and is the starting point for Webb's further analysis.

Asset Confiscation through The Great Taking

Webb's theory is that, as in the 1930s, after fifty years of constant private and central bank inflation, we're now entering a new phase of debt deflation that will result in a financial crash and a confiscation of all property titles which have collateral character. What are the mechanisms he predicts? Webb focuses on the clearing institutions of the financial system, the members of the Central Clearing Parties (CCP).

The CCP members are clearing institutions which act as intermediaries between two parties trading foreign exchange, securities, options, or derivative contracts by taking on the transaction risk and providing clearing and settlement for the trades. For example, the Luxembourg based Clearstream International SA is a clearing counterparty for the central storage and the settlement of securities transactions for securities across all asset classes. The securities are stored in digital form at the company which acts on behalf of the owners of the titles. Clearstream changes the ownership titles when trades are closed. In 2018, it held collateral worth more than eleven trillion dollars and performed more than 48 million transactions. The main task is to guarantee a flawless change of ownership when a deal gets closed. Essentially all financial transactions involving collateral assets, loans, and their numerous derivatives are now performed using CCPs. Therefore, a lot of risk is concentrated in that sector of the financial system.

Clearing institutions take the risk that one of the parties defaults on the transaction which the clearing house has taken onto its balance sheet. The clearing institutions are massively under-capitalized for a situation in which such defaults occur more frequently. If this happens, their equity is wiped out and they go bankrupt. This endangers the Central Clearing Parties in which they are organized. If these are unable to bail out their members because too much equity is wiped out, they go bust themselves. Then, according to the Fed, *"if the securities intermediary is a clearing corporation, the claims of its creditors have priority over the claims of entitlement holders."*

This means that if the debtors are institutions which used collateral from private investors, these will lose their property to the creditor of the clearing corporation. Such collateral can be bonds, shares, life insurance or retirement entitlements and many financial derivatives created from collateral by the clearing corporation's debtor party, for instance a bank, an insurance, or a wealth fund. The owners of these property titles, private investors and companies who believe that their titles are safe with the issuer, which can be their bank, life insurance, or pension fund, lose all of the property titles because the creditors of the clearing institutions have precedence over them.

They can take all the assets, even if these are debt-free and represent the owners' savings. For example, if a bank has issued an exchange-traded fund (ETF) savings scheme in which private persons have invested their savings, and this bank defaults in a clearing deal, the creditor of the clearing institution has precedence over the collaterals held by the defaulting bank and will receive these collaterals including the shares held in the bank's ETF. The ETF share owners, small and large, will lose their savings as if they had savings account in a bankrupt bank and could not withdraw their savings in time.

Webb supports his argument by scrutinizing the standardization and harmonization of the US and EU collateral administration schemes as well as the regulation of clearing institutions. To test his hypothesis that big creditors can have precedence over the natural persons who actually own the assets, he is reviewing the 2008 financial crisis. For example, when Lehman Brothers went bust, during "the lead-up to the failure, JP Morgan (JPM) had taken client assets as a secured creditor while being the custodian for these client assets" (p. 34). Later, courts ruled that this had been legal because JPM is a member of the privileged party under the safe harbor regulation. *Webb believes that this dispossession scheme will be heavily used upon the next debt deflation-induced crash, which is unavoidable and factored into the thinking of the Fed and its plutocratic owners.*

I disagree that the clearing institutions must necessarily constitute the breaking point of the system; this may well occur in another area, for example a collective panic with mass sales of life insurance contracts, shares, or treasury bonds, or derivatives thereof. But the effect of bankruptcies on the issuers of digital collateral (asset) titles will be the same, and the asset confiscation by the central banks will occur in the same way and have the same consequences. It is also certain that the system will collapse, and the Fed as well as the private banks and other corporations of the financial system know this.

Webb argues that we are already in the beginning of a debt deflation which is ending a fifty-year inflation period that led to the largest relative and absolute debt bubble in human history, well above three hundred trillion dollars at the time of writing. In the US, house prices and the rate of real estate transactions have been falling since the end of 2022, and the same is true for Europe. Interest rates are still rising, Fed rates are now close to five percent. At the same time banks are affected by the deflation as bond prices are dropping with rising coupons, wiping out an important collateral class in their balance sheets. This was the main mechanism for the small spring 2023 banking crisis, which was solved by bailouts. These are symptoms of the beginning of a debt deflation. It seems that the Fed is now lowering rates to prevent a debt deflation from materializing, so that we might see one or more cycles of easing before the crash occurs.

But at some point, a crash of the economy with mass defaults will be unavoidable. But this time, unlike in 1933, bankruptcies will not only lead to the confiscation of debt-loaded collateral such as mortgages or business loans which have real estate of machines as collateral. *This time, Webb predicts, the confiscation will also be extended to collateral that is debt-free and legally owned by those who invested their savings (private persons) or profits (corporations) into assets.* This is a confiscation of debt-free assets by the creditors and ultimately by central banks and its owners and the banks they own by which all owners of non-physical assets are affected, *so that all fortunes denoted in digital property titles can be wiped out and transferred to the part of the banking system chosen by the central banks.* These will undoubtedly be those with dominating plutocratic ownership structures. According to Webb, it is likely that, as in the aftermath of 1933, market conditions will be made difficult by the central banks to prolong the recession in order to squeeze more owners out of their property.

This could be reinforced by taxation schemes on real estate owners or regulations enforcing 'green' renovation of houses. Along with the beginning of debt deflation, we already see such policies which have now passed in Germany and other European countries, forcing small home owners who cannot afford the expensive regulation out of their property. Another way to destroy private non-oligarchic property is business regulation, but more importantly, deliberate energy shortages. The main gas line from Russia to Germany was cut off by the US according to Seymour Hersh (2023), and Germany is switching off nuclear plants in the middle of an energy crisis and keeps on raising energy (so called carbon) taxation, driving small business into bankruptcy; as of February 2024, such business failures increased by 40 percent as compared to the previous year. These policies offer no benefit whatsoever to 99 percent of the population, and neither do they in any way help the environment, on the contrary, they increase pollution (see Chapter 2). These policies are yet still vigorously pursued and huge propaganda efforts are made to justify them. Their real aim is clearly to reduce non-oligarchic distributed property and to concentrate wealth in the hands of very few families even further.

This would make it possible to confiscate eighty to ninety percent of the property not yet owned by the plutocrats, driving their property share from today's 60 to 70 percent of all means of production (Piketty) to over 90 percent of all property, including real estate, to reach the dichotomy levels of feudalism (when a thousandth of the population owned everything). We do not know whether Webb's predictions will become true, but the analogy to the

1930s carries to some extent; *what we can certainly learn from his speculations is that our dichotomized financial and economic system is rigged towards the plutocrats, even if the scenario he envisages will not materialize.*

Given the huge global debt levels, the central banks can initiate the crash of the financial system via interest rate increments anytime. In this way, the previous inflation phase can be seen as a preparation for this step. When will it happen? What will be the equivalent to the gold confiscation we saw in the 1930s? All major global banks are preparing an infrastructure for central bank digital currencies (CBDCs), which will replace the current currency system when the crash happens. This money will be digital, it will be used via computers and phones only and will be issued directly by the central banks (or its distributing agencies) without private money creation by commercial banks. Like the money of the Soviet Union, it will be a full currency (without partial reserve) fully under the control of the central banks, but because it will be digital, this will allow the tracking of all transactions, which was not possible in the USSR. After the crash, any time it is more suitable for the owning elites, it can be converted back into a partial reserve currency with private banks enabled to create digital money again.

But CBDCs have another interesting property. Because each unit of the CBDCs will have a unique identifier, it can be tagged with metadata that can be adjusted depending on the receiver of the unit. For example, one could tag the unit with an expiration date or a restricted validity of the unit, so that it can only be spent in certain jurisdictions or for certain classes of goods. This would allow total control of the transactions of all businesses or private persons in which the state takes an interest. Once the debt deflation reaches its peak and distribution problems with black markets and illegal makeshift currencies set in (as occurred after World War II in Europe before the currency reforms of the late 1940s; see Carol Reed's movie *The Third Man*), the public could be switched to CBDC, which will appear as a deus ex machina type of salvation. It would require quite an upheaval to end such a system, even if it is unlikely to fully work, because human transactions are too complex to be fully covered with digital means alone.

If the ongoing dichotomization continues at the current pace and the introduction of CBDCs occurs, Klaus Schwab's famous prophecy 'You will own nothing and be happy' will become reality, at least the first half of it.

Why Is There Globalization Hype?

Globalization Hype is an ideology that pursues so-called 'global governance'. This is a type of political decision making in which nation states, which have been, since the seventeenth century, the traditional jurisdictions of sovereign political will formation by princes (absolutism) and later the people (democratic age), are replaced by transnational political will formation and legislative bodies.

These international entities prepare policies and legislation which is then merely executed by national governments. Examples are the EU, which is producing more than two thirds of the legislation of its member states, the WHO, which is currently preparing a treaty to deal with future 'pandemics', or the United Nations with their agenda 2030 program, which is a meta-political agenda-setting system to enable systematic dispossession of everyone not belonging to the plutocratic elite.

None of these organizations has any democratic legitimacy, and they have no accountability towards the sovereign peoples of the democratic nations. They are not controlled by bottom-up political will formation in accordance with the principles of democratic rule, but by the interest of tiny minorities. This is the same minority that performed the confiscation policy during the Great Depression and that is now pursuing a policy of increasing dichotomization.

The ideology is justified with two main arguments:

- **We need Globalism to deal with international problems the nation states cannot solve — mainly the fictional anthropogenic climate change and the pseudo-pandemics.**

- **We need Globalism to remedy the injustices we committed towards the Third World historically, during the age of colonialism, and by our 'carbon footprint' — which supposedly damages their countries.**

Both are used to justify the transnational governance to which the plutocrats aspire. Their ownership structures have extended beyond nation states since the end of World War I, and the League of Nations was the first attempt towards global governance. It was renewed with the United Nations, the EU, and many so-called NGOs which were founded and funded by the plutocrats over the last sixty years, such as the WWF (World Wildlife Fund for Nature), founded in 1961 under the leadership of the eugenicist Julian Huxley (Aldous Huxley's brother), the Rockefeller-financed Club of Rome or World Economic Forum, and the many 'philanthropist' plutocratic funds as well as state-funded NGOs also serving the interests of the plutocrats. All of them are working towards global governance to supersede the democratic political will formation at the national level in accordance with global ownership structures.

Both of the above main arguments are ideological and misleading. The first is nonsensical because, as we have seen in other chapters, there are only very few problems which require transnational solutions; among these are long-term international conflicts (such as the conflict in Palestine), heavy metal or plastic pollution issues, or rain-forest destruction. These can be solved by international agreements modeled on the classical Westphalian sovereignty model, but do not require a global governance. As to the second argument, this is an application of the idea of social justice to the historical past, an ideology even more absurd than the ideas we will discuss in Chapter 13.

No one but the plutocrats needs a global governance. Its sole goal is to remove democratic will formation to align politics with the property structures. We have gone down this path for decades now, and we're witnessing the progression of this tendency which destroys individual freedom and the traditional processes of community and society formation.

8

War Hype

War is nothing but the continuation of policy by other means.

—CARL VON CLAUSEWITZ, 1834

War has not had a good public image in the West since World War II, especially in Europe, which lost tens of millions of its population in the worst war in mankind's history. Not so in the United States, which won the war with the help of the Soviet Union, did not experience significant damage domestically, and emerged as a global hegemonic power.

The United States was directly and indirectly engaged in fifteen mid-sized or major wars between 1945 and 1990, of which the Korea and Vietnam wars were the most prominent. Furthermore, the US has been engaged in the following major wars since 1990:

- **Bosnian war and Croatian war (1992–1995)**
- **Kosovo war (1998–1999)**
- **War in Afghanistan (2001–2021)**
- **Iraq war (2003–2011)**
- **Intervention in Libya (2011)**
- **Intervention in Iraq (2014–2021)**
- **US intervention in the Syrian civil war (2014–present)**
- **US intervention in Libya (2015–2019)**

- **Ukraine war (since 2022)**

- **Greater Isreal War (since 2023)**

In addition, there were many smaller interventions, mostly related to the War on Terror.

These wars were generally depicted as necessary and beneficial, and supported by a heavy barrage of media messaging. For example, a massive propaganda effort was used to launch the War on Terror after the attacks on the World Trade Center and the Pentagon on September 11th 2001. And though the US population was not really interested, the War on Terror cost taxpayers and state creditors five trillion dollars from 2001 until today, not counting interest payments.

But only the Ukraine war has been Hyped to an extraordinary extent that we have not seen in the West since World War II. We saw Ukraine flags everywhere in the public space, and the Hype was so strong that many private persons were flying Ukrainian flags on their houses. There were Ukraine flags, fund-raising, solidarity, and refugee welcoming events everywhere from San Francisco to Dorpat (Estonia), which is just forty miles from the Russian border. Public institutions, but also private clubs and associations, fueled the Hype. The West has spent hundreds of billions of dollars on this war.

The war propaganda needed to create this War Hype was prodigious. We were told that this was a war for freedom and democracy, a war for values in which a free country, Ukraine, fights against an autocratic oppressor, Russia. This was untrue, as both countries are autocracies suppressing minorities and disregarding the rule of law or democratic separation of powers. This never was a war of a democracy against a tyranny, and in fact Ukraine became steadily more oppressive, canceling elections, outlawing the Russian language (spoken by the majority of Ukrainians), and outlawing the Ukrainian Orthodox Church.

We heard that Ukraine, backed by Nato, was easily winning and would soon take back Crimea, defeating Russia and restoring the pre-2014 borders. We were also told that the bellicose Russian government would rapidly collapse under the sanctions so that it could be replaced by a pro-Western alternative. While at the time of writing, the war is not over, it is abundantly clear that *none* of the Nato goals will be achieved and that Russia will prevail and achieve its stated geopolitical goals.

Why have we witnessed a Hype about the Ukraine war that had no precedents in the West since World War II?

War is a mode of politics which is used by a state to exert power over an opponent by employing organized physical force. In classical warfare, this opponent is another state, but there is also asymmetric warfare in which the opponent is not a state, but a militarily acting group with or without political ties to the state it is acting on behalf of. We exclude from this chapter civil war, which is an armed conflict between opposing political groups involving military units fighting on both sides.

War has always been a major instrument of politics. Politics is the process concerned with the partitioning of power in a society and between societies. Modern societies are politically organized in nation states or trans-national contract structures (such as the European Union), but today armies able to wage successful wars are in most cases under the control of nation states so that war is waged at the national level. In post-Roman medieval western Europe, from which the current West emerged, modern warfare originated in the Crusades. These had the following components which required a high degree of organization and bureaucracy: (i) War propaganda, consisting of the identification of an enemy and the call to arms and support for the war. (ii) War financing, the collection of funds for warfare via donations, taxation, and war loans. (iii) Warfare logistics and equipment. (iv) The gathering of armies and the conduct of war.

All of these components are still characteristic of warfare today, and all of them are constantly ongoing as long as wars continue. The only change which has occurred since the First Crusade is that today, the war is planned and conducted by nation states, while in the late eleventh century, it was financed by feudal lords.

Causes and Consequences of the Ukraine war

From the perspective of the aggressor, *wars are generally waged for three major reasons: To stabilize international power (which includes pre-emptive warfare when an attack by an opponent is expected), to intensify it, and to stabilize or strengthen domestic power.* The Ukraine war was initiated with all three motives, but not with equal distribution on both sides. Though Russia's invasion was against international law, it was certainly not, as the Western press has portrayed it, an "unprovoked and unjustified attack of Russia against its neighbor." Neither is it a conflict unilaterally planned and executed by Russia.

It is rather a conflict over supremacy in Eastern Europe, at the border of Russia, a major hegemon. The West after 1991, led by its declining global hegemon, the United States, pursued the goal of expanding its sphere of control to the Russian border. In 2008, Russia ended the further expansion of Nato by successfully waging war in Georgia to stop the erosion of its sphere of influence. By then, it had recovered from the collapse of the USSR sufficiently to reassert its role as a regional hegemon. But the West did not give up its own hegemonic plans for Eastern Europe. The United States and its allies supported a coup in Kiev in 2014, which removed the elected Russia-friendly government that had refused to terminate its trade with Russia in exchange for a trade agreement with the EU. The CIA-led coup replaced it by a pro-Western government. Soon thereafter, the Ukrainian army based in Crimea seceded to Russia, which explains why the Russian annexation of the Crimea occurred without military conflict.

Since then, the West and Russia have been engaged in a continuous escalation involving the Donbas situated by the Russian border. The Ukrainian government has revoked the minority rights of the ethnic Russians living in the Donbas and by the Black Sea and has regularly shelled the Donbas region, killing up to twenty thousand civilians between 2014 and 2022, before the Russian invasion. The West planned to integrate Ukraine into Nato and the EU. In the meantime, Ukraine was turned into an outright dictatorship, dissidents were jailed and competing political parties suppressed, media were shut down, the rule of law and democratic division of power were abolished. At the same time, Nato trained and equipped the Ukrainian armed forces, building up a force supposedly capable of invading Crimea.

From the fall of 2021, Russia amassed troops at the Northern and Eastern Ukrainian borders, Putin proposed a non-military resolution of the conflict to US president Biden in November 2021. The content of this proposal was a Western guarantee to uphold the main assertions of the Minsk I and II accords. However, as we learned from ex-chancellor Angela Merkel in fall 2022, the West's intention was never to enforce the accords, but to use them as a tool of deception against Russia, to win time to arm and equip Ukraine for a military conflict (Mearsheimer).

In February 2022, Russia invaded Ukraine to militarily enforce its political interests which were also documented in the Minsk Accords: A demilitarization of Donbas, firmly established minority rights for the ethnic Russians in Ukraine, and a guarantee that Ukraine would not become a member of Nato. With the invasion, Russia expanded these goals to include absorbing into Russia the ethnic-Russian eastern and southern parts of Ukraine, demilitarization of the country, and a removal of the regime installed by the West (which Putin polemically calls de-nazification, a term that is overblown, though there is some appreciable influence of neo-Nazis—followers of Stepan Bandera—in the Ukrainian government). The main strategic goal of Russia is to prevent a buildup of Nato military equipment and troops on its Eastern border.

Russia's overall political goals were to stabilize and intensify its position as a hegemon, but also to solidify domestic power via a successful military campaign. The goals of the West in arming Ukraine and inducing the Russian invasion were to increase its economic and military power domain to include Ukraine and to extend the reach of Nato towards the Russian border in order to threaten and weaken Russia as a regional power. The first Western goal is likely to fail, but the second has already partially succeeded with the inclusion of Sweden and Finland into Nato. In the northwest, Russia now has a Nato border with Norway and Finland.

Some observers say that Nato pursues goals beyond the integration of Ukraine into Nato and the EU, namely a participation in the exploitation of Russian natural resources, which it had established after 1991 but lost

when Putin came to power. And indeed Western politicians, think tanks, and commentators declared in 2021
that a goal of the war was to induce a breakdown of the
Russian government through the combined effect of the
confiscation of Russian assets in the Western banking system, sanctions, and warfare.

The idea was to replace Putin and his staff with a pro-
Western government comparable to the Yeltsin government of the 1990s. The West was relentless in pursuing this
goal. Once Russia began its "special military operation," it
became clear that the West, though it was not technically
the original aggressor (attacks on Donbas civilians using
Western equipment, 2014–2021, aside), was not interested
in ending the war. A peace treaty draft that was negotiated
in April 2022 with the help of Turkey, just two months into
the war, was suppressed by Western diplomats to keep the
war going. The West was convinced that it could win this
war and overthrow the Russian government by military
and economic attrition.

This goal, however, now seems unattainable. The
West underestimated Russian resilience and its ability to
export its commodities to other partners, some of which
re-export them to Europe thus circumventing the sanctions. Russia's GDP has grown strongly over the entire
period of the war (by five percent or more) and its public
debt has remained stable and under twenty percent of
GDP—while the US debt to GDP ratio is now above
100 percent, and only 20 percent of its GDP is real
economy). Russia's gold reserves (more than 2,330
tons) were stable over the war, and the Russian gold
reserve to GDP ratio is 3.5 times higher than that of the
US. Russia's inflation rate is somewhat higher than international inflation due to war-economy-caused overheating.

Already now, Russia is economically profiting from its
newly acquired territories by exploiting mines in the
Donbas. Once the war is over, this exploitation will reim-
burse Russia for its military investment in a short period of
five to ten years. The war will pay off for Russia. This is the
opposite of what the West was aiming for, and much more
than the Russians would have obtained under the Minsk II
accords or the Istanbul treaty if either of these had been
accepted by the West.

Causes of the War Hype

It now looks likely that Russia will defeat Ukraine and realize its war goals. What will be the consequences of this
defeat? Why did the West start this war to begin with? Why
did Western elites so totally miscalculate the outcome?

Western elites had just achieved a major success with the
Covid vaccination campaign. Though the coupling of free
movement to vaccination status was not permanently
established, which would have been a maximal success,
billions of humans were injected with a somatic gene therapy that has only negative effects (as I explain in Chapter
5). The lockdown policies and the massive creation of
money led to a further redistribution of property rights
from the middle-class to the tiny minority of multi-billion-
aires, who bought market shares in logistics, distribution
and other sectors in which mid-sized companies failed
under the pressure of supply chain disruptions and a combined supply and demand shock.

Furthermore, huge tax revenues and state loans were used
to buy pharmaceutical and medical products (such as Covid
test kits and masks), so that public funds were privatized. This
success gave the elites a sense of strength and victory and
nourished their illusion of invincibility. *The pattern of privatiz-
ing public funds for large corporations and their plutocratic
owners is the same in Covid and warfare:* the goods produced
are used for a non-productive effect—in Covid, for harmful
and useless drugs, a pattern that the pharma industry wants to
repeat in future pseudo-pandemics.

In warfare, the pattern is to make weapons that are
meant to be destroyed upon use so that replacements are
required. This guarantees a constant flow of public funds
into the pockets of the owners of the pharmaceutical and
military industries, a form of indirect taxation. This was
a major motive for operation Covid, and the main motive
for the various US-led War Hypes, which did not achieve
lasting military victories, but often led to humiliating
defeats (as in Vietnam and Afghanistan), while the privatization of public income via military spending always
worked out well.

Secondly, it was planned to implement a US and EU
policy of economic control over commodities in Russia

that worked so well for decades in Latin America, Africa and the Middle East, and that had worked for the chaotic years in Russia after the breakdown of the USSR, before the election of Vladimir Putin. This attempt was based on a misjudgment of the state of the Russian economy, military-industrial complex and the maturity of Russian relationships with other emerging economies. While the Russian GDP is usually reckoned to be thirteen times smaller than the US GDP (though only four times smaller by the more illuminating purchasing power parity method), its industrial economy is only 2.5 times smaller than the US, because US GDP is 80 percent services.

When Russia invaded Ukraine, it had developed a huge military-industrial complex able to produce all the military equipment from its domestic commodities and to obtain components not produced in Russia from non-Western partners. Also, the production capacity seems to be above the total Western capacity, because the US and EU countries have been largely de-industrialized. Though there are attempts to recreate a Western domestic military high-and surge-capacity production, this is a long process which is in contradiction with the long-term trend of de-industrialization since the late 1970s. While the West certainly hurt Russia by confiscation of dollar- and euro-denominated assets in the Western banking system, it underestimated Russia's flexibility and the maturity of its ties to China, India, and many other emerging economies. Thanks to these relationships, Western embargoes do not hurt Russia, but rather increase its GDP because the prices for its commodities rose much faster than the general inflation rate, while the exported volume was unaffected.

Furthermore, the US and its allies underestimated the logistical advantage of Russia, which can easily bring equipment to its Western front, against Ukraine which was struggling with the logistics of the war under Russian attacks on its infrastructure. The Armed Forces of Ukraine and the West were not able to seriously retaliate against these because this would have required systematic attacks on the Russian territories (excluding Donbas), which Western generals saw as too risky for the West to engage in. Also, Russia has a demographic advantage over Ukraine, since the West was unwilling to commit troops to the war and become an openly active war party beyond the equipment, training, and intelligence, and strategic support for the Armed Forces of Ukriane. At the time of writing, Ukraine counted at least one million war casualties (dead or maimed to an extent that return to the war theater is not possible), probably many times more than Russian casualties. Unless the West decides to commit to hundreds of thousands of casualties by directly becoming a war party with its own troops, the war will end when Ukraine is bled out of men or the influx of war materiel from the West becomes insufficient.

Thirdly, Western elites are nowadays culture blind. They neither understand their own culture nor the differences between themselves and Slavic culture. Our own culture makes it very hard or impossible for us to wage and win direct wars involving mass casualties of our own soldiers. Modern mass societies function by the creation and distribution of goods; they are essentially consumer societies. The cultural ideals are self-realization and individual authenticity, which are thought to be obtained via consuming certain goods depending on the social status and subcultural orientation.

Despite this individual consumerism, the values propagated by our education system and the media are essentially collectivist. But neither postmodern hedonistic individualism nor Woke collectivism can motivate the mobilization of millions of young men to die at the front in the way religious or nationalistic ideologies could (Amoghli and Meschnig 2018).

While it was the *cultural norm* in Europe for both the military commander nobility and the rank-and-file soldiers *to die for God*, the King, or the Prince and since the eighteenth century, for the Nation, *postmodern culture has eroded these norms.* While this process was delayed in the US compared to Europe, the US is now culturally as incapable of manning the ranks and leading them into major battles as European states. Even Israel is incapable of waging an effective war in Gaza because it carefully looks to keep its own casualties as low as possible. With an average of less than one son per family, Western nations no longer produce the male surplus that is essential to wage and win boots-on-the-ground wars. In contrast to this, Slavic countries such as Russia and Ukraine have still preserved some of the culture that enables warfare, though they have the same demographic problem as all countries of the Northern Hemisphere, which limits the intensity of Russian-Ukrainian warfare. While the US clearly factored in the willingness of the UAF to fight, they did not expect the Russians' strong war motivation.

Given this cultural context, *Western War Hype is a Hype around wars not to be conducted by themselves, but by peoples still capable of fighting and sustaining the losses while using Western equipment*, which is employed by both sides in the Gaza war, and by one side of the Ukraine war.

The War Hype was created to justify the engagement in a war from which Western elites planned to obtain economic and hegemonic advantages in Eastern Europe. The Hype broke out exactly when the Covid Hype abated due to general exhaustion of the public. The West is now politically governed using a series of Hypes, the intensity and frequency of which has continually risen since 2001.

As the Ukraine Hype lost momentum, a new Hype around the conflict between Israel and Arab militias in the Middle East broke out. All major Hypes we have seen since 2001 have induced military spending, justified money printing, and increased the dichotomization of Western societies into a tiny minority that owns an increasing share of the means of production and a majority of the population owning nothing. The ten percent small owners in the middle are losing political importance, as in the Feudal age, they are now mainly managing the rest of society on behalf of the real owners.

War Hype was not dangerous for the US and EU elites as long as losing a war did not matter and wealth could be transferred from the taxpayers to the owners of the military-industrial complex. The American loss in the Ukraine war will change this. The power of deterrence of the US military presence around the globe will continue to dwindle, and threats of military interventions by the US will have less and less impact. The West is not prepared for an escalation of the current Middle East conflict or another later conflict.

The pattern of Hype around wars fought by foreign soldiers will not work if the West gets truly drawn into a war that endangers its economic structures to an extent that requires the use of masses of its own populations to man the fronts. The West is neither culturally nor economically prepared for such wars, and it would be wise to end the current policy of warmongering. War can only be an instrument of politics if you're ready to accept the destruction it brings, even when the outcome is victory. Europe and the US are no longer ready.

9

Multicultural Hype

... the idiot who praises with enthusiastic tone
All centuries but this, and every country but his own

—W.S. GILBERT, *The Mikado*

Conventional and elite opinion in the West strongly favors the view that large-scale immigration is highly desirable. Any move to cut back on the huge inflow of immigrants is branded as xenophobic, racist, or even fascist.

In support of this advocacy of subsidized mass immigration, we're treated to Multicultural Hype. In the US, the migration topic was traditionally less debated than in Europe, though it has recently become a big topic in America too.

We're told that migration leads to a multicultural society and that this is a desirable state of affairs, superior to the monocultural societies of traditional nation states. We're also told that the immigrants have no responsibility to adapt to the ways of the natives, and have a right to express their own cultures, while the natives have no right to cling to their traditional cultural practices—a doctrine the late Christopher Hitchens called "one-way multiculturalism."

Multiculturalism and virtually (if not candidly) open borders are propagated by numerous NGOs and philanthropic foundations such as Kellogg, Getty, Soros, or the Bill and Melinda Gates Foundation. This is an issue where the elite is permanently at loggerheads with the great majority of the population. At the time of writing, the US federal government is trying to enforce an open border policy against the state of Texas—tens of millions of people have been encouraged to come into the US illegally, and then subsidized and pampered on arrival, a ruthless and remorseless policy which no one ever voted for. Sam Houston would not have campaigned for Texas to join the Union in 1845 if he had known that it would be coerced into not protecting its territory against illegal mass migration 175 years later.

Migration has been a big topic in Europe since decolonization in the 1950s and 1960s. Former colonial powers such as France, Belgium, or the UK experienced major immigration, at first from their former colonies. Germany, which had received an influx of German refugees from the territories confiscated by Russia and divided among several states of its sphere of influence (mainly Poland), started to receive non-German migrants from abroad in the 1960s, at first mainly from Turkey in the context of the resolution of the Cuban missile crisis—to motivate the Turkish government to relinquish the nuclear missiles stationed there, Turkey was given the opportunity to send migrants to Germany. Southern Italian and Greek migrants came later, and a constant stream of international migrants trickled in until 2015. Then, Germany experienced a flood of migrants, amounting to millions. While Germany consisted of close to 100-percent native German speakers in 1960, the population now has more than twenty-five percent migrants, most of them with an education level well below the necessities of the German labor market.

They now consume more than sixty percent of non-medical social welfare payments (their share in medical consumption is hard to obtain and is not reported by the public health insurance system). It's estimated that the total cost of migrant payments of the German state amount to fifty billion euros a year, not counting increased law enforcement costs. Germany is like a magnet for migrants from the Middle East, Africa and Asia (Afghanistan, Pakistan and many other countries) because it pays the migrants so well and tolerates a lifestyle that is forbidden in Germany for Germans, but allowed for the migrants (for example, polygamy). It's popular for migrants because equality before the law has been discontinued there. Other European countries face similar challenges.

A big proportion of the migrants to Europe are Muslims. In total, Western Europe now hosts approximately twenty-five million Muslims, which is close to ten percent of the population. Some towns in France and Britain now have more than seventy percent Muslims.

The United States has a similar situation with forty-five million non-US-born residents in 2021. Both in the US and Europe, many of the recent migrants are not families, but young, uneducated males, a circumstance with explosive potential. Something like two thirds of the migrants across the Mexican border are now non-Mexicans, and many of them come from faraway locations such as Africa or Asia; various organizations are financing and actively managing an illegal international migration to the US via the Mexican border. Populists call this an 'invasion'.

But despite Migration Hype, which took on grotesque forms in Germany in 2015 with the *Willkommenskultur* (culture of welcoming), the migration is not acclaimed by any of the Western populations: two thirds or more of the voters are against it, as polls repeatedly show.

The Nature of Migration

According to the economist Paul Collier, migration occurs because of the gap in standards of living between Western countries and poor countries. The former are economically successful due to many factors (which can be subsumed under 'Western social norms and culture'). The latter, the poor countries, have a culture that currently does not lead to economic success; they are also disadvantaged and hampered in their economic evolution by the US-led international trade and loan regime. This state of affairs leaves many of their young people without much opportunity, but with a clear appreciation of the advantages of a life in the West. This 'economic' migration constitutes the bulk of the global migration we see.

The migrants form what Collier calls diasporas in the countries into which they migrate. These are the communities of non-integrated migrants. Given an income gap between the country of origin and the target country, the migration increases with the size of the diaspora, because bigger diasporas make it easier for migrants to live in the foreign country and attract more migrants. *Therefore, migration is self-reinforcing and only slows down either if the income gap disappears* because the target country becomes as poor as the countries from which the migrants originate, *or if it is controlled and discouraged*, for example by adapting the quality of life for migrants to their contributions to the host society.

Collier's broad conclusion is that migration is economically advantageous and beneficial for the society of the target *countries if the number of migrants per year equals their assimilation rate*. The bigger the diaspora, the lower the assimilation rate. Assimilation, as opposed to mere integration, is the process after which a migrant becomes a full citizen of the country he has migrated into, which means: mastering of the language at the socio-economic level of this social stratum, acceptance and affirmation of the country's values and customs, active legal economic contribution, and possibly participation in the biological reproduction of the population.

An integrated migrant participates in legal economic production, but does not fulfil any of the other criteria. A non-integrated migrant merely receives social benefit payments or participates in the illegal economy (for instance pimping, drugs, illegal arms, or protection rackets). Depending on the culture and composition of the migrating groups, their willingness and aptitude to integrate and ultimately assimilate differs. While East Asians have a very high propensity to integrate well into European nations, the US, and Canada, Muslims and African blacks have a much lower ability or willingness to assimilate. Only a low proportion of the descendants of the former black slaves in the US assimilated, the majority is merely integrated or even— though this is a minority—not integrated, but state-dependent or criminal. *This means that the lower the aptitude to integrate and assimilate is, the less migrants can be let into the country without harming it economically and socially.* In other words, the migration capacity, which is the number of migrants that can be accepted in a Western country without harming it, is lower, for example, for Muslims than for East-Asians or Hungarians.

If migration exceeds the assimilation level, it becomes harmful; we call it damaging migration.

Beneficial Migration

Why is this so? Let's first look at the advantages of beneficial migration. For the receiving country, migrants who actively contribute to the economy increase the output of the society (GDP) and demand, because they consume goods. If the country is in demographic decline, that can be very beneficial to make up for some of the loss in workforce. However, actively contributing to an economy with high levels of productivity and low labor unit costs requires a high level of education and the ability to adapt to the culture of the environment. This is because not only many types of work, but social interactions at the workplace are highly complex as well. Furthermore, migration does not solve the problem of demographics, because demographic decline is a structural problem of rich postmodern societies. If the migrants contribute to the productive sector, they will adapt to the reproduction strategy of the target country and have as few children as the average couple of the autochthonous population. Only the non-integrated reproduce as highly as in their countries of origin, which aggravates the problems of the social insurance system.

The effect of mass migration on the target countries' economy is to provide cheap labor for the low-productivity sectors, which are of marginal importance for advanced economies, and to provide more workers at higher skill levels if these are available among the migrants. In the real estate property market, the most important real asset market for the middle class, migration has the effect of driving up prices for homes as migrants become able to purchase houses. In the social accommodation sector, migrants may crowd out the domestic destitutes. For example, in Germany, social elderly care homes are now emptied of their frail inhabitants to house migrants. These yield higher profits for the landlords because the state remunerates their accommodation at a higher rate than for the elderly. These perverse incentives impact private, public and state-owned homes.

For the migrants, migration is beneficial because they can obtain a higher standard of living in the target country than in their country of origin. Even if they do not contribute to the legal economy, the social security payments they receive may be sufficient to pay remittances to their relatives in their countries of origin. If they contribute to the legal or illegal economy, they are able to increase remittances or to get their relatives to join them.

For the migrants' countries of origin, migration causes a drain of labor which is usually destructive despite the remittance payments, because often the most eager, talented and courageous men of the lower and middle classes leave exodus countries, creating a shortage of talent and labor there. Unless migrants flee from an active war zone or from ethnic cleansing, primary migration is a male phenomenon, women follow thereafter.

Damaging Migration

Damaging migration, which occurs when the migration rate is higher than the assimilation rate, harms the target society as a whole. If non-integrating migrants dominate, as is now the case in Germany, the US, and many other Western countries, this leads to short-term benefits to several groups: Landlords who let cheap accommodations to migrants, producers of fast-moving consumer goods which are purchased by the migrants, or the migrant administration industry, which is a mix of state institutions and NGOs financed from tax revenues. *All of them benefit from migration at the expense of the taxpayers; they privatize public income.* But the *overall effect* of damaging mass migration *is utterly destructive*, as we can see in the US and Europe.

Public infrastructure such as public transport in bigger towns and cities becomes overwhelmed. Public institutions such as hospitals become over-used and dysfunctional. Emergency wards, often the only resource which migrants in health distress can use, become overcrowded and fail. Triage becomes necessary, but is met with active resistance by migrants, who now often physically attack nurses and doctors in German emergency rooms.

Schooling becomes harder or impossible with classes almost exclusively made up of migrant children who do not speak the target country's language—in big German cities, there are hundreds of such classes with over ninety percent migrant children. It becomes impossible to teach these children reading, writing, and basic arithmetic and geometry during the four years of primary school, let alone cultural knowledge that is supposed to be imparted to six- to ten-year-old children in Western education systems.

In social insurance, unfunded systems in which the contributor base of the system pays the expenses for the recipients are called PAYGO systems. The US Social Security system (Medicare, Medicaid, OASDI, TANF and others) and the German public social insurance systems for health, pension, unemployment and work-related accidents are both PAYGO systems. In funded systems, such as the US pension system, the members of a fund pay money into the scheme to obtain a pension upon retirement.

Both systems are disrupted by damaging migration—the first type because the contributor base is too small to fund the expenses for the migrants who do not contribute to the system, the second type because they have never paid into the system and should not be entitled to receive anything. In that situation, the expenses are covered from tax revenue. In any case, the quality of the system declines or has to be subsidized out of tax revenues at the expense of the general population.

In the course of damaging migration with an increasing number of criminal migrants, the crime rate increases, there is more illegal drug trade, more prostitution, there are more armed felonies, rapes, homicides, and robberies. Public safety declines, and novel forms of crime are established which are unprecedented because they occur due to an interaction effect between migrant activities and the way the postmodern state reacts to them.

The Rotherham child sexual exploitation scandal, which went on for decades, illustrates the problem, and it is just the tip of the iceberg; there are Rotherhams all over the West. The essential structure is that migrant criminals com-

mit systematic felonies: in the case of Rotherham, systematic sexual abuse of girls from the native underclass. Many
of these girls were abused by their offenders for years for
their own sexual satisfaction or for enforced prostitution.
From the perspective of the Muslim migrants, white
Christian girls are legitimate prey because they are seen as
culturally inferior, in the same way that during the Ottoman
empire, it was seen as legitimate practice to capture white
slaves in eastern Europe, to use them domestically or to
export them to their Islamic trade partners. In today's structures of hidden slavery in the West, the authorities, including the entire legal enforcement system, know about the
systematic felony committed against weak members of the
native population. But they do not prosecute them, either
because they believe that they have to respect the culture
of the migrants or because they're afraid of being publicly
labeled racists.

Both attitudes are incompatible with the rule of law,
equality before the law, and more generally a functioning
republic or state, but in the Rotherham schema, the postmodern, ethically challenged magistrates let the felony go on
and on. Protests by the public or even criminal charges submitted by private persons or lawyers are ignored by the
public prosecutors and not followed up, while media
refuse to report the incidents or disguise them to an extent
that the migratory root cause of the crimes is not disclosed.

As Collier describes, in a process of damaging migration,
the non integrated migrants segregate into relatively
homogeneous urban communities (diasporas or ghettos)
where they can live in a micro-environment of the culture
and social norms of their home countries. In Berlin and
Cologne, for example, immigrants now dominate many
entire neighborhoods. They continue to speak their
mother tongue, refuse to learn the language of the target
country or use it as little as possible, build their community or miniature society (once the ghettos get bigger than
a thousand inhabitants) based on the social norms of their
cultural provenance, do not respect the rules and norms of
the target country, contribute insufficiently to its economy
or taxation base, but use its infrastructure and benefits as
well as the wealth of the host society for their own ends.
They are typically hostile towards the majority of the soci-

ety and look down upon the native inhabitants; in Germany, they call us 'white rolls' or 'potatoes'.

Collier summarizes that damaging migration reduces the social capital of the target country by the erosion of trust, mutuality, co-operation, and social norms. This can ultimately lead to social unrest and violence between migrant groups (which we are already witnessing, for example in France and the UK) or between the native population and the migrants.

Damaging Islamic Migration

If the migrants who do not assimilate, but segregate, are Muslims, they tend to pursue the goal of transforming the host society into a part of the Ummah, the community of Muslims. At least this is what they pray for in their mosques and discuss in their parish assemblies.

Islam is traditionally a theocratic religion which, unlike the creed of Western societies based on Christianity and humanism, does not distinguish between state and church, but sees both as one. Therefore, the law of such societies is Divine law, the law of Mohammed rendered in the Quran and Sharia, which forms an integral part of Islam. These laws require politics to be based on religious laws and on religious ideas regarding the ideal structures of society, which in Muslim teaching is the Califate. The Western concepts of natural law, rule of law, democratic participation, republican citizenship, and civil magistrates are alien to them. No state in the world that has Islam as its majority religion is a Western-type republic. The aim of Islamic rule is the establishment of a global Ummah by subjugation of the world population (Spencer 2005; Nagel 2014).

The Western idea that there can be a reformed Islam, a humanistic Islam, or an Islam-based rule of law in the Western sense is the product of Western misunderstanding of Islam and a projection of the West's unique history and cultural evolution onto other cultures. This universalism, which aims to impose on everyone the ideas formulated in Northern Italy, Scotland, the Netherlands or Königsberg, is a classic failure of Western thinking (Nagel 2014). This critical view of Western universalism, however, as being naive towards Islam, is not to be confounded with postmodern philo-islamic views such as the influential Edward Said (1978), who criticized the Western view of Islam from the point of view of metaphysical anti-rationalism.

As long as Islamic migrants are in a minority or the ruling minority can prevent them from taking control of the state, the degree of harm they can inflict on the host society depends on how the society deals with the migrants. If it fully applies the rule of law to Muslim migrants and conditions social welfare benefits on contributions, the damage can be limited. But both principles are not applied in Europe or the United States.

Why the Elites Want Migration

It is rarely officially stated, but the ruling class of the West is pro-migration, in fact pro-damaging-migration, because damaging migration erodes the formation of political will, and today's globalist elites want to rule via transnational organizations reducing or abolishing political self-determination at the national, regional, or local level. Peter Sutherland, who was the UN Special Repre-sentative of the Secretary-General for International Migration from 2006 to 2017, openly stated that the purpose of migration into the Western hemisphere is the inhibition of democratic political will formation by undermining national homogeneity.

The formation of political will by the sovereign requires cultural homogeneity; this is also true for societies before the Enlightenment defined the people as the republican sovereign. When feudal princes became very powerful in the late Middle Ages, the slow process of the evolution of their kingdoms into nation states began. Absolutist rulers needed a culturally homogeneous population to rule effectively. For example, the enforced homogenization of language and culture under Henri IV laid the foundations for the hegemonic role that France held for centuries in continental Europe. Effective law enforcement required a population willing to accept the rule, pay taxes, and obey the magistracy. A bureaucracy was build up that was able to enforce this type of modern rule, and its magistrates had to be culturally homogeneous as well.

Powerful nation states based on a culturally homogeneous class of ruling nobility, magistrates and politicians (from the emergence of constitutional monarchy onwards) and a homogeneous ruled population were able to colonize the Southern Hemisphere and to wage nationalistic wars against each other which culminated in the age of World Wars (1914–1945).

Then, globalist elites recognized that a transnational order would be much more attractive to achieve their goal of global power and rule. First-generation globalists such as H.G. Wells, George-Bernard Shaw, Bertrand Russell, Walter Lippmann (all of them also eugenicists, and many of them members of the Fabian society), or Count Richard Coudenhove-Kalergi, after whom the globalist Charlemagne-Price of the European Union is named, sketched ideas of trans- and super-national rule in the 1920s, and the League of Nations was formed as an initial attempt to achieve supernational governance. But the interests behind the leading nation states concerning Europe were too strong, and the League of Nations failed.

The period of 1914 to 1945 can best be explained by the Halford Mackinder theory published in 1904, which states that global geo-strategic dominance by Britain (and its Western hegemonial successor, the US) depends on who controls the heartland: continental Europe and Russia. His followers concluded that it should be prevented at all costs that Germany would dominate Russia or that the two countries would become partners. Indeed, during the entire century from 1914 to today it can be observed that the Mackinder theory is an important factor in US diplomacy and warfare in Europe: Both wars and the US policy after the Second World War from the cold war to the attempt to dominate Russia after 1991, Nato expansion and the systematic transformation of Ukraine into an opponent of Russia after the break-up of Russia and the West in 2008 are all influenced by this theory.

After the Second World War, the United Nations was created, and though it was mostly regarded as a forum to prevent war and foster international collaboration, we can observe beginning in the 1990s that an important group within the UN started to pursue a post-national agenda.

The UN evolved from a coordination forum of the nations to an NGO pursuing the interests of its private donors representing huge private capital managers and foundations. This evolution was catalyzed by the withdrawal of the US government as a payor to the UN, which resulted in the UN lobbying for and accepting private funding. Other privately funded influential organizations, such as the Club of Rome or the World Economic Forum, both founded by the Rockefellers, and the Trilateral Commission, a private-public-partnership institution, were pushing global governance from the early 1970s. All of them, and many other foundations created by global plutocrats, have always aggressively promoted migration.

The goal is to break the power of the nation states which is based on cultural homogeneity. Globalist left-wing activists openly advocate multiculturalism as a way to erode the national state which they hate so much. The globalists advocate two types of multiculturalism: In the first "The nation is reconceived to be a geopolitical space in which separate cultural communities peacefully coexist with equal legal and social status" (Collier, p. 97). The second is a fusion of migrants and native populations to create a new race of mixed ancestry, which is what many multiculturalists in Germany, for example, are hoping to achieve: the eradication of white Germans, a goal which they have inserted into their official party programs, thus engaging in a strange reverse racism mirroring the racial purity ideology so popular with their grandparents from 1933 onwards. Both visions are unrealistic and indicate ignorance of both history and anthropology.

The Medium-Term Consequences of Migration

In the medium term, large-scale migration can lead to precisely four possible outcomes:

1. **destruction of the culture of the target country,**

2. **ghettoization of the immigrants, possibly with the creation of an apartheid state or a continuous asymmetric warfare,**

3. **forced expulsion of the non-integrated migrants (ethnic cleansing), or**

4. **mass killing of the non-integrated migrants (genocide).**

There is no other possibility because human societies need a common set of social norms and will spontaneously do everything to maintain or re-create shared social norms. There are no examples of stable multicultural states in the strict sense, though some degree of cultural co-existence may be possible if there is a very strong uniting idea which has the function of a set of social meta-norms for the different cultures—the Austro-Hungarian Empire is an example, the USA until 1980 as well to some extent. The current flow of migrants to the USA and Europe will lead to one of these four outcomes in the mid-term, a grim prospect.

To illustrate the four different outcomes, let's look at some historic examples.

Outcome 1: The Langobards destroyed the West Roman culture in Italy so thoroughly that the remainders of the Roman culture were preserved and passed on North of the Alps rather than in Italy from the seventh century onwards (though the Langobards were also influenced by Roman culture). Of course, they were conquerors, not modern migrants, but their movement was part of the migrations during the Migration Period (300–800 A.D., also known as the Barbarian Invasion).

Outcome 2: Jewish populations migrating into Europe from the Middle East and Asia under increased migration pressure following the Islamic expansion. These populations were ghettoized, and they had fewer rights than Christian citizens, so this was a medieval form of apartheid. Other examples are gypsies in Europe as well as numerous minorities living in ghettos and with fewer rights than the citizens belonging to the ethno-cultural majority of a jurisdiction. The South African apartheid is an impressive example since the oppressed citizens were in the majority. The state of Israel is the most important contemporary example; the Zionist state gives systematically fewer rights to its Arab citizens than to ethnic Jews.

Outcome 3: Ethnic cleansing via forced expulsion is a regular pattern by which majority populations assert their social norms and culture in an aggressive fashion. Recent examples are the ethnic cleansing in the former Yugoslavia after 1992, the expulsion of Armenians from Nagorny Karabach in the fall of 2023, or the efforts of the Israeli state to cleanse the Gaza strip after October 2023. Sometimes this outcome is hard to distinguish from genocide.

Outcome 4: Genocide is the most aggressive way of asserting the social norms and culture by a majority population. Famous examples are the Armenian genocide by the Ottoman empire during the first world war, the Holocaust of the European Jews conducted by the Nazis, or the Rwandan genocide in 1994.

No one can predict which of the outcomes will occur, but the more non-integrated migrants are allowed to establish themselves, the faster the standards of living will drop and create economic and social distribution conflicts. At some point, one of the above outcomes or a combination thereof will occur.

What can be done?

It's not too late to stop the influx of immigrants attracted by higher living standards in the West. Furthermore, Western states can remove incentives for the non-integrating migrants to stay. If these policies were introduced now, the above outcomes could be avoided. But if the migrations continue, they will either destroy Western culture or the native populations under pressure will react, bring to power new leaders, and execute one of the last three solutions mentioned above.

We can only hope that this outcome will somehow be avoided.

Death Hype

Nascentes morimor. (As we are born, we die).

— *Carmina Latina Epigraphica*, ed. F. Bücheler

Death Hype—the glorification of death for its own sake—has usually been a marginal phenomenon in Western culture, but it is now clearly moving into the mainstream.

We find Death Hype among members of the military in nomadic cultures such as the Jihad warriors during the emergence of Islam, but also in urbanized societies with an established state and bureaucracy focusing on military rule such as Sparta, Rome, or Nazi Germany. In these cultures, the death cult is usually restricted to elite soldiers such as the Spartiates or the German Waffen SS. The social norms of such warriors involve the duty to defend their own group and culture, obedience, gratitude towards the ancestors and persons of respect, a strong sense of solidarity within the group, and, most importantly, the willingness to sacrifice your own life.

Dying in battle is seen as a form of honor, the funerals of fallen soldiers are elaborate, and their memory is cultivated by the military institutions. In the Waffen SS, the death cult was radicalized to the abandonment of individuality in favor of the combat units' group identification with a readiness for suffering and death combined with a perverted form of intense aggression and hatred against both enemy combatants and civilians selected for elimination.

Naturally, such death-worship typically exists within a context of birth and rebirth for the race, the nation, or the religious denomination.

Exulting in the killing of other human beings is a recurring topic in all civilizations. In post-classical European history, bureaucratically and systematically organized violence and a radical collective will to kill started with the Crusades, organized by the Catholic Church. In 1095, Urban II proclaimed the first Crusade with the goal of liberating Jerusalem from Muslim rule. These Crusades focusing on the Holy Land lasted for two centuries and were of extreme violence. Other Crusades were conducted against pagans, for example the Nordic Crusades against the Wends, Finns, and Balts. Yet another type of Crusade was directed against domestic religious dissenters, such as the Albigensian Crusade in the Languedoc, the Crusades against the Waldensians in Savoy, and against the Hussites in Bohemia. Violence and aggression are basic motives of human behavior, as are love and compassion.

By Death Hype, I mean the systematic organization of aggression by the state to obtain political outcomes. This need not necessarily be military violence. Ultimately, the love of death which is expressed in radical aggression with the goal to kill is pure evil, it is the opposite of love, which is the good. The military death cult is currently very subdued in Western culture and only survives in some platoons and on the fringes of our cultural sphere, for example in Russia. Instead, we have a *Civilian Death Hype*. What is this?

Our Civilian Death Hype

Death Hype has now entered the political mainstream. Let's see how.

As we've seen in Chapter 5, in 2020 all major states of the Northern Hemisphere started a panic campaign about the mildly pathogenic respiratory virus SARS-CoV-2. The virus was at least three times less lethal than the influenza strains which had been endemic in the winter of 2017–18, namely B-Yamagata and A-H1N1pdm09. No one would have even noticed the presence of the virus without a colossal Fear Hype.

After preparing the population using epidemiologically nonsensical lockdowns and other crushing restrictions, our governments proceeded to poison billions of humans with the injection of nucleic acids that force the body cells to make a toxic protein, the SARS-CoV-2 Spike protein. It was clear from autumn 2020 onwards that these nucleic acids would not have any efficacy against contagion by the virus, but would be dangerously toxic, because the nucleic acids encode for a protein highly homologous to the SARS-CoV-1 SPIKE protein that was tried and failed as a vaccination antigen ten years earlier. Among those injected in the global roll-out since the end of 2020 there were many young people at reproductive age or younger not endangered by the virus in the least.

As a consequence of the campaign, reasonable estimates reckon that globally ten to twenty million died from these injections, among them many children and young adults as well as unborn children of injected mothers. Five to ten times as many are now chronically ill or disabled. We don't know yet whether damage to the reproductive system of the young is temporary or irreversible. Some estimate that two to four percent of the injected face a severely reduced life expectancy. The whole vaccination campaign was a eugenicist, transhumanist program which resulted in mass homicide.

From January 2021 onwards, when it became apparent that the 'vaccines' were highly toxic, mass killing was consciously accepted. Nevertheless, the campaign is still painted as a great success of modern genetic-recombination-based medicine.

We witness other examples of deadly evil. We have constantly high abortion rates which range as high as twenty-five percent of all pregnancies on average in the OECD countries. The abortion rates are much higher among the socioeconomically disadvantaged: In the US, the Hispanics, blacks, and singles show much higher rates than the middle class and the wealthy. Furthermore, abortion is now mostly used as a form of belated contraception. In Germany, for example, ninety-six percent of all abortions in 2021 were undertaken for non-medical reasons. Medical reasons in the strict sense are fetal malformations not compatible with continued life or significant health hazard to the mother.

Abortion for non-medical reasons is a form of murder, the murder of unborn children. Societies could find alternatives to this practice, such as foster parents or care homes for unwanted children. Instead Western societies are advocating abortion and making it ever easier to obtain. So-called philanthropic NGOs, funded by ultra-rich individuals fiercely promote it. For example, the Ford Foundation believes that "access to abortion is not only a fundamental human right, but a key pillar of democracy and a pivotal step on the road to equality."

So killing unborn children as a form of contraception is a human right? Certainly not if human rights are seen as the modern form of natural law. And what is its relation to democracy or social justice supposed to be? There is none, the statement by the NGO is empty and evil; murder is linked to positive ideals without evidence. *Instead, the net effect of abortion is to kill unborn children of women from the underclass so that women from this layer of society reproduce less.* Organizations such as the Ford Foundation and other well-financed NGOs argue in favor of euthanasia, social selection via abortion.

We also have an unprecedented *mutilation of adolescents* and young adults under the cultural pretext of transsexuality. Everywhere in the West, thousands of them receive chemical castration with substances such as leuprorelin that block the release of testosterone and estrogen. Many of them are also surgically castrated, an irreversible mutilation which in the past was a fate reserved for slaves in slaveholder societies. Children not only receive chemical castration, but also sexual hormones of the opposite sex in the proclaimed attempt to 'transform' their sexuality, which is biologically impossible.

At a very young age and under the influence of evil adults masquerading as benevolent, like the Devil in the synoptic gospels (for instance, Matthew 4), these children are crippled and deprived of their reproductive function for life. The vast majority of them will regret it later: only a tiny minority has an indication for sexual-appearance-altering surgery. These mass mutilations are an expression of pure evil.

Another domain of Death Hype is euthanasia. As an example let's consider Canada's medical assistance in dying law (MAID). This law enables the euthanasia of adults under the condition that they have public health insurance and make a "voluntary request that is not the result of external pressure, give informed consent to receive MAID, meaning that the person has consented to receiving MAID after they have received all information needed to make this decision, have a serious and incurable illness, disease or disability, are in an advanced state of irreversible decline in capability, have enduring and intolerable physical or psychological suffering that cannot be alleviated under conditions the person considers acceptable."

It is currently under deliberation whether the euthanasia law should include the mentally ill as well, and it is still a matter of debate whether they must consent themselves or whether consent of their relatives is sufficient to have them killed. Other Western countries such as Switzerland, the Netherlands and Belgium have similar laws; overall the euthanasia quotes are increasing in the West. If Canada introduces the euthanasia of the mentally ill, this would be the first state-driven euthanasia program for mentally ill in the West since the end of the Nazi state terror. Under the rule of natural law, it is undisputed that the mentally ill need compassionate care, not killing by the state.

Another example of deadly evil is the *trafficking of children* on an industrial scale for sexual abuse and murder. The United Nations organization for migration (IOM) and its labor organization, the ILO, currently estimated that fifty million people live as slaves, meaning that they have lost the ownership of themselves and are possessed by someone else. Among these, more than six million are sex slaves owned for sexual exploitation and abuse, of which 1.7 million are underaged. Other estimates range as high as ten million children abused as sex slaves. The Economist Intelligence Unit estimated that four hundred million children worldwide are exposed to sexual exploitation and abuse.

The demand is high in Western countries: 0.4 percent of male Germans reported their experience of child sex abuse in a sample of over eight thousand males questioned. An unknown number of children get killed in abuse situations every year. If they're unregistered migrants, which is not uncommon in the US, they simply disappear without anyone noticing.

We also see a death cult in the Western pro-Ukraine propaganda, which has led to the death of hundreds of thousands of Ukranians, who are not given such prominence in published opinion. This is an interesting case of an implicit death cult. Of course, those who order, produce, ship and pay for the armament of Ukraine know that these weapons do not only kill Russians, but mainly Ukrainians who are in an inferior position. But the killing is willingly accepted and the process leading to it, the proxy war, is lauded.

As a last example, let's consider the twenty-first-century *opiate war* against Western societies. In the nineteenth century, the British conducted opium wars in China to protect the highly profitable export of opium into China, which increased the consumption by a factor of ten over a generation and had devastating consequences for the functionality of Chinese society. Today, we face an opioid crisis in the West which is much worse than during the nineteenth century.

In the US, we now have fifty thousand deaths from opioid overdoses per year, up from a couple of thousand per year in the 1980s. The poison is often synthetic (fentanyl), but refined opium products such as heroin also cause many deaths. The sources of the opioids vary over time. During the occupation of Afghanistan by US and Nato troops, heroin production increased by a factor of 25, and the number of heroin addicts in the US rose from under 200 thousand in 2000 to 4.5 million in 2016, an increase facilitated by the massive increase in the availability of the drug. Since the Taliban took over the government after the US lost the war, production of heroin has plummeted again.

Where do the opiates come from now? From Mexico, which obtains more than ten billion dollars in cash every year from the illegal trade. This money is laundered with the help of Western bank affiliates in Mexico, which are essential to the trade—without the money laundering activity of the banks, the money would have to be stored as cash, but it is impossible to protect such vast amounts of cash. Without the support of the Western dominated banking system, the supply of opioids to the US would decrease, and the opioid crisis would recede. But Western financial elites do not care for the public good. The flow of opioids into Western societies and the lives wasted in this terrible addiction, as well as the atrocious deaths the opioids are causing, are consciously accepted.

All these examples of evil have a common property: *hatred of life and devotion to murder*. This devotion to death and evil is now so dominant in mainstream culture that speaking up against it or naming it is called 'hate crime', 'conspiracy theory', 'trans hate', 'Covid denial' or 'denial of women's reproductive rights'.

Given these developments, it's hardly surprising that there are growing movements, both academic and grass-roots, explicitly aiming at the abolition of humankind. The most notable scholarly work in this vein is David Benatar's book, *Better Never to Have Been: The Harm of Coming into Existence*. At a more popular level, there is a following for Les Knight's Voluntary Human Extinction Movement (www.vhemt.org), which emerged out of the environmentalist movement, where it has become a cliché that humans are "the cancer of the Planet" and the Planet would be better off without them.

The Theology of Evil

Where does this evil come from? There is no clear philosophical answer to this. Many thinkers tend to deny the existence of evil. For example according to Konrad Lorenz it is just an expression of biological aggression—Lorenz does not make the traditional metaphysical distinction between man and all other animals. Nietzsche also tends to diminish the significance of evil, writing that malignity (evil behavior) is not done "for the sake of the suffering of the other, but for one's own delight," and sees in this the "innocuous character" of evil. On the other hand, Kant describes malignity as an attitude in which evil is taken as the dominating force of one's main maxim, the fundamental principle of action. Schopenhauer summarizes this maxim as follows: "Omnes, quantum potes, laede" (Hurt everyone whenever you can).

Today, our high culture seems to have lost this knowledge of evil which was typical of Christian civilization; it is currently neither a cultural topic nor a concept at the core of the modern individual's concerns, which instead focuses on lip-service to values of hyper-morality that do not have to be lived in personal practice, such as diversity, inclusion, 'equity' (now superseding equality, as we will see in Chapter 13), or selective tolerance (Marcuse) for propositions of the 'true [Marxist] consciousness' (Adorno).

This cultural blindness to the reality of evil enables malignant institutions such as the CDC, the FDA, or the MHRA to proceed with their large-scale malignancy. The deeply evil bureaucrats working there and the politicians who oversee their malignancy maximize harm for everyone by approving and promoting the distribution of poisons such as the Covid-nucleic acids or ineffective and toxic drugs such as Nirmatrelvir/ritonavir (Paxlovid). They are acting according to the malignancy maxim postulated by Schopenhauer.

From a theological perspective, evil is the denial of God. Luther calls it the theft of the deity of God, the evangelist John calls it the "murderous lie" (John 8:44). It is ultimately the denial of life and the cult of death. Pagan, pre-Christianization mythical nightmare figures of evil which contributed to our cultural mainstream, such as witches, ghouls, vampires, or zombies are indeed allied to the Devil. So are undead monsters bringing death and contagion to the living—confirming the view that evil is ultimately the lust for killing and death.

However, the really difficult question is: what's the difference between sin and evil? According to the New Testament, our existence is sin, which Luther characterizes as forgetting God (*Gottesvergessenheit*). We are all sinners, and each of us is always in need of God's grace which is freely given to us if we turn to him. So if sin and evil were the same, we would all be evil. But obviously, not all of us lives according to the maxim 'omnes, quantum potes, laede'.

But then how does evil arise? Rudolf Bultmann was maybe the first theologian to provide an answer. According to him, evil comes into the world via sinning but then induces more sinning. The individual gets into a cycle of evil which corresponds to Schopenhauer's maxim. The sin itself is a *privatio veri* (deprivation of truth). The life lived in lies leads to the absence of freedom, the slavery of the soul. The enslaved soul then lacks faith, love, and hope, which would enable it to escape the cycle of evil. Instead, the malignant human falls into 'relationlessness'; he has no relation to other humans and God any more, or, speaking in medieval terms, he is now possessed by the Devil and totally alone, like the fictional archdeacon Claude Frollo in Hugo's *Hunchback of Notre Dame*.

All of this is very characteristic of the classical Christian view of our existence as an individual relation (or non-relation) to God. Evil is nothing else than complete detachment from God. But Christianity does not say much about evil as a phenomenon in society. John of Patmos, the author of the Book of Revelation, is an exception among the Christian canonical texts.

John describes an epic battle of good and evil according to the scheme of Gnosticism which influenced him. This battle involves the whole of humankind which is divided into the faithful and those following the Devil. John describes how society (as we would call it today) is shaped by this battle. The leading Christian (Lutheran and Catholic) teaching acknowledges theologically important and beautiful aspects of *Revelation*—such as the ultimate promise of grace for the faithful in 21:4—"And God shall wipe away all tears from their eyes; and there shall be no more death, neither sorrow, nor crying, neither shall there be any more pain."

But for both the Lutheran and the Catholic reading of the New Testament, the world is not shaped by an epic antagonism of good and evil. Rather every Christian is asked to see the world from the perspective of my relationship to God, which concerns only me and God and excludes an inspection of or speculation about the next person's relationship with God. *In other words, the perspective of society is outside the scope of the core concern of the New Testament*. It does not give us any means to explain historic, social, and political developments.

And so, from the point of view of Christian faith, what we are witnessing today is not a Manichean battle between good (God) and evil (Satan), but the default evolution of human nature freed of faith and thus rebelling against God. Evil always prevails in the fallen world, but its extent can vary over time and society. If the number of members of a society devoid of faith become the overwhelming majority, secularly speaking, social norms erode. Theologically speaking, there is not enough "salt of the earth" (Matthew 5:13) left.

Culture and state power become dominated by individuals who are indulging in riotous, unrestrained sinning in total self-syntony—these evil individuals are totally penetrated by malignancy but experience this state of mind and the thoughts, intentions and emotions belonging to it as something natural. Such a collective state of malignancy of those who shape society via public utterances and their decisions as rule makers and executive power regularly recurs in history. It was clearly present, for example, during the 1620s in Germany in the Thirty Years' War at the pinnacle of the last witch-hunt period, and certainly also during the peak of fascism in the early 1940s, before a silent majority became disenchanted by Hitler and the Allied victory put an end to the Nazi regime.

In each of these periods, we saw what we see again today: Western mainstream churches are full of leaders who live in a state of malignancy. For example, they praised measures that preceded the Covid 'vaccination' campaign and prepared the population to accept the mass poisoning as 'Christian duty', and they support abortion or fail to stand up against euthanasia. In Germany, both leading congregations raise funds to support human trafficking which leads to human misery and increases death rates both on the migration routes and in the societies which have to host the migrants.

Certainly, many church leaders believe that they are acting in accordance with morality, but they fail to see that they are massively misinterpreting faith and are ultimately active in an idiosyncratic and proud rejection of life and God as its creator by supporting evil policies directed against life and creation.

Because contemporary postmodernism which now prevails in our culture is unconcerned with evil, published opinion fails to recognize what's going on, but rather participates in the indulgence of evil: Public voices are competing in applauding the obvious malignancy of our politicians and magistrates. This is a remarkable state we have rarely witnessed before, in such a homogeneous form across the entire domain of Western culture, though the Crusades and the witch hunts come to mind.

The Political Philosophy of Evil

Because the New Testament deals with the relationship of the individual to God, to understand the prevalence of evil in our society, we need to look at political philosophy. From this perspective, evil prevails in society when the elites which control it try to accumulate too much power and for various reasons the mechanisms to control and reduce the abuse of power fail.

In urbanized societies, power is always organized as a state monopoly, because the alternative is chaos and civil war. Since the beginning of urbanization five thousand years ago, there has been a permanent struggle for the prevention of the abuse of state power by politicians (formerly the nobility) and their underlings (today, the administrative bureaucracy) via the cultural, economic, social or political control of power. Whenever this control fails, power leads to evil because from the perspective of the individual who holds the power, the absence of control brings a temptation to use power for his own purposes.

Today we see a multi-layered failure of control of power. Our culture fails to demand control of power and, as we have seen, to properly recognize and name evil. The traditional economic control of power via a broad distribution of property is failing because we have a massive dichotomy of the ownership of the means of production which has become more pronounced at an accelerating speed since the 1970s. This dichotomy is itself the main reason for the exacerbation of power abuse. Social control of power is failing because the interest groups which bring forward the demands and needs of the dependent masses, such as trade unions or classical left wing labor parties, have weakened or entirely lost their connection to the weaker members of society.

Political control of power is seriously reduced because the plutocratic elites have bypassed democratic procedures for the formation of political will by compromise. This has brought us into a situation where unrestrained power enables the triumph of evil in Western societies, and it's not yet clear when or how this process will be stopped. Unfortunately, there are many historic examples for such phases to last for more than a generation.

Gender Hype

In the day that God created man, in the likeness of God made he him. Male and female created he them; and blessed them , , ,

—Genesis 5:1–2

Up until the 1950s, in the English-speaking world, the word 'gender' was used only to talk about grammar, mainly the grammar of foreign languages. If you were learning French, you had to know that the gender of *manteau* (coat) is masculine, while the gender of *maison* (house) is feminine. All that began to change in the 1950s, when, rather suddenly, speakers of English started using 'gender' to mean something much broader. The result has been a lot of confusion, because now people often say 'gender' when what they really mean is 'sex'.

'Sex' is an objective fact of biology. Ideologues of the Wokish persuasion like to say that sex is 'assigned' at birth, but this is only true in the sense that age, blood group, or medical condition are 'assigned' on admission to hospital. The person doing the 'assigning' is really ascertaining and reporting a fact, an independent reality out there in the world, and it's not up to that person to make their own decision about what classification to assign. They can do this job accurately or they can make mistakes.

A person's sex, male or female, is fixed at conception, and can be observed, recognized, and recorded at birth or earlier. We now know that this binary distinction between male and female is determined by the genes. Females have XX chromosomes while males have XY chromosomes.

Proponents of gender indeterminacy like to mention cases where the chromosome is other than XX or XY. But such cases are rare, and furthermore, most of them can still be subsumed under the general rule of male and female. For example, a male person with an extra X chromosome, XXY has the Klinefelter-syndrome, leading to hypogonadism; this is the most frequent hereditary aberration of the sex chromosomes. The few cases where there is some ambiguity are even rarer; you can work all your life in a maternity ward and never come across a single example.

Biology Is Binary

And so, gender is not sex. Sex is the genetically determined reproductive identity of all sexually reproducing animals or plants, which is either male or female. Isaac Asimov once wrote a science-fiction story (*The Gods Themselves*, 1972), which features a parallel universe with different physical laws to our universe, where there is an intelligent species with three sexes, all three having to act together to reproduce. On planet Earth, due to the contingency of evolution, wherever there is sex there are always and everywhere precisely two sexes.

In vertebrates, male animals provide sperms and female animals provide eggs; these two fuse during the sexual act to create new life. In mammals, female sex is characterized by having two sex chromosomes of type X, while male sex has one X and one Y sex chromosome. This genetic property is unalterable, and so is sex. Gender, on the other hand, in its new, broadened meaning, is understood to be your subjective attitude towards your own sex and the way that you relate to other human beings with regard to their sex. For example, a homosexual male is a man with an XY chromosome desiring sexual interaction with other males, each with XY chromosomes. A bisexual female is a woman with an XX chromosome desiring sexual interaction with both sexes (though not necessarily at the same time).

A transsexual man (called a 'trans woman' by current fashion) is a man with an XY chromosome subjectively seeing himself as a woman; he may or may not undergo surgery and hormone treatment to change his bodily appearance to look more like a woman. Doing this doesn't change his sex; his chromosomes remain the same. Surgery may destroy his ability to produce sperms, but nothing can give him the ability to produce eggs. Nevertheless, legislation in many Western countries now classifies the act of calling a 'trans woman' a man and using male pronouns when relating to him as a crime. It has become a crime to tell the simple, literal, scientific truth.

The Changed Usage of 'Gender'

What has changed with regard to the cultural phenomenon of 'gender'? The change began in the 1950s but did not really affect most people until about 1968. Before the late 1960s, gender was tightly coupled to sex. Heterosexuality leading to reproduction in families was seen as the cultural norm. Until the 1970s, the American Psychiatric Association defined homosexuality as a mental illness. Homosexuality and bisexuality were punishable criminal offenses (which they were not in ancient Greece or Rome). The prohibition of homosexuality and bisexuality represented a social norm which was first perceived and put into written form by Augustine, and evolved further in the early Middle Ages.

Over the last sixty years, these customary attitudes have changed. First, homosexuality and bisexuality were decriminalized in the 1970s, and then there was a burst of gay emancipation in the 1980s which exalted this sexual preference. Feminism then focused on the idea that traditional sex language is oppressive, is the result of male domination, and needs reform to overcome the oppression of women.

A theory of gender as a 'social construct' was formulated, drawing upon postmodern philosophy, which proposes that gender is constructed by society. This is of course nonsensical. Society does not 'construct' anything, but social norms or customs spontaneously evolve. They can't be ordered top-down; rather, they emerge. As Hegel pointed out, they are already there when they are put into writing. The core of the Gender Hype, we see now is, sadly enough, the outcome of a spontaneous process. Gender focus, in other words, is a cultural trend which may or may not lead to stable social norms or may go out of fashion as will many other ephemeral trends in the age of postmodernity.

Sex Appeal Is Not Fooled

Incidentally, the vast majority of normal heterosexual men are turned off by trans women. Heterosexual men want real women, not pretend women, however much the pretend women might have been mutilated and rewrapped. And the same goes for gays. Homosexual males want real men, not trans men. This conclusion is based on extensive questioning of male homosexual acquaintances of myself and some of my associates. The same presumably

applies to heterosexual and homosexual women, though I can't
support that with similar empirical evidence.

There has been much talk about 'the LGBT community', now
often expanded to 'LGBTQIA+', which stands for Lesbian Gay
Bisexual Trans Queer Intersex Asexual plus'. The 'plus' encompasses
human sexual relations with other animal species and with the legendary fairy folk. We can now see that the LGBT population, what
Dave Chappelle calls Alphabet People, is not truly a community, but
a collectivity riven by class divisions. Gays want partners of the same
sex, not the other sex masquerading as the same sex, so there is an
essential tension between the 'LG' and the 'T'.

What Is Gender Hype About?

Everywhere, we see advertisements and movies showing gender
minorities in positive roles or showing despicable behavior of
white males oppressing women and gender minorities. In the
West, public sector servants, politicians and magistrates as well as
large enterprises, big business service providers such as accounting
organizations (the Big Four) or law and consulting firms, many
publishers, and almost all the mainstream media require their
employees to use what they call 'gender-inclusive' language. But
they also force it upon the public. For example, in many German
universities, students are automatically downgraded if they do not
use such language. Often, the institutions of the public administration now use gender language in their communication to the public, and mainstream media journalists now use it not only in
writing, but also when they speak.

Generic Masculinity

The vast majority of languages have masculine and feminine genders, and where this is the case, there often occurs the grammatical
feature known as generic masculinity. What this means is that, in
many contexts, the masculine form can be used to denote both
masculine and feminine. So, when Aristotle said, "Man is a political
animal" or when Rousseau wrote "Man was born free, and everywhere he is in chains," everyone immediately understands that
these are not references to the masculine gender or to male
humans, but to all adult members of the human species, male or
female. Traditional teachers of English grammar would sometimes
express this by saying, with gentle wit, "'He' embraces 'she'."

In German, which like English has the generic masculine, the recent Wokish upsurge in gender awareness has led to absurd verbal constructions. In German, the denotation of the feminine is most commonly done by adding the suffix -in. So, *Fahrer* (driver) becomes *Fahrerin* (female driver). This is similar to the English suffix -ess, as in 'shepherdess'. Wokish Germans now feel they have to add the suffix '-in' where it traditionally wouldn't be considered necessary. So *Richter* means 'judge', male or female. But now Wokists feel they have to add the '-in' to denote a female judge. But instead of just adding it, which in this case would seem unnatural, people add it with a colon, and speakers make a pause before adding the feminine inflection to the word 'Richter': it becomes 'Richter:in'. While this looks absurd in writing, it sounds crazy when spoken: speakers pause between the noun and the '-in' suffix or produce a click consonant, which is part of the speech of the Kalahari Bushmen, normally not used in Indo-European languages.

In English the process has worked in the other direction. At one time British female managers, for example managers of stores, would be given the title 'manageress'. But this suddenly become viewed as demeaning to those women, and 'manageress' was effectively outlawed. Along similar lines, a female actor used to be called an 'actress', but it is now considered ideologically correct to call female actors 'actors', just like men.

Many end consumer service providers such as Apple or Spotify or social media platforms such as YouTube, Facebook and Twitter aggressively promote this language in their communication to their customers. At the same time, an excessive propaganda is produced to indoctrinate the public to use this type of language and to blame those who reject is as right-wing extremists, conservatives, sexists, refuseniks, haters, or enemies of humankind. In other words, the West is awash with this artificial neo-language and propaganda promoting it.

The second big phenomenon in the gender area is the Hype about non-heterosexual orientations, sexual perversions, and personality disorders of sexual identity: The LGBTQ Hype. I look at this in Chapter 14, where I also discuss sexuality in our post-reproductive culture.

Gender language Hype is primarily a Fear Hype, the fear of signaling dissent from the required opinion, and also the fear of perpetuating a grievance, the suppression of gender minorities or women via so-called 'sexist language', an invented phenomenon that does not exist—though there are, of course, sexist speakers

(language users). It is therefore tightly interwoven with Wokeness
Hype: it's supposed to mend a postulated grievance, the systematic
oppression of women and minorities.

Gender Language

So called gender-inclusive language is vehemently propagated with
the goal of eliminating assumed grievances from society. The first of
these is Sexism, a postulated systematic discrimination and oppression of women and of so-called non-binary persons. The idea is that
language determines the attitude of the speakers and the contents of
their thoughts and that, if we eliminate certain language patterns, we
will change these attitudes and contents. In a language which has a
gender system distinguishing between the genders by using pronouns and gender-specific nouns, and possibly gender-specific inflection (such as actor and actress in English, though English has far
fewer such gender distinguishing nouns than other Indo-European
languages), one of the forms, the *unmarked form*, is used to desig-
nate both genders. Very often, the unmarked form is the masculine
form. For example, for Indio-European languages such as French or
German which have masculine (grammatically indefinite, unmarked)
noun forms combined with their respective masculine pronouns, it
is argued by the Wokists that the usage of these nouns encodes and
fosters a permanent discrimination against women. In English, this
is postulated for the nouns designating professions with the suffix
man (like policeman or chairman), but also for personal and possessive pronouns in singular, because the male form is usually the
default in the English that spontaneously evolved from Old English
(Anglo-Saxon).

Gender theories of language hold that a language system where
the masculine gender is used as the common gender causes and
maintains a patriarchal society, often dubbed 'phallocratic'. If these
'gender-discriminating' elements of language are removed, the
ideology proposes, we obtain a better society and heal the grievances we observe today.

There are several major problems with this belief system:

1. **The alleged discrimination and oppression of women,**

2. **the theory that language shapes reality,**

3. **the claim that we can engineer a better society by prescribing a neo-language.**

The attempt to implement this ideology has a consequence and a true nature:

1. **The language becomes dysfunctional.**

2. **Language is used as an instrument of rule.**

Discrimination, Suppression, and Language

All Western societies have been patriarchal, and the same applies to all historical and prehistorical societies without exception, as shown by Steven Goldberg in *Why Men Rule* and by Cynthia Eller in *The Myth of Matriarchal Prehistory*.

What 'patriarchy' means is that power-related positions tend to be held overwhelmingly by men. Usually men have also dominated in the productive professions, while married women are mostly occupied with family duties and house-related work. Only non-married women worked in professions, for examples in convents (agriculture, manufacturing, charity work) or as prostitutes.

This traditional division of labor between men and women has many advantages from the point of view of an effectively and efficiently organized society. But it also subjugated women to men and kept women away from worthwhile avenues of social life, especially politics. With very few exceptions (such as the English monarchy which traditionally allowed female succession under unusual and rare conditions) women could only influence political decision indirectly. Women who intended to enter a profession or politics were suppressed; there was little possibility for women to contribute to arts or sciences. Many linguists believe that this male dominance in society has led to the evolution of the masculine as the unmarked form and that it reflects the cultural state of the past. This view is probably valid.

With the Enlightenment it became clear that isonomy ought to be extended to women, and the introduction of universal suffrage almost everywhere in the West ended the suppression of women, a process that had achieved all its goals by the 1970s. Today, systematic discrimination and suppression of women have disappeared, there is no grievance left with regard to women.

That women still get raped is a matter of intractable human evil, just as weak, unarmed, or conspicuously wealthy people are more likely to be targets of robbery. This kind of behavior can probably never totally disappear, and requires to be deterred and thus minimized by severe punishments. But it is not the result of structural suppression of women, which has been overcome in the West (though it is coming back to some extent with Islamic immigration). Therefore, there is nothing more to be done but to maintain the equal treatment extending to all mentally normal adults.

The structure of our language is no longer entirely in phase with the status of women in society. It is the result of the spontaneous evolution of language, but the generic masculine form no longer has meaning today. Historic evolution of language means that isonomy or sensibility for the needs of certain groups, which are culturally new phenomena, are not encoded in the very old morphologic or syntactic structure of language, but are cultural phenomena that evolve as social norms change. Germany, with a language that uses generic masculine nouns, now has a culture of deeply rooted equal treatment and equality of opportunities between men and women, at least in its indigenous population. Turkey, with a language that has female generic nouns, is the Nato-member with the worst and most systematic oppression of women, which is far worse than it ever was in Europe since the eleventh century, when the ban on polygamy was achieved in the culturally evolved areas.

There certainly is an intimate relationship between the evolution of culture and language, but the discrimination of women was overcome while the classical Western languages were still used. It is a matter of the evolution of social norms, and nothing else. These norms evolve much faster than language. The emancipation of women evolved and succeeded since the Suffragette-movement at the turn of the last century without any change in the use of language. *The politicized gender language was invented only after the success of the emancipation movement.*

Does Language Shape Our View of Reality?

The idea that language causally determines the contents of our thinking was proposed by Edward Sapir in 1929 and Benjamin Whorf in 1956. The Sapir-Whorf hypothesis says that language determines our view of reality so that different languages create different universals. An absurd trivialization of this theory, which Whorf would probably not have subscribed to, is the view that by changing our language, we can change the way we think about reality. You sometimes hear people talk about changing 'our reality' or even 'reality' by the way we think about it. This is obvious nonsense: reality exists and has its own properties and qualities, independently of what we think about it. In our thought and speech, we attempt to comprehend that independent reality.

There is a dialectical relationship between language and culture. As cultures evolve, the language changes, and both together shape the content of our thinking, the mental concepts, our relationship to reality, and what we can achieve as individuals and as a society when interacting with nature. For example, a culture without written language cannot build up a bureaucracy that is needed to maintain a city, and without arithmetic and geometry, only limited architectural technologies are possible.

The invention of calculus, a special way of thinking and writing in mathematics, by Isaac Newton and Gottfried Leibniz, is an even more extreme example, because it laid the foundation for tremendous advances in science and for the industrial revolution. But the evolution of language also enables extensive social change: From the late seventh century B.C. onwards, Greek thinkers formulated the inventory of concepts and thought patterns required to transform Athens into a democracy under the rule of law. Another example is the radical change of religion brought about by the first Christian theologians Paul, John, and the three synoptic evangelists (Matthew, Mark, and Luke), which fundamentally changed society after Christianity had been adopted as the religion of the Roman state.

However, such changes are the result of a spontaneous cultural evolution and not of planned interventions. Social norms cannot be invented and postulated or enforced in the absence of social substance. There is a long tradition of state power aiming to change reality by prescribing a certain language. The most extreme examples are the French Revolution, the German Third Reich, and state Communism as in the USSR, its satellite countries, or China.

Victor Klemperer and George Orwell both analyzed this type of language in the 1940s, Klemperer using the real language of the German government, Orwell creating a fictive language modeled on his experience with socialism. Both are characterized by the repetitive use of buzzwords, phrases, and slogans that are highly ideological and often designed to mislead. The language is detached from reality, its function is not to establish a relationship to the social and natural reality, but to exert power, it is propaganda language. Its propositions are not always false or mendacious, rather, they are formulated with the sole purpose of establishing or maintaining power structures with no interest in the truth-value of propositions.

In other words, they are fraudulent or mendacious when it is necessary from the perspective of political rule, but can also happen to be true in some cases. In totalitarian societies, contradicting publicly and often also privately the content of official propaganda, no matter what their truth value, is not tolerated. Mild criticism is punished with social exclusion, fractious or recalcitrant rejection of the propaganda contents is punished using penal law, in the most extreme cases including the death penalty (France under the Revolution and Napoleon I, Germany under the Third Reich, the USSR under Stalin). In all its forms, such political language becomes a part of the political change of reality. But such intervention into language cannot alter non-political social reality.

This can be observed in the field of psychiatric disease nomenclature. Because mental diseases are seen as a stigma, they are regularly renamed with the aim of avoiding insults to the patients—but the stigma does not vanish. For example, transsexual psychopathy, was renamed 'transsexual personality disorder', then 'gender dysphoria' (in the diagnostic manual DSM-V), or 'gender incongruence' (in the disease classification schema ICD11).

However, this has not changed the mental illness condition of individuals affected by this disease, nor has it changed the way they are seen by the majority of the population. Fear of, mistrust of, and revulsion for individuals displaying a gross deviance from the norm, especially if this is caused by mental disease, are hard-wired emotions of humans. By careful education, humans can be cultivated to mild manners and politeness, so that they can control these emotions or not show them too openly, but the primordial reaction has a deep neurological foundation. (See the movie masterwork, *The Elephant Man*, by David Lynch.) This state of affairs cannot be changed by using new terms, as little as the diseases themselves, which have biological causes, can be changed by renaming them.

The idea that we can change nature by renaming it is a modern form of magical thinking, whereby the invocation of a name is thought to cause a transcendent entity to change reality. But the structural encoding of therapy-invariant personality disorders or oligophrenia (mental disability) cannot be overcome by renaming them. Nor can any other entities be altered by renaming them, though some can be changed by engineering.

Engineered Society

Since the middle of the eighteenth century, when Étienne-Gabriel Morelly published his *Code of Nature*, the idea that society can be engineered like a machine was born, and obtained more and more traction. In the tradition of French rationalism and materialism, Claude-Henri de St. Simon and Auguste Comte, among others, advanced the idea that society is a machine that can be modeled mathematically. Comte called the science tasked to achieve this 'social physics' and later coined the term 'sociology'. Such models, he was certain, would enable rational changes to the machinery of society and cause it to move towards the goals set by those who apply the changes. This way, it would become possible to achieve progress and deliver a superior type of society. In Britain, Jeremy Bentham maintained that rational interventions into society would maximize happiness; these ideas were refined by nineteenth-century liberalism, which was strongest in Britain.

Nineteenth-century socialism and liberalism both believed that true historical progress can be achieved by a certain reconfiguration of society. While socialists believed in central intervention, liberals thought that a certain framework for society must be set so that spontaneous market forces could achieve a happiness optimum. Both movements firmly believed that state power can be harnessed by law and utilized for the benefit of society—in socialism, via planned intervention and the permanent redistribution of wealth, in liberalism, by setting a framework for spontaneous forces, while using the state to create and maintain a legal order which could underpin the free operation of the market.

Certainly, liberals did not attempt to directly engineer society as socialism proposed, but the idea of achieving a total utility optimum for an entire society by way of ensuring the proper functioning of market mechanisms was nevertheless an expression of a rationalistic, positivist, and mechanistic view of society. Liberalism in its pure form, however, was never really realized in Western societies; the nineteenth century was full of old structures inherited from feudalism. Keynesianism, a variant of neoclassical economics advocating more intrusive state interventions into markets, was adopted by Western governments after the 1930s. It was combined with fiat currencies and a partial reserve monetary system, creating a system in which state and the private economic sector have merged.

Socialism and all attempts to rationally plan society have always failed more obviously and immediately than liberalism, because we

220   *Gender Hype*

cannot manipulate complex systems in a way which guarantees the outcomes we want. If we use an intervention of which we think it can cause a certain effect and apply it to society or even isolated natural entities, there are always side effects of the intervention we do not expect. This is due to the fact that in reality, the intervention has immediate and long-term multiple effects on the system that we do not understand and cannot predict. But haven't rulers always intervened into society using legislation, taxation and the executive arm of government? Haven't they used various types of power to get what they want?

Certainly. But outside brief phases of tyranny, the repertoire of power measures was provided by established social norms that regulated which type of power could be used under what circumstances. New techniques and measures were tried slowly and one at a time, because in unindustrialized societies, changing too many variables rapidly led to production chain disruptions with famine and protests. *Only with industrialization* and its massive increase in output, reliability and the emergence of industrial food processing and preservation and higher resilience of production chains thanks to fossil fuel abundance, *it became feasible to try to change social conditions radically*. This has encouraged dreams of social engineering and to the present day has led its proponents to believe that engineering societies is a valid, feasible option for rulers. But this is an illusion. Only measures that are in harmony with the spontaneous evolution of society can be implemented, maintained, and have a lasting effect. Social engineering against evolved social norms causes waste and chaos and cannot be sustained.

Gender language is an attempt to engineer society. Because language is the means of communication that differentiates humans from other animals, the attempt to engineer language is one of the most fundamental interferences with our mode of existence. Like all other forms of social engineering planned in conflict with established social norms, it's bound to fail because it is not adopted by the general population and disrupts social interactions. In the case of language, because it is the primary means of communication, the disruption is fundamental and harmful. Speakers realize this and evade the artificial rules contrived by the planners. Gender language establishes a perverse kind of rule. Let's now turn to these consequences of gender language.

Dysfunctionality

Languages like German with generic masculine nouns are harmed more by gender language than languages like English which do not have gender-specific articles ('der', 'die', and 'das' are merely 'the' in English).

In English, gender language focuses on the use of personal pronouns (he, she) and possessive pronouns (his, hers) and the rare cases when male forms are parts of composite nouns, such as 'policeman' or 'spokesman'. While replacing the latter by composites ending on 'person' is unnecessary and ridiculous, it does not cause much harm to the language. The usage of plural pronouns to avoid using gender-related pronouns as in 'A judge must certify that they have familiarized themselves with the record of the proceedings', however, reduces the functionality and introduces more ambiguity into the language without necessity, it harms language parsimony and functionality.

Deixis, the usage of parsimonious language to refer to a specific temporal or spatial fact or a person in context, such as the words 'tomorrow', 'there', and 'he', is hampered by the replacement of singular with plural forms to avoid gender. Even worse is the newer trend to require the usage of gender-specific pronouns for arbitrary genders, here is a typical list: 'zie, zim, zir, zis, zieself sie, sie, hir, hirs, hirself, ey, em, eir, eirs, eirself, ve, ver, vis, vers, verself, tey, ter, tem, ters, terself, e, em, eir, eirs, emself.' It goes without saying that this is absurd and makes it impossible to address those who chose such pronouns for themselves correctly.

Personal and possessive pronouns have two genders because human beings have two sexes that are phenotypes corresponding to their karyotype (XX or XY chromosome). This allows us to spontaneously refer to humans we encounter in a way which is practically adequate. This ability to refer to fellow human beings rapidly is crucial for our communication. The attempt to disturb or abolish it will always fail. In English, gender language using artificial pronouns or the plural forms when referring to single persons decreases the understandability of the language.

In German and other languages with generic masculine nouns and a predominance of gender-specific noun forms and demonstrative pronouns, gender language makes it impossible to use the singular form and destroys the language economy, which is required for efficient communication. Therefore, the political program of the Greens, a Woke German party inadvertently pursuing the goal of implementing the Morgenthau Plan of deindustrializing the country eighty years after it was seriously proposed, does not use the singular form. While this can be done in political propaganda texts, it is impossible to do it in everyday language without seriously diminishing people's ability to communicate.

An Instrument of the Ruling Class

The real reason for propagating gender language is not to promote equality or to abolish power exercised through language, but to solidify domination through language. How does this work?

The usage of gender language signals the rise of a new class of rulers. Those who use this artificial, dysfunctional language show their distinction and their ability to master the code of the elites. At the same time, the inability to use gender language leads to the demarcation of such groups as sociolect-speakers not pertaining to these elites: the so-called 'deplorables'. Even more so, the active refusal to use gender language by linguistically powerful, educated speakers leads to autostigmatization. For example, many authors and journalists refuse to use this dysfunctional form of language because they can only express themselves effectively and efficiently using natural language or because they want to convey that they reject this form of authoritarian language. They become excluded from the circles of power and are not allowed to deliver their services to this class anymore.

At the same time, gender language is almost always used together with the language of 'political correctness'. This language, which seeks to ban certain spontaneously created lexemes and idiomatic expressions and replace them with neologisms, has, as we saw, a similar formal function to the *lingua tertii imperii* studied by Victor Klemperer. Such artificial languages, interspersed with language bans, neologisms and striking, often propagandistically used neo-idiomatic phrases and slogans, always serve to establish or maintain a usurpatory order.

Usurpatory orders are arbitrary power relations imposed by a small group at the expense of the general public by overcoming established power relations. If the usurpers are revolutionaries, they seize power by force, like Napoleon, Lenin, or Hitler. Their language, bursting with expletives, acronyms and apotheoses of violence, is characteristic of their style of rule.

However, a usurpation can also be carried out with little or no violence. For example, in his usurpation of the Roman Republic and its transformation into the Empire, Augustus was scrupulously careful to maintain the appearance of the Republic by means of pseudo-institutions. The senators and other groups of the formerly republican elites could continue to indulge in the illusion of still being involved in power. *Today, the seizure of power by the global elites is also taking place insidiously, coming along in the guise of the old constitutional republican order.* The creeping usurpation is only possible because of the high level of prosperity in the West and the very high security of supply of the population. Another precondition for the silent usurpation we're experiencing is the need for state institutions to actively respond to social change, which has been massively accelerated by the industrial revolution; change has been so rapid and so extensive for over a hundred years that a spontaneous social response to it can only have a partial effect. The language regime of gender language and 'political correctness' are merely cultural symptoms of this political process. The usurpation that many people are not aware of in other areas becomes visible and tangible for a very broad majority of people in the area of language (70 to 80 percent of the population reject gender language). They fight back by not letting the state dictate the most important instrument of their actions.

Intuitively, citizens know that their language has emerged spontaneously and only changes and develops autonomously. It is a form of expression and a means of communication of social norms. Language is one of the most fundamental social norms, which makes many other norms possible in the first place. All social norms that are exclusive to humans, and which other higher mammals do not have, are language-bound. These include many implicit, non-codified norms of behavior such as subtle rules of politeness and conduct that can only be communicated through language, but also all explicit social norms expressed in language such as law or the Ten Commandments.

Linguistic innovations can originate in the vernacular usage of language and then spread into the standardized high language spoken by the elites. Many idiomatic expressions and proverbs have arisen in this way, for example from Luther's translation of the Bible, Schlegel-Tieck's translation of Shakespeare, or Goethe's Faust. But the spread of such high language is also a spontaneous process that cannot be controlled. No one really understands how it works; the development of language by the community of speakers is a system of complex systems.

Prescribed language such as gender language or the language of political correctness have just as little chance of spontaneously sustaining themselves as the *lingua tertii imperii* or the political language of the German Democratic Republic with its absurd abbreviations like 'Diamat' (dialectical materialism) or slogans like 'Socialism will prevail because it is the truth.' Political artificial languages are already dead while they are spoken and written by members of the political elites or their minions at the supreme summit of domination; anyone can decode this language and expose its mendacity, hollowness, and falsehood. The population does this through irony, reversal of terms (a politically correct term like 'handicapped person' is turned into a swear word), disregard, or satire, and jokes.

It's painful to the point of disgust to have to read and listen to this mendacious, presumptuous language of domination that violates the sense of language and hinders the freedom of expression, and meanwhile also to have to speak and write it as a state or corporate employee. But it is inconceivable that this misanthropic nonsense can persist in the long run. No usurpation lasts long, and no *lingua tertii, quatri* or *quinti imeprii* can endure permanently.

Race Hype

> The government cannot be permitted to define one group as being privileged over another group of people. It was wrong in the days of Jim Crow; it is wrong in the days of affirmative action.

—CHARLES A. MURRAY

R ace Hype has been growing in the USA for some decades, but it reached a new peak during the Black Lives Matter (BLM) riots in the summer of 2021. Cities seriously considered 'defunding the police' because politicians apparently bought in to the rhetoric that the police are inherently racist and are systematically killing Blacks.

The result of defunding the police has to be a reduction in the safety of Blacks, in part because most homicides with Black victims are committed by Blacks, and one result of the existence of the police is to reduce the number of homicides. At the same time, Whites were expected to accept that they were guilty of 'systemic racism'. Meanwhile, the socio-economic status of the Black population was declining, following earlier gains. Interracial marriages in the US between Whites and Blacks are only ten percent of all interracial marriages (14 percent, according to a 2008 Pew Research result), so overall about 1 percent of marriages are Black with White. What is this all about?

For many years, we have read in numerous publications in the humanities that human races do not exist. Such assumptions are 'social constructs' of racists and an expression of racism (Guess 2006). Many biologists have also agreed with this view and have recently claimed that human races do not exist from a biological perspective either. The "concept of race is the result of racism," says the German Zoological Society (2019). There are now calls for the term 'race' to be removed from Article 3 of the German Constitution, and one German state recently implemented this. But unlike racism, a cultural concept that is mind-dependent and constitutes an attitude which tends to contradict universal human rights, races are not merely a 'concept' but part of the factual reality that surrounds us.

Biology of the Human Races

Everyone knows from personal experience that there are human races, because there are Caucasians, black Africans, Asians, Indians and Aborigines, all of whom have group-specific, externally distinguishable characteristics such as skin color and facial features. Because people have known for thousands of years that external characteristics are hereditary, it has long been clear that racial membership is hereditary. The sequencing of the human genome has confirmed this. Based on the genetic variance associated with external racial characteristics, at least the following races can be genetically distinguished from one another: Asians, Black Africans, and Caucasians and, with smaller but still significant genetic differences (phylogenetic distance) Indians, Aborigines and the inhabitants of the ancestral lands of the Semitic languages (Jorde 2004).

It's important to be aware how the variance is calculated. In order to make a meaningful comparison between the genomes of different races and, for example, to be able to measure the phylogenetic distance between the races, so-called polymorphic gene loci must be compared. These are sections of the genome that show a high variance between individuals. As Edwards (2003) explains, biomathematical comparisons must consider larger groups rather than individual polymorphic gene loci in order to classify individuals by race.

Considering that complex racial traits such as facial skull shape, heel bone length, and melanin content of the skin are inherited polygenetically, this is obviously true. Witherspoon et al. (2007) have confirmed this and shown that when using larger polymorphic gene locus sets, an almost perfect classification by race can be calculated and the variance between individuals drops to almost zero compared to the variance between races.

If, on the other hand, the variance between individual gene loci is measured, the inter-individual variance is always greater than the variance between the races. This clearly proves at a molecular level what humans have always known: that races are real and are transmitted by the biology of reproduction. The data from the International Genome Sample Resource project, which continued after the decoding of the human genome, has generated large amounts of genomic sequences that can be used to repeat this calculation at any time (Clarke 2017).

Where do the genetic differences between the races come from? They were essentially caused by geographical segregation of humans after the first humans left Africa more than five hundred thousand years ago. Such differences increase when groups of individuals of a species live in isolation from each other for long periods of time.

Mutation and selection change the genomes of the separate populations; genetic drift occurs. We measure this drift when we determine the genetic differences between the races. Social segregation can also lead to measurable genetic differences. For example, this is the case with the Indian castes, which are also externally distinguishable after thousands of years of social (but not geographical) segregation (Jorde et al. 2004). The castes lived side by side but without cross-caste mating.

In terms of physical performance, hereditary diseases, drug effects and metabolism, there are objective differences between races. If physicians do not take these differences into account in pharmacotherapy, they may endanger the lives of their patients. In sub-Saharan Africa, for example, ten percent of the male population suffer from favism, the X-chromosome linked recessive glucose-6-phosphate dehydrogenase deficiency. Although this enzyme defect causes a natural resistance to malaria and has therefore spread in the population through evolution, it also has disadvantages. If, for example, a Black African is treated with aspirin (or certain other drugs) without being sure that he does not suffer from favism, there is a ten percent risk of killing him; the patients die in agony from haemolytic anaemia.

For this reason, international clinical trials for the authorization of drugs strictly observe minimum quotas for the
different races when compiling the sample. Without
knowledge of the genetic differences between the races,
modern pharmacotherapy is just as impossible as rational
and targeted diagnostics in human genetics or successful
competitive medical support for athletes.

New Findings on Racial Differences

In *Facing Reality*, Charles Murray updates and refines his
most important theses from his classic *The Bell Curve* on
the subject of racial differences in mental abilities. He sets
out two key findings. The first is that there has been a
constant structural difference in the mean intelligence
quotient between blacks and whites in the USA for around
three decades, amounting to one standard deviation (SD,
15 IQ points). IQ is biometrically standardized so that
100 is the mean value.

The difference between blacks and whites was even
greater in the 1970s (around 1.3 SD) and fell to 1 SD by the
end of the 1980s, but has since stagnated at 1 SD. The difference between Latinos and Whites in the US was slightly
less than 1 SD in 1970, but is now only 0.75 SD, and the
trend is towards a further reduction in the gap. Asians in
the USA, on the other hand, are 0.25 SD superior to
Whites in IQ (3–4 points more), and this trend has been
increasing since the end of the 1990s.

The evidence for these differences is clear, even after adjust-
ing for all social and cultural covariates, which is very important and a social-science task at which Murray excels. First of
all, this means that there are millions of Black people in
America whose intelligence is higher than that of millions of
white people, namely in the range of average intelligence up
to one standard deviation (67 percent of the population).

But at its edges, the Bell curve has only a tiny surface
under the curve. Therefore, starting from two SD (IQ 130)
due to the small proportion of humans in this range and the
shift of the Bell Curve for Blacks by fifteen points, there are
very few highly gifted Black people at the right edge of the
curve: Around one Black person for every fifty white people
at two SD and then fewer and fewer at three (IQ 145) or

four SD (IQ 160) marks—and this difference is exacerbated by the smaller proportion of Black people in the US
population by a factor of 5. As a result, very few Black people are structurally able to perform jobs that require a particularly high IQ (3 SD or more, such as research at an elite
institution like MIT or Cal Tech).

These differences have been known for a long time.
Michael Levin also worked them out meticulously three
years after *The Bell Curve* in his well-known book *Why Race
Matters* (1997); his methodological part is a masterpiece of
scientific method control. In this book Levin not only
proved that there is a difference in IQ, but also showed that
Black people are less able to control their emotional
impulses than white people.

This fact is also closely related to the second finding that
Murray presents: that, on average, Blacks in the US commit
eleven times more violent crimes than Whites, and Latinos
three times more than Whites. As a result, these groups also
commit the majority of murders and are the dominant
populations in prisons for felons. In Washington DC,
Blacks commit ninety times more murders than Whites, in
Los Angeles, Chicago, and New York City, they commit
about twenty times more. The second finding is likely to
have clearer social covariates than the first, but the poorer
impulse control of Blacks described by Levin also plays an
important role in violent crime.

*Both findings are extremely well documented empirically
and must be regarded as part of social-psychological factual
knowledge. They have nothing to do with racism, but they do
challenge postmodern dogmas and taboos around human
race.*

Equality before the law implies that individual members of different populations, however defined, are treated
the same when all the circumstances of the case are the
same. There is no discrimination against members of particular populations as compared with members of different populations. To attempt to shape the law so that a
particular preconceived pattern arises with respect to
members of whichever population, for example to aim for
the outcome that the same percentage of people in one
population are convicted of burglary as in another population, would be unfair and unjust.

The Causes and Effects

Are these differences of genetic origin? The causal contribution of inheritance versus socialization for the findings of Murray and Levin cannot be clearly identified because there are too many covariates and intelligence is inherited omnigenetically anyway (meaning that many or all genes, not one or a few genes, effectively collaborate to influence intelligence; Boyle et al. 2017). This means that causal relationships cannot be determined. However, the fact that intelligence variation among individuals is inherited to a high degree and that there are clear racial differences in average intelligence strongly suggests that these differences have genetic causes. However this may be, the fact that the differences described by Murray do exist plays a major role in social reality, even though active attempts have been made for sixty years to change them by political measures.

Now what do these differences mean in terms of intelligence and violent crimes? The USA has been pursuing affirmative action since the 1960s, which was originally intended to compensate for the real racial disadvantage of Black people in the education system and the labor market. Over time, however, the program has been expanded and tightened, and other minorities have been added, including so-called LGBTQ minorities during Obama's presidency and then under Biden. As in Germany, US companies were obliged to implement state equality requirements in their employment policies.

Supporters of the programs assume that all people are biologically equal, and that this equality can be addressed by state programs in such a way that equality of results is achieved. However, equality in the legal sense as a fundamental right has always meant equal treatment by the state executive and judiciary, not the achievement of material equality of all citizens through activities of the state.

The utopian goal of equality for all citizens goes back to the early socialist ideas of Morelly, who first formulated it in 1755. Today it is referred to as 'equity' and pursued with aggressive programs. However, this does not lead to more equality, but instead creates frustration among talented White and Asian candidates who are no longer considered for jobs because less talented Black candidates have to be preferred to comply with the legislation. It also lowers the performance of organizations when weak candidates are given management positions for which they are not mentally suited, a recent example is the now resigned Black and antisemitic Harvard president Claudine Gay, a political scientist specialized in Afro-American Studies.

Many moderately talented Black people are placed in positions that they are not suited to and in which they come under pressure and become unhappy. Conversely, professions in which Blacks are superior because of their racial characteristics, such as many sports, would never apply quotas for Whites. At the same time, as Murray points out, the situation in neighborhoods with a majority of Black inhabitants is not improving despite decades of such measures; the security situation there is often catastrophic, and those who cannot leave such neighborhoods for economic reasons are almost defenseless against the rampant violence.

Murray does not point out the only solution to the problem. It would be to bring the low-skilled inhabitants of these neighborhoods back into work by relocating simple jobs from overseas back to the USA. There have been initial attempts to do this since 2016, but there is also great resistance from the financial sector, which has acquired fabulous wealth through the deindustrialization of America.

However, a reindustrialization of America is possible, but would take at least ten years.

Murray's Conclusions

Murray concludes the following from his excellent empirical observations.

1. The denial of objective racial differences among US elites is a denial of reality and a delusional aberration. Cultural Marxist identity politics which are now practiced in educational institutions, especially in the universities by younger faculty members and students, is comparable in its delusion to the actions of Mao's Red Guards. He cites some

terrifying examples of the use of violence against profes-
sors by students and junior staff.

2. Identity politics divides society into groups competing
   against each other for the state's favor and corrodes
   freedom of expression and equal treatment, the most
   important foundations of liberal societies. It will destroy
   US society if the White elites continue to enforce these
   policies against natural racial differences. Murray
   assumes that even today's escalation—here he also
   refers to the Black Lives Matter protests and looting following the death of George Floyd—will lead to society
   being plunged into chaos and civil war if it continues
   unabated. According to Murray, highly aggressive White
   minority groups are already forming. They are aggressively fighting for preferential treatment from the state,
   for example as part of the transgender movement.

3. As the general population clearly realizes how nonsensical and damaging the elites' racial and identity
   politics are, the legitimacy of the government rapidly
   declines as a result, especially among members of the
   functional and leadership class who do not receive
   secure places in the top echelons of power through
   inheritance (such as the children of top politicians and
   billionaires), as Murray explicitly points out. Without
   these fifteen percent or so of society, no system of
   rule is stable (George Orwell called them the "Outer
   Party"). This loss of legitimacy is already leading to a
   spiral of fear, disobedience, repression, oppression,
   and dysfunction that is spinning ever faster.

4. Murray sees the solution in an end to identity politics and
   a revitalization of the American Creed.

With the help of Murray's investigations, we can therefore recognize the truth of racial differences also in mental abilities.
In view of this, how can it be that there are calls for the concept of race to be understood as a 'social construct'?

The New Nominalism and the Loss of Epistemic Norms

How can we explain the fact that attempts are now being
made to present the reality of race as nothing more than

a 'concept' and 'construct' and to turn it into a taboo? As Max Scheler described a hundred years ago, we are living in a time of Nominalism. According to Scheler, this school of thought 'rejects the existence of an objective reality and world of forms'. It always comes to life when 'a given world of forms of human existence and culture comes into dissolution'. We are living in such times. We are witnessing a phase of neo-nominalism, in which the bourgeois-participatory democracy, founded in the nation state and the pinnacle of modern realism, is drifting towards dissolution.

The first great representative of this new nominalism after the Second World War was Martin Heidegger (1948). Under his influence, it has spread throughout the West since the 1970s via French deconstructionists such as Foucault and Derrida. It rejects the Western culture of logos, Aristotelian-Kantian realism, and the classical theories of truth (consistency and coherence). In contrast to Kant's critical realism, for this school of thought there is no objective reality beyond our understanding; rather, it claims that reality is 'socially constructed' with the help of 'concepts'. This rejection of classical rationalism and epistemological norms negates the foundation of our civilization, as all the achievements that led to the industrial revolution and liberated people from the misery of a static agrarian society are based on rationalism and instrumental reason.

Nominalists believe that reality is determined by concepts. The predominance of this way of thinking can be seen everywhere today: It began with the deconstruction of the humanities, which Himmelfarb (1994) has vividly described. Initially, it reached education, literature, and other cultural studies and ridiculed the classical concept of truth as "phallocentric" (Derrida). Today, the negation of logos culture is also affecting the sciences, wherever scientific thinking can have political implications, as we saw in several chapters in Part I of this book. Nominalism thus serves political goals and interests. It serves power. At least in this respect, the theories of the deconstructionists are confirmed. Some of them would probably oppose the use of their thoughts as an instrument of power as we see it today, because it was not their intention to justify a new ideology of domination.

We can also see the new nominalism at work in the concept of race. Racism is abhorrent and must never emanate
from the state; this is also the meaning of the principle of
equal treatment (Article 3 of the German Constitution).
However, eliminating the term will not make the biological reality of race disappear. There are individual racist acts
by state officials, but state-induced racism is by no means
systemic (anchored in institutions and laws) in Western
industrialized nations. It is rather a sad and exceptional
phenomenon. It is not possible to prevent such offences
and crimes ex officio. But of course they must be severely
punished when they occur.

However, it's impossible to completely eliminate subtle
racism that does not originate from the state and does not
constitute a criminal offense. Level-headed politicians,
journalists and social scientists should be aware of this. In
reality, anti-racist activists in the media, politics and education sector are not concerned with preventing subtle
racism, but with the sovereignty over discourse in the
selection of topics that are discussed in the media. This
allows them to expand their own position of power and
prevent criticism of their own mistakes. Totalitarian
demands are being made in the name of anti-racism, such
as complete state surveillance of data traffic.

Neo-Racism

So what is anti-epistemological, nominalist anti-racism all
about? Biological knowledge is negated in order to
crudely remove the basis for racism. It's argued that dis-
criminating against people on account of their race is nonsensical, as there are no races. However, the anti-racists
fail to recognize the mechanisms by which strangers encounter each other.

Communities and societies define what is their own
through tradition and demarcation from what is foreign
(Eibl-Eibesfeld 1989). Tolerance towards racial minorities
cannot therefore be achieved by denying their otherness
and foreignness. Rather, the foreign must be recognized
so that the fear of it can be overcome and tolerance made
possible. We must face up to foreignness. Trying to erase
the foreignness of other races reinforces racism, especially

when society is economically destabilized. In that case, distribution struggles emerge and spread to the middle class.

At the same time, nominalist anti-racism is a form of neo-racism. This is because its champions view racial minorities as victims of social conditions. Since social mobility in Western societies is high, anti-racists deny the autonomy of the socially disadvantaged: the implication is that anyone who is designated as a victim in a socially mobile society obviously lacks initiative and the will to succeed. *So all the victims are implicitly marked as lacking autonomy. Autonomy, however, is the essence of human dignity* (Immanuel Kant). Anyone who denies it to another person dehumanizes them and robs them of their dignity, making them, in Kant's words, "a mere means." For White nominalist anti-racists, Black people are just that: a means to the end of securing those Whites' sovereign control of public discourse. Labeling Blacks as victims robs them of their dignity.

Based on this thinking, anti-racists can justify their demand for a state ban on discrimination. The deconstruction of the Western scientific ideal corresponds to social constructivism, which assumes that social structures can be rationally planned and enforced by the state. As Oakeshott pointed out in 1962, paradoxically, social constructivists, although often deconstructionists and anti-rationalists in cultural terms, use rational thought patterns to realize political goals—precisely where they are almost always ineffective and destructive in the medium term.

The nominalist anti-racists thus fall back on Rudyard Kipling's pattern of argumentation; Kipling saw the indigenous inhabitants of the British colonial empire as weak people in need of education and guidance from the white man and wanted to impose the moral obligation of the 'white man's burden' upon us. In this way, he provided politicians with the moral justification for exploitative colonial policies. This pattern of thought is returning today. The left-wing anti-racists, anti-fascists, anti-nationalists, and anti-capitalists are concerned with acquiring power secured by the state. Their hyper-moral thinking is dishonest, inhumane and directed against the ideals of the Protestant Enlightenment. It denies the autonomy of members of certain races and turns them into a tool to serve the elite's political agenda.

Is there a way out? Once social constructivism clearly fails, perhaps the social elites will return to epistemological norms, realism, and political reason. At present, however, it looks as if we will have to live with the nominalist self-contradiction consisting of epistemological deconstructivism in conjunction with social constructivism for some time to come.

13

Diversity Hype

In nova fert animus, mutatas dicere formas. (It pleases the mind yet again to narrate about the changing forms,)

—OVID, *Metamorphoses*

The Outer Party never stops preaching Wokism.

"The Outer Party," in *Nineteen Eighty-Four*, comprises the people responsible for transmitting the dictates of the Inner Party to the broader public. So it encompasses the management and administration class—the bureaucracy—the politicians, pundits, and journalists, but also NGO and think-tank leaders, artists and scientists, as well as the free professions such as lawyers and physicians. Members of the Outer Party are expected to promote Wokism at every opportunity—or at the very least never to openly contradict it.

Big philanthropic foundations support Wokism with billions and pay for activists in movements such as Black Lives Matter or LGBTQ in Western countries and in those countries which the West wants to add to its sphere of control. Wokeness flags are flying on public and corporate buildings; we have Woke messages and propaganda on movies, billboards, in songs and everywhere in our culture, it has become a massive complex Fear-Hope-Fear Hype: Fear of the alleged massive social, racial, and sexual-orientation related 'systemic' injustice and oppression. Hope because it seems to support positive goals, and Fear again because those who

237

dissent from this Hype are afraid of the consequences of their opposition.

At the core of this Hype is the belief that, in the West, we live in societies characterized by systemic injustice and oppression. Those Hyping Wokeness pretend that the primary characteristic of our societies is social injustice which they believe is baked into the institutions of Western societies. For example, Critical Race Theory, a Woke ideology masquerading as an academic field of research, claims that United States institutions are deeply racist and systematically harm racial minorities.

This 'systemic racism', so the ideology proposes, is not a property of individuals, but of institutions. The disparate rates of incarcerations by races are, we're told, a consequence of bias and institutional racism. Race, the ideologues tell us, in denial of genetic reality, is a 'social construct'. Therefore, it can be 'deconstructed' using the appropriate measures to obtain a racism-free society.

Critical Race Theory is the ideology behind the BLM movement that rioted and plundered after a polytoxicomaniac African American man who had overdosed himself on fentanyl and methamphetamine died under the grip of a policeman in summer 2021. In the aftermath of these protests, cities and towns run by ideologues removed their police funding leading to a surge in crime and homicide rates among the poorest citizens. Police funding had to be restored. Certainly, the idea of changing genetic properties of human beings using deconstruction with words is magical thinking.

So what is Wokism? How do such absurd ideas emerge and get so much prominence in our culture?

Wokism is a perverted form of humanism, also called humanitarianism. Its proponents conceive it as an awareness of matters such as social injustice, racism, sexism, suppression of minorities. Wokism encompasses identity politics such as the transgender movement, but also other political ideas, such as Zero Carbon or Zero Covid. It implies support for policies which propose to mend these perceived problems of society by realizing various goals, the most important of which are Diversity, Equity, and Inclusion (DEI).

Support for the Woke goals can range from simple verbal assent to these goals and the policies derived from them to the introduction of new social norms in private and public corporations, to donations for interest groups or political activism. Often, state institutions now champion and support these goals and use the public monopoly on violence to enforce them, for example, when the police suppress various forms of protest against Woke policies while facilitating protests against non-Woke activities. At the most extreme, Woke institutions justify, promote, and pay for private violence, as the example of BLM shows.

To appreciate how omnipresent and dominant in our culture this movement has become, consider that many private and public employers now demand that their employees undergo regular training on topics such as gender diversity, 'white supremacy', slavery reparations for Blacks, or environmental sustainability. The minimum duty for an employee is to participate in these training sessions, which often involve tests to verify that the participants have learned the contents of the trainings.

In a typical questionnaire after an online training session, the correct answer to the question: 'What is systemic racism?' will be something like 'Our entire society supports a permanent unfair advantage to whites and discriminates against other ethnic groups'. Some institutions already mandate the participation in internal events in which a collective confession to imaginary sins like racism is required. This can be combined with collective chanting and the playing of rhythmical instruments, practices well known from totalitarian societies and religious cults.

Such corporate events aside, it's still possible to remain silent about Wokism, but those who contradict its principles, seem to act against them, or participate in political activism against Wokism can face serious consequences. The proponents of Wokism call such practices 'call-out culture'; its critics describe it as Cancel Culture. It's a form of public attack against the persons who dissent from the goals and methods of the Woke ideology and its policies, often followed by a drastic reduction in their social and economic prospects.

As an example of radical execution of the Woke agenda consider that recently, in the United Kingdom, purely verbal critics of the migration agenda on social media have been sentenced to twenty months in prison or longer without parole; the British government is clearing out the prisons of felons to make room to imprison thought criminals.

Such critics of Wokism, often classical liberals, conservatives, Christians, or just unaffiliated people who tend to abide by common sense, are then branded as 'far right extremists' or 'Nazis'. There are many prominent examples, such as the *Harry Potter* author J.K. Rowling, who was publicly attacked by Woke journalists and activists because she mildly criticized the transgender ideology. She received hundreds of death threats. Thousands of public figures, but also nameless local dissidents have been removed from their jobs or had their bank accounts canceled or blocked by agents of Woke institutions.

In the most extreme cases, we already see imprisonment of such dissidents as the above example from the UK shows. But similar developments also occur elsewhere in the West. Michael Ballweg, a leading organizer of the German protests against the Covid measures, was kept in detention pending trial for more than nine months in a high-security prison usually reserved to terrorists and high-intensity felons. Both the duration and the choice of location were unwarranted and of a political nature. Though Covid is not a primary topic of Wokeness, the Woke movement made Zero Covid one of their goals during the pseudo-pandemic and supported the use of force against Covid dissidents.

Another striking example of Wokeness is the Hype around transsexuals, whose condition is now called 'gender dysphoria', 'transgender', or simply 'trans'. Woke ideology calls genetic males declaring themselves to be women, with or without surgical and hormonal treatment to acquire a female-like outer appearance, 'trans women'. In Canada and Scotland, such 'trans women' with fully functional male sexual organs and hormone systems were convicted of the felony of rape; these pretend women raped real women. They were sentenced to serve their sentence in female prisons because their lawyers demanded it and the courts accepted it.

Proponents of the Woke ideology maintain that this is necessary to promote equity and inclusion. But upon imprisonment in these facilities for females, the felons would have the opportunity to sexually molest and even rape other inmates. Certainly, the women detained in a prison do not want such perpetrators among them, and there is clearly a reason why our penal system has separation of prisoners by sex. Such cases exemplify the craziness of the Woke ideology which turns perpetrators into victims and gives them the opportunity for new crimes. As we shall see, the deeper, underlying reason for this is total negation of compassion in the Woke ideology, and a positive view of bottom-up violence.

Wokeness Goals and Grievances

POSITIVE GOALS OF WOKISM

Wokism has many goals, but most of them are not values like the over-arching goals of classical value systems such as Humanism or Christianity.

What are the *positive goals* of Wokeness? Proponents of the ideology name *diversity, equity, and inclusion*. But also social justice, impartiality and fairness. How are these defined and related? The University of Washington defines them with a focus on the workforce, but the definitions are very characteristic of the Woke creed:

1. "*Diversity* is the presence of differences that enrich our workplace. Some examples of diversity may include race, gender, religion, sexual orientation, ethnicity, nationality, socioe-conomic status, language, (dis)ability, age, religious commitment, or political perspective in our workplace. There are many more. We acknowledge that our American culture is rife with systemic racism, sexism, agism, and classism that negatively impacts diversity in the workplace."

So we learn that diversity is a state of affairs in which a population (in this case, employees) can be categorized into identity groups which have different properties.

Why is this a state of affairs that is seen as desirable and positive? Because it's depicted as redress or atonement for a situation of systematic suppression of groups based on some of their characteristics, such as their race, sex, age, or 'class', a term that is not defined. The definition is circular, because this suppression prevents the desired state of

Diversity Hype

affairs, which is not positively described. But it is worth noting that the *necessity for diversity is derived from the postulated omnipresence of suppression.*

> 2. In the same text, *equity* is defined as "ensuring that access, resources, and opportunities are provided for all to succeed and grow, especially for those who are underrepresented and have been historically disadvantaged. The goal for equity is to promote justice, impartiality and fairness within the procedures, processes, and distribution of resources within our workplace."

So equity, we learn, is a modern term for social justice, combined with *fairness* and *impartiality*. The latter is the classical legal principle of isonomy (equal treatment) first defined on the basis of an emerging social norm by Cleisthenes of Athens, the principle that a judge should not disadvantage a party based on their characteristics, traditionally class membership. Fairness in the sense in which it is mostly used today was defined by John Rawls. At a highly abstract level he defines fairness as the universal validity of human rights in combination with distributive justice. So *equity* is really social justice in combination with a state of affairs in which natural law applies to everyone and institutions adhere to equal treatment of all groups. Rawls is not a postmodernist, but he is a contractarian socialist. We see in his thinking a mixture of fundamental social norms (natural law, isonomy) in combination with social justice, characteristic of socialism.

> 3. The University of Washington goes on to explain that *inclusion* "is a workplace culture that is welcoming to all people regardless of race, ethnicity, sex, gender identity, age, abilities, and religion and everyone is valued, respected and able to reach their full potential. Inclusion means our employee standards, policies, and opportunities are updated routinely to ensure all voices are heard. . . . Inclusion means we use language that acknowledges diversity, conveys respect to all people, is sensitive to differences, and promotes equitable opportunities."

From this definition, it seems that inclusion is a form of culture that results from the realization of diversity and equity. Its consequence is supposed to be that everyone gains respect, is valued and can reach their potential. This sounds like a utopian scenario, a promise to realize the realm of God in our earthly existence. 'Inclusion' is a desired state of affairs that is in total contradiction to human nature, as we shall see.

By analyzing the definitions, *we have learned that the core contents of Woke thinking can be reduced to a set of goals that are supposed to redress or provide atonement for a postulated status quo of ubiquitous oppression and social injustice.* Diversity and social justice (combined with classical natural law and equality before the law) are supposed to achieve this redress, while the state of inclusion is merely a hypothetical consequence of achieving diversity and equality.

All the goals of Wokism are imagined as goals not only at a local or national level, but as global goals. For their proponents, constant intense political activity, legislation, and law enforcement are required to achieve these desired states which, like a mirage in a desert, can never be reached.

All of this is, of course, utter nonsense, but before analyzing it, let's look at the grievances assumed by the Woke ideology because without them, there is not even a need for the redress expected from diversity and equity.

Wokeness Grievances

The grievances and deplorable state of affairs that Wokeness postulates read like a synopsis of the evils of the Western world: sexism, patriarchy, phallocracy, paternalism, racism (only of whites against other races), white supremacism, racist pollution (only the pollution caused by Caucasians is problematic), anthropogenic climate catastrophe, European culture, Eurocentrism, the West, white European males, colonialism, and imperialism. And also religions and entire systems of thought: Christianity (but not Islam), transcendence, metaphysics, rationalism, classical humanism.

From these, the Woke creed believes, result ubiquitous oppression, cruelty, violence, exclusion, and injustice, all caused by these evil forces of Western culture. So Wokeness is mostly about a rejection of European culture, its social and epistemic norms. If Western culture is not marred by the grievances and defects described by Wokeness, then the positive goals of Wokism are obsolete and the redress to be obtained by striving for diversity and equity is not needed. We know that although the West has witnessed power abuse in its history, it is also the source of the values that make life in modern societies pleasant and tolerable.

CONSEQUENCES OF WOKENESS

Wokism is a self-destructive ideology. Though based in Western thought, it rejects the West's values and erodes the prevalence of social norms, removing the glue that holds our societies together.

It supports most of the irrational forms of Hype described in this book and damns those who critically oppose its creed. Its core goals lead it to support uncontrolled mass immigration, which is very damaging to our societies. It also calls for the destruction of the industrial base of Western economies and the restriction of free movement using various forms of carbon taxation and a radical prohibition of individual traffic within so-called fifteen-minute-cities in the name of the absurd and physically impossible goal of Zero Carbon.

From 2020 to 2022, Woke ideologues demanded the anti-scientific, irrational biosecurity state measures that were set up to achieve the nonsensical, biologically impossible Zero Covid goal during the pseudo-pandemic, measures which did nothing but harm to humankind. Wokeness proponents are lobbying for and implementing identity politics undermining the formation of a collective political will and consensus at the national level, leading to the dismantling of meritocracy and its replacement with minority quotas entailing technocratic failure (modern societies need a component of competent technocracy).

Wokism also demands the damaging of families and effectuating the irrevocable physical damaging of children under the transgender agenda. It calls for political censorship with mass surveillance of Internet communication to suppress the freedom of expression. In the name of social justice and even more absurd goals, it is also demands the suppression of human rights, for example, the freedom of assembly and the invulnerability of the body (vaccine mandates).

Overall, it is self-damaging and weakening the West to an extent that may well lead to its dissolution and to the falling of Western states under foreign rule, in a manner comparable to the falling of Spain and the Balkans under the rule of Islam during the Middle Ages.

Wokeness is, in other words, the syndrome that shows us the deepest cultural crisis of the West since the fall of the Western Roman empire and the start of the early Middle Ages.

Arguments Against Wokism

Wokism is utterly nonsensical, because the state of affairs it describes, the grievances it bemoans, do not exist in the way that the Woke preachers depict them. Therefore, they cannot be redressed in the way the Woke ideology proposes it. Diversity and equity are thus pseudo-goals.

Man, Community, and Society

Wokism lacks a valid theory of man, it has no anthropology, and it does not have a coherent view of community and society. At the peak of the evolution of Western thought, thinkers like Georg Simmel, Max Weber, Arnold Gehlen, and Talcott Parsons formulated the following account of human social relations, which is still valid today.

Humans are social beings, who depend on communities and, since urbanization evolved approximately five thousand years ago, societies. There are two major foundations that enable social relations in communities: First, *intersubjectivity*, the ability to feel and understand the intentions and perspective of another person or group via communication. Second, the respect for *social norms* which are internalized and in most cases unconsciously followed by the individuals. Social norms are learned via the process of socialization in families, other communities and, in the case of societies, in wider institutions.

The most elementary community is the family, whose shape varies in different cultures but consists of the parents and their children at its core in modern, industrialized societies. Other communities are the larger family with more distant relatives, the clan, the village, the parish, or various clubs in which people associate. They all have in common that the social relationships inside communities are dominated by mutual trust. In communities, everyone knows everybody else personally, which leads to a very tight mutual control of the adherence to social norms.

In communities of all animals, including humans, there are *hierarchies* which enable communities to function. There is no community without hierarchies anywhere in the realm of higher animals. A hierarchy is a structure of relationships which gives certain individuals more power than others. *What is power?* The ability to realize more possibilities than others given that resources are limited. Power is ubiquitous, and it is not problematic, but rather an anthropological constant common to all human beings of all times, part of the human condition (*conditio humana*).

Societies are social structures which arise when the number of humans living together and depending on each other gets too big to allow complete mutual acquaintance. Social relations in societies are to a large extent anonymous, so that they are characterized by mutual mistrust. Societies function because they have institutions which formalize and enforce social norms. Like communities, societies are hierarchical and always will be. Because power relations are normal for humans, those with more power will have more possibilities to realize their goals. This can indeed take the form of oppression and cruel tyranny. These grievances exist. But Wokeness fails to understand their nature.

The dilemma of power is the following: Power is a necessary condition of human existence, but those who hold it can easily abuse it. In communities, the abuse is tightly regulated by the network of mutual acquaintance. But in societies, where power is anonymous, centralized, and a privilege of the institutions (state monopoly of force) those who hold it are in constant temptation to abuse it for their personal gain. The history of urbanized societies can be understood as the struggle to control the abuse of power. Multiple concepts and methods have been developed for this purpose, and they are always the same over the last five millennia as far as we can tell. The most important are:

- **natural law (human rights),**

- **isonomy (equal treatment before the law),**

- **the rule of law,**

- **norms limiting the scope of authority—such as separation of powers or federalism,**

- **norms regulating procedures of power—such as the code of criminal procedure,**

- **norms of holding office—election, term duration,**

- **norms for the public sphere—freedoms of speech and assembly, and**

- **political participation, which in modern mass societies is the participation of organizations representing the interests of the major associations of a society in the formation of the political will. It can be, but need not be, realized as democratic participation.**

Societies vary in the degree of realization of these means for the control of state power, but those in which they fail totally become tyrannies and are internally and externally dangerous states. They are also unstable, like France under Napoleon Bonaparte, or Germany in the first half of the 1940s.

The political fight for the control and limitation of power is the main driver of political history, and methods listed above form the core of social norms at the politico-institutional level.

Though the Woke ideology picks up two important methods, isonomy and natural law, it presupposes that the level of control of power essentially fails in the West and that the West has no tradition of the control of power, but is a culture of unrestrained power abuse. *The opposite is true.* Some of the norms for the limitation of power have also been developed in other cultures, especially the rule of law, competence-limiting norms, procedural norms and norms of holding office. But equal treatment, norms for the public sphere and democratic participation as well as natural law, which is a refinement of the Greek and Roman system of civil rights, were invented in the West and refined here over many centuries.

It is evident that these norms have not always been adhered to. It is clear that they are ideals for balanced societies which are never realized fully in any society. We know that the West has internally violated them badly in many phases of its history since the birth of democracy in Athens, and that towards its colonies and vassal states, Western empires have often been excessively cruel.

But the West introduced Magna Carta and the Bill of Rights and abolished slavery, and Western jurisdictions were the first to allow universal suffrage and democratic participation.

There's no reason to believe that the state of affairs in which we found the Western states between 1949 and 2020 was in any way worse than most of human history. To the contrary, the period from 1950 to 2000 can be seen as a golden age of democratic participation and rule of law in most Western societies. *Power struggles are natural, and the difference between good and bad societies consists in the way with which they are dealt with.* The West was indeed better than the rest as a place to live for normal citizens for most of the last seventy years.

Now that we have seen that the allegations of the Woke ideology are wrong, and that therefore there is no foundation for the goals of 'diversity, equity, and inclusion', what substance remains? The aspects of Wokism that deserve a closer look are social justice, diversity and identity.

Social Justice, Diversity, and Identity

Justice is one of the oldest ethical values of Western thinking and a social norm in all human social systems. It was already defined as a virtue in classical Greek philosophy, and was a core concept of all ethical theories before Max Scheler revolutionized the way we see values in 1913 in his book on value ethics.

Justice is an ideal, never fully realizable state of affairs in which each individual has the same duties and rights as every other individual. An individual who acts according to the sense of justice defined by Plato or the ancient Jews respects the freedom, property and social relations of all other individuals in the way that the right-hand side of the Ten Commandments (from "Thou shalt not kill" to "Thou shalt not covet . . .") requires it. Anyone who acts against these rules of justice will nevertheless always require that he himself is treated by others in accordance with these rules, which shows how fundamental they are. Justice is therefore the precondition of any social order. It is also related to law in the sense that the legal system, the positive law, though it cannot realize justice, is a system of rules to enforce the rules of justice even if individuals choose not to adhere to them. Justice in this sense is equality of men before the law. But it is not distributive justice, which is at the core of the idea of *social justice*.

Early socialism started a hundred years before Marx's *Communist Manifesto* with Étienne-Gabriel Morelly's book *The Code of Nature* (1755). His radical socialist ideas of social justice, centralized state property, central planning and regular redistribution of property in the sense of distributive justice to obtain equal outcomes was refined in the late eighteenth century by protagonists such as Henri de Saint-Simon, Robert Owen, or François Noël Babeuf. All of them added to the concept of justice the idea of *social equality*. Justice according to this view implies equality of social outcomes, or, in a weaker version developed by social democrats in the twentieth century, equality of opportunity. This understanding of justice is not a personal ethical value anymore, but a social goal, since individuals cannot strive for it, want it or achieve it. *But only goals that the individual can intend can qualify as values.* Rather, only a central authority can define and try to realize the goal of social justice. What can we say about this?

Human societies can never achieve a state of material equality. Human beings are different by nature and education and will always form power structures in societies where those at the top will have more opportunities than those at the bottom. In societies in which this inequality is not too extreme, and those at the bottom do have the means to survive and reproduce at a tolerable level, or the chance for social mobility based on talent, material inequality must be faced as an inevitable part of reality.

Due to the variance among human beings and human striving for the maximal realization of the individual's intentions, no society can avoid material inequality. Modern societies have mitigated material inequality, but cannot eliminate it. All attempts to do so lead to the manifestation of new forms of power structures. Every

Communist society had massive inequality, and we observe power structures even among the inmates of concentration camps and prisons.

So the question of Wokist 'social justice' is not whether it can be realized—it most certainly cannot. The question is, to what extent we should or can create trade-off policies that mitigate social inequality without causing too much harm in other areas? Woke ideology, however, does not want to accept this, but strives for a goal that can never be achieved. Every attempt to realize full equality of outcomes leads to tyranny, with the group tasked with achieving equality at the top of society suppressing anyone else—much in the way George Orwell describes it in his fable *Animal Farm*.

Norbert Elias showed that what counts as high culture, the arts and sciences, is always dependent on social inequality and the presence of an elite with the necessity for social differentiation via this type of cultural achievements—and the means to pay for it. Soviet-style 'Communist' societies did not achieve equality of outcomes, but they did try to suppress basic human nature in order to approximate that ideal, at least for those who were not part of the Inner Party. This thwarts a significant part of the spontaneous evolution of high culture. The Cultural Revolution in China destroyed works of art and killed (and even ate) those who owned and produced them, and though the Soviet Union maintained some of the classical culture of Russia (opera, ballet, music, and some parts of science), most of its own cultural production was dismal and often pathetic—though there were a few notable exceptions in literature and cinema.

Foolishness and the Abyss

Wokeness is an anti-rational, anti-epistemic, nihilistic, and anti-human ideology. The basis of Wokeness was developed by postmodern philosophers who rejected the foundations of Western thought. We sometimes hear that philosophy is an expensive but useless hobby of society which was funded by the princes who maintained universities in a semi-private peer competition until the end of the nineteenth century; thereafter funding came from the education and science

── **Sidebar: Identity, Diversity, Isonomy** ──

Identity and *diversity* are two major concepts of Woke ideology. The political concept of *identity* is needed to define the groups that are supposed to be oppressed and require redress via the realization of Woke goals. Identity in this sense is not the concept of numerical identity, which means that an entity is qualitatively totally equal to itself (the same thing). Rather, in the context of Wokeness, identity is the totality of characteristics specific to a human being, making him distinguishable as an individual distinct from other individuals.

In identity politics, it is the alleged shared experience of injustice of members of certain social groups, for example 'systemic racism' against Blacks or 'ubiquitous discrimination' against transsexuals. Identity is not a value, but a formal relation used to define targets of political activation and systematic privileging, often in the form of positive discrimination by the state in contradiction with the classical principles of justice and equal treatment.

Diversity, a goal which is supposed to provide a redress of 'systemic injustice', is another formal relation. "It is therefore difficult to understand why anyone could think that they have value-properties" (Kevin Mulligan). Diversity thus cannot be good or bad.

While identity is a political concept used to define alleged groups of victims, diversity is a political goal, but not a value.

ISONOMY

The Woke goal of 'equity' encompasses isonomy, a fundamental norm for the control of power. But Woke ideology fails to understand the concept of isonomy.

Isonomy means that the state has to treat all citizens equally when its bureaucracy, usually the executive power or jurisdiction, is interacting with the citizens. For example, a policeman should not treat suspects differently because of their race, but only because of their behavior. A suspect offering resistance needs a different treatment than a compliant subject, but the offender's race or social stratum should not play a role in the actions of the policeman. Neither should a British judge treat a member of the landed gentry differently than a clerk not belonging to the nobility.

The principle of isonomy does not mean that the state should actively try to make the citizens equal in any way: isonomy is a purely negative, defensive goal which historically evolved against the systematic discrimination of non-noble citizens by the feudal and absolutist state institutions.

The Woke ideology redefined isonomy to mean that the state should actively promote the equality of its citizens, and thus moved the concept close to the idea of social justice.

As employers, Woke public institutions strive to promote equal outcomes among their employees. However, this is not possible given the differences in qualification and performance of the employees. Because of the division of labor in organizations, differentiation of talent and ability are a necessity to build, manage and run them effectively. A workforce uniform at all levels could not achieve anything; hierarchy and specialization are inescapable.

Furthermore, the ideology also asks non-public employers, such as private companies and non-profit associations, to strive for equality among their employees. The state and big financial corporations are already starting to mandate Woke policies via so-called "environmental, social, and corporate governance," which is also promoted through the United Nations' so-called "sustainable development goals." These goals ask companies to pursue activities which are not related to producing goods and services and making profit, but to the realization of the Woke agenda. Access to capital markets is now linked to the fulfillment of ESG goals, so that there is systematic pressure for enterprises to implement Woke policies including Zero Carbon', the most expensive of the ESG goals.

But private companies exist to produce goods and services from mining ore to providing insurance contracts or legal services. Their goal must be to produce these goods at maximal quality and minimal costs to maximize profits. This is incompatible to achieving any kind of equality or identity-specific diversity and inclusion in the workforce. Rather, companies are compelled by the market environment to optimize their workforce for the task at hand irrespective of the identity properties of the potential employees.

Of course, managers know this, and while they pay lip service to diversity, equality, and inclusion, they strive to fulfill ESG regulation solely because they need access to capital markets. The ESG policy can be seen as a social credit system for corporations designed by Woke NGOs, the state, and the big money collectors and fund managers, to enforce Woke goals in society. Enterprises that really implement ESG policies will have a competitive disadvantage because they have a higher cost of doing business—reducing carbon dioxide emissions is costly—and their workforce and leadership will be less effective and efficient than those of ESG-free competitors in Russia or China.

Isonomy is a purely defensive right essentially meaning impartiality of judges and magistrates. It was established in the bourgeois revolutions and reforms to protect citizens against the feudal state biased in favor of the nobility. In Germany it has been transformed into a positive right to be enforced by the state, beginning in the early 1960s, when the German supreme court ruled that it is the obligation of the state not only to be impartial, but also to actively achieve equality of the population. Before this ruling, in the 1950s, Ernst Forsthoff argued that isonomy is a defensive right and the welfare state is not an instrument of justice, but merely of protection against hardship and misery for a small proportion of the population. With the ruling of the supreme court, he lost the argument against Wolfgang Abendroth, a socialist. Other Western states have followed a similar path.

The welfare state has been a great source of state legitimacy, but also of chronic and unsustainable public debt. It has entailed the establishment of an entrenched, socially immobilized layer of recipients of welfare payments who hand on their parasitic behavior across the generations. ESG is the destructive attempt to implement the pattern of the welfare state within corporations. Because ESG-compliance is expensive and non-compliance leads to exclusion from capital markets, it leads to further concentration of the means of production in fewer hands. We discussed this and related problems in Chapter 7.

Isonomy is a goal that is not applicable to private corporations. If it would be enforced fully, it would destroy what remains of the market economy.

budgets of the respective republics. But it turns out that theology and philosophy, from the seventeenth century onwards, are still crucial for the way we understand our lives.

What are the foundations of Western thought which Wokeness rejects?

From the perspective of classical Western thought, humans, though they are of course emotional, are rational beings who have the ability to understand their environment and themselves and to arrive at true statements about reality. We can do this based on observations (induction), as it is done in physics or chemistry, or starting from abstract objects (deduction), as it is done in mathematics, to build structures of true statements called knowledge.

What is true and false is arrived at by cognitive norms which were developed in classical Greece and refined since the Renaissance to also encompass scientific experiments. Based on these norms, we have developed the sciences and the technology derived from them, which allowed us to transform the world we live in to the extent that today, urban citizens regularly contact only one substance that is not man-made or processed by the tools of man: the air we breathe. Everything else we drink, eat or touch is man-made or man-processed unless we walk in a virgin forest or a weed patch. It's fair to call the world we now live in a technosphere in which raw natural items play a minor role, even if they are the foundation of all technology.

Furthermore, we have social norms which tell us how to behave: elementary norms which guide our behavior in communities and more elaborate ones which are specific to societies. An important part of these are ethical norms based on ethical values. Our feeling for these values indicates to us which behavior is morally right in a given situation. While these social norms are subject to change and also culture-specific, the West has existential ethical norms.

These were formulated in the Ten Commandments, which came from Jewish into Western culture via Christianity and have been accorded fundamental validity until recently. But some ethical and social norms which are now basic to us arose later and constitute the highest level of humanism only fully developed towards the end of the eighteenth century: a natural law grounded in human reason and autonomy protecting everyone's freedom and rights, which also led to a rejection of slavery and, another hundred years later, to a rejection of the death penalty.

Wokism is a nihilistic ideology which rejects all Western norms that evolved through the end of the nineteenth century. It negates Western rationality, the ideas of truth and knowledge, and Western metaphysics. It is deeply ambiguous towards science and technology. It also negates fundamental social and ethical norms of the West, especially the valuation of autonomy.

In the eyes of the Woke ideology, there is no truth, no knowledge, no rationality, every sentence can be true or false. Instead of knowledge, there is only power, but this is not power seen from a traditional point of view of power as hierarchy. Classically, it is the ability of the stronger to subdue and dominate the weaker in order to realize more of their intentions than the others. But in postmodern Wokism, power becomes a flow of energy through the human beings who struggle against rationalism and its products. The notion of oppression and oppressed vanishes, and we're taught that what matters is the rebellion against the culture of rational understanding of the world.

At the same time, Wokism does not embrace the ethical values embodied in modern humanism. These are (according to Hartmann): the good, the pure, plenitude, and the sublime, as the most fundamental values. As specific values classified by their historical origins: justice, wisdom, courage, and self-domination; classified as values of antiquity; compassion, truthfulness, loyalty, and humbleness as values of the Middle Ages; authenticity, love, as well as the values discovered by Nietzsche, the donating virtue and charity for future generations as modern values.

Most of these values are not considered by Wokism, or are rejected as 'white virtues' or seen as the expression of 'white supremacy'. Among these virtues, Wokeness is mainly concerned about justice as an ideal, but only social justice, which, as we have seen, is an unrealistic, totalitarian ideal that can never be realized, is directed against human nature, and requires expansive coercion in every vain attempt to obtain it.

Woke humanitarianism pretends to advocate social justice, but the real object of Christian compassion, the neighbor, is never in focus. Those in focus are minorities who are supposed to be given privileges at the expense and detriment of the majority, as the 'trans woman' prison sentence in a female prison illustrates. Or, the focus is on large groups never or hardly encountered by those who advocate open borders for humanitarian reasons, so that masses of migrants cross the US and EU borders every day. But those who support and co-finance this migration never encounter them or turn to them in true affection, and certainly, they are not distributed to Bel Air, Los Angeles, or the Hamptons.

The Western value system was massively shaped by Christianity. In Christian faith, the ability to love the neighbor and turn towards him in affection is the result of the insight into one's own sinning and the turning towards God for forgiveness and in obedience. This obedience enables Christians to feel and act upon the values embodied in Christianity. From the Christian point of view, compassion, charity and enacting the good has a transcendent source, and cannot exist without it—a view not maintained by many in our secular age. But the huge charity efforts made in the West since the early Middle Ages, when the first hospitals and poorhouses emerged, were the result of the view that the Church has three major functions in society: preaching, teaching, and organized charity.

Why does Wokism reject the norms and values that have resulted in the historic miracle of the West, the invention of natural law and modern technology? Because it is a form of *foolishness*. The leaders of Wokeness are not stupid, they are fools. Foolishness is not stupidity. Stupidity is the inability to understand complicated states of affairs such as syntactical structures or mathematical equations. Foolishness, by contrast, is a vice to which an emotional state, an affective attitude is attached: it is the hostility or indifference to cognitive norms, which is either grounded in an inability to see them (value blindness) or in emotions which are stronger than the adherence to the value. For the fool, other values have priority over the cognitive value truth, and these are often: vanity, in the form of overestimation of one's own importance or the overvaluation of one's own vulnerability (snowflake mentality), but also aggression, or sexual desire.

These values are what Scheler calls personal values or material values. Affections related to such values can overrule the feeling of cognitive values and out-compete them in the process of will formation. Mulligan gives the example of a vain, rich old man with a young poor mistress convincing himself that she really loves him rather than desiring his wealth, and quotes Nietzsche who said that the vain man "rejoices in every good opinion he hears about himself (quite apart from all considerations of usefulness and quite apart from truth or falsity)."

Wokeness, in this view, is a decadent form of foolishness which overturns cognitive and ethical values to fulfill intentions linked to material or personal values. What are these? In contemporary Western societies, *Wokism is linked to material privileges, higher education, aggression against one's own provenance and culture, and the over-valuation of an impossible goal, social justice.* But while privileged members of our society make Woke statements and support Woke policies, they never live with their consequence which have to be experienced elsewhere, mostly by the less privileged. The Woke rather use their wokeness as a social status symbol, in what is called virtue signaling.

Why Wokism?

In 1944, Aurel Kolnai coined the term 'humanitarianism'. As a religious man, he asked whether "humanitarianism is essentially capable of maintaining itself in actual reality or is fated to defeat its own ends, thus marking a brief transition towards disintegration and anarchy—coupled, of necessity, with new phenomena of tyranny and new forms of gross and superstitious creeds."

This, to my knowledge is the earliest description of wokeness, without, of course, mentioning the term, which came into use much later. Kolnai defines humanitarianism as an ideology starting from human needs and seeing all these needs as equally legitimate. The role of society is to enable every individual to live out these needs by giving equal possibilities to each of them thereby maximizing the total utility for all individuals. Kolnai thus emphasises that humanitarianism is utilitarian, hedonistic, and that it is of course not realizable because no central planner or spontaneous process can achieve this end.

Another early critic of wokeness was Arnold Gehlen. In his book *Moral und Hypermoral* (*Morality and Hypermorality*, 1969) he hypothesized that German culture was transitioning into a state of hypermorality characterized by a unipolar focus on social justice, which he described as a fanatical will for planet-wide charity. Charity in the traditional Christian sense is a personal value with a local range extending to the neighbor, which is the person one encounters personally (Mark 12:31: "Thou shalt love thy neighbor as thyself.") But in the form of social justice, as a nationwide and then global goal encompassing not the personal encounter, but mankind as a whole, it is not a value any more, but becomes a self-destructive goal.

Though Wokism was not yet a mature ideology at the time of Gehlen's writing, Germany was one of the first cultures to develop humanitarianism, as Gehlen called it, a precursor to full-fledged Wokism, especially in the circles of Lutheran theologians and social democrats of the 1960s.

Nowadays, Wokism has become the dominating ideology of the West, with the Protestant countries leading and the Catholic countries somewhat lagging behind, especially in Eastern and Southern Europe.

What are the reasons why the West as a whole and so many individuals and institutions adopt this irrational goal?

Wokism as Pseudo-religion

Human beings have a need for transcendence, the need to imagine or believe in the existence of entities that cannot be empirically experienced. Such entities comprise: God in monotheistic religions, the gods in polytheism, or the spirits and ghosts inhabiting or embodied in rivers, mountains or trees in primitive religions. In modern secularized societies, religion is only one of many options for transcendence, others include esoteric world models, pantheism, or panpsychism. Traditional religious thinking always addressed the question of the natural end of our physical existence via some form of eternal life or rebirth. Another recurring topic is the punishment of the evil non-believers and the rewarding of the faithful in the afterlife.

But when the need for transcendence can't be fulfilled by faith in eternal life, the earthly existence must fulfill all the hopes of the individual. This explains the hedonism and the profligate, radical will for self-optimization of modern individuals. God, as Max Stirner already put it in the mid-nineteenth century, is dead, and the individuals own themselves and are each their own God to themselves, given and tasked with the opportunity of hedonistic self-optimization.

But what is this individual supposed to believe in that goes beyond himself? In mankind, explained Auguste Comte, the French inventor of the 'religion of humanity', during the same period. This idea is one of the origins of Wokism as a new secular creed. Wokism allows its believers to radically self-optimize while giving them the feeling that they are applauding or fighting for a good cause, that they have a morally superior and compelling view of the world and how humans should live together in societies. However, the humanitarianism of Wokism is not a religion, but a pseudo-religion.

Humanitarianism, and its contemporary form, Wokism, have no notion of evil. Evil is merely seen as human impulses "which in given conditions are likely to interfere with the fulfillment of more imperious, general and permanent needs" (Kolnai). Therefore, Wokism knows no individual sin, but only grievances of society as a whole, which are termed 'systematic racism' or 'white cis-male transphobia'. *Not knowing the reality of evil and sin means to be blind to what they cause in the world, and ultimately to become evil oneself.* As Daniel Mahoney puts it, Wokeness is an "idol of our age," that does not lead to the living of values, but quite its opposite, as we have seen above when we looked at the destructive consequences of Wokism.

The ideology of Wokism leads to an aggressive, unstable self-affirmation. Proponents of Wokeness cannot tolerate opinions deviating from their own, they cannot accept pluralism and the open exchange of opinions, but develop an open hatred against their critics which they are intellectually and judgmentally unable to cope with. Therefore, they are forced to label their opponents as far-right extremists or 'Nazis', even if these critics merely demand a return to the elementary principles of natural law and the rule of law.

Wokeness is part of the Western consumerist attitude that has evolved in almost eighty years of a constant increase in per-capita income at least for the upper twenty percent of society engaging with the Woke pseudo-religion. True morality involves gratitude for the world that our ancestors built, and a willingness of the individual to sacrifice benefits, including his own life, for the benefit of the society he is a member of (soldier bravery) or for his faith and convictions (martyr bravery). Wokism has no notion of sacrifice, and is therefore no religion at all.

Wokism as an Ideology of Domination

An ideology of domination is a system of thought that presents a narrative to the population which promises a set of positive effects bound to a certain behavior. Its goal is the stabilization of power structures lacking spontaneous attractiveness and legitimacy. It is doing this by facilitating the masses to internalize its maxims and goals so that the individuals pursue the contents on their own, make them their own. This is what Max Weber called the iron shell of bondage within an overarching context of rationalism and demystification of the world.

A historical example of such an ideology is the commercialized indulgence which the Catholic church propagated around 1500. The faithful were promised salvation under the condition of buying 'indulgences', letters giving them absolution from their sins. The goal was not to help the faithful or to strengthen their faith, but to exploit the faith of the masses to fund Church spending for political and cultural matters while keeping them in a state of constant terror, urging them to renew the payments for indulgence. Those who invented these schemes were of course aware of this and did not themselves believe in these ideas, but used them to dominate and suppress the population. The Church went too far, because after more than a hundred years of unanswered and successfully suppressed demands for reformation, this practice finally provoked a breakthrough for Protestantism, which gained support from important parts of the European nobility, with a focus on Northern Europe.

Wokism is an ideology of domination. Many of those who fund Wokism via their huge misanthropic foundations do not believe in it themselves, but see it as a method to convince the management and support layer of society (the management and bureaucracy class, the Outer Party) to adhere to the ideology so that it can be used to legitimize and cover the neo-feudal evolution of society we are witnessing. The education system is now submerged in Woke ideology, with only few institutions and individuals dissenting. While Wokeness is usually rejected by the working class, many of those with an academic education embrace it.

Those who enact Wokeness fail to recognize that they are damaging society via particularization and leading it ever more into a state which privileges a tiny minority at the cost of everyone else. Wokeness is so compelling to them because it seems enlightened and morally superior. But its promise of social justice is empty, and nowhere does it propose how to deal with economic inequality and the consequences of the abuse of real power structures. It merely provides a way to use virtue signaling as a method to demonstrate the moral self-justification of a pharisee and fosters radical egoism. It is a toxic ideology of tyranny and self-destruction.

Postmodernism and Wokism

In Western societies, postmodern thinking is not the only cultural force, but is a major force dominating political discourse and published opinion. It is so dominant now that it makes no sense to say that the postmodernists are 'left wing' and those supporting classical Western thought are 'right wing': The entire political spectrum is dominated by postmodern thinking. The founding thinkers of postmodernism have at least the following in common:

- **A rejection of Western rationalism, metaphysics, truth, knowledge. Knowledge is redefined as an amorphous, emergent property of the undercurrent of society.**

- **A self-contradictory view of language and cognition: Language is seen only as a game or the mysterious 'house of being' (Heidegger), but at the same time, it is used with an ambivalent, insecure claim of the truth of the statements of the postmodern author.**

- **A radical critique of modern rationalism and the demystification of the world it entails.**

- **A longing for an archaic, primordial culture that is in harmony with nature; this culture embraces open violence, which is seen as positive by all postmodernists. It is supposed to be based on healthy, pre-rational myths, while rationalism is seen as rotten and sick.**

- **A strong rejection of compassion, charity, and love of neighbor, combined with an indifference towards material injustice and the suffering of the destitute.**

- **The view that modernity will be overcome by some cataclysm, an annihilation of our society.**

- **A self-portrait of the postmodern thinker as a heroic mastermind and outsider.**

- **A redefinition of power, which is not the ability of an individual or a group to achieve more of what they want than others, but a diffuse, esoteric pattern of energy. Archaic power is glorified; there is no understanding that power structures in the sense of Hobbes are part of the human condition.**

- **Malthusianism, the view that the resources of the world cannot support mankind.**

- **A self-contradicting mish-mash of the concepts and views of postmodernists, which culminates most clearly in Heidegger's forgetfulness of being (Seinsvergessenheit), from which there is no way out. The other postmodernists have similar irresolvabilities, as they can no longer appeal to rationality, the core of the Western adaptation pattern to the world.**

In postmodernism, three thinkers stand out: Jünger, Heidegger, and Foucault. The only major difference between Foucault and the two German postmodernists (Jünger and Heidegger) is that the latter reject Globalism, while he supports it. Foucault is not by chance the dominating teacher of today's postmodernism: His teaching is fully compatible with a rational, cold, and merciless oligopolistic carving up of the world that his Neocon disciples are striving for.

At first glance, it might appear that Wokism differs from postmodernism in that it embraces social justice, which we do not find in the fathers of postmodernism. But that is an illusion, because social justice is not a type of compassion, but a sterile, impossible goal which serves the moral narcissism of the modern day pharisees who pay lip service to this goal as virtue signal, but do not live compassion in their lives.

Nevertheless, though Wokism developed from postmodernism, it is not an academic style or system of thought, but a practiced cultural movement and thus differs in many ways from postmodernism. Though postmodernism is a self-contradictory, absurd ideology, Wokism has even more self-contradictions. At its heart, though, we find the same derogation of compassion, rejection of social and epistemic norms, and ignorance of human nature: *dangerous foolishness*.

The redefinition of power allows both postmodernism and Wokishness to look away from the real power structures of society and focus on minorities, but not with the goal of helping them to improve their participation in democratic processes, but with the goal of particularization. This clearly undermines the formation of a political will from the bottom and fosters top-down global, centralized political will formation and implementation.

Like postmodernism, Wokism also rejects natural law, therefore it was no problem for the Woke movement to demand the cessation of human rights and the employment of raw public power against protesters under the absurd Zero Covid regime. It is also willing to support measures directed against carbon emissions which trample over natural law, for example in the negation of property rights and the right of free movement. As practiced postmodernism, Wokism also acclaims bottom-up violence as the primordial, positive form of power, which is the reason why the movement embraced the violence of Black Lives Matter or the massive violence against public infrastructure committed by the so-called climate activists. Wokeness is, as Preparata said about postmodernism, an ideology of tyranny.

Sidebar: The Origins of Wokism

Wokeness is a postmodern humanitarianism with anti-rational, anti-metaphysical, anti-religious, anti-transcended, deeply skeptical, hedonistic, and ultimately anti-human core convictions. Its historical sources are the Young Hegelians, socialism, and postmodernism.

The Young Hegelians were a movement of followers of the German philosopher Georg Hegel, from the 1830s to the late 1840s. The three most important of them are Ludwig Feuerbach, Max Stirner, and Karl Marx. Unlike their teacher, but like the French Enlightenment philosophers, all three of them (as well as others from their group) denied the existence of God. But the French Enlightenment thinkers like Voltaire were more novelists than philosophers in the Greek, German, or British sense, or they were political philosophers like Jean-Jacques Rousseau or Benjamin Constant. Their metaphysical thinking in the rejection of God was less rigorous than the reasoning of the Young Hegelians, who had a more decisive effect on philosophy: Since then, Western philosophy has become atheist. But they did more than dispute the existence of God.

They also formulated the program of *hedonistic self-utilitarianism* (Max Stirner). The ideas expressed by Max Stirner evolved into the cult of the self, mass-consumerism, and hedonism as well as an individualism devoid of cultural individuation. The latter is a result of careful, conscious self-cultivation, it can never be a mass phenomenon.

Socialism, with the goal of social justice at its core, to which Karl Marx gave a philosophical foundation with long-lasting effect, became a powerful political movement. Even after the end of the Soviet Union, it survived as Western Marxism and has always inspired the European and American left, which is no longer 'left' in the classic sense. Since the 1980s, this former left has become the social center of Wokeness, which comprises both hedonism and the idea of social justice.

However, both hedonism and socialism are not anti-rational and anti-metaphysical, and neither were their Young Hegelian sources. So where did the nihilism and skepticism and foolish negation of epistemic norms that is so characteristic of today's Wokeness come from?

Nihilism arose in Europe with Nietzsche, who questioned the foundations of rationalism, metaphysics and ethics in a radical manner, though it can be argued that he saw himself in the tradition of Enlightenment. While Nietzsche defended the idea of perspectivism which, to some extent is related to hermeneutics, views knowledge a matter of perspective, he also affirms the truth of his own ideas. Therefore, he was no skeptic like Sextus Empiricus who denied any form of truth. But the way his thinking was utilized led to *postmodernism*. From the 1920s onwards, three thinkers developed the foundation of today's postmodernism, the *source of the Woke nihilism:* Martin Heidegger, Georges Bataille, and Ernst Jünger.

Martin Heidegger (1889–1976)

Martin Heidegger's thinking is characterized by a deep and fundamental negation of rationalism, metaphysics, knowledge, and Christian transcendence. He was opposed to Western thinking both in philosophy and science, which in his view had led to individualism and the modern technical world, which he despised.

According to Heidegger, rationalism and science have led modern man into a state of 'forgetfulness of being' (Seinsvergessenheit) and destroyed his being (he uses the neologism *Seyn* with a 'y' to replace the classical *Sein*) and essence. Cartesianism led to the illusion of the calculability and feasibility of the metaphysical being, with a false 'Sein' destroying the 'truth of the beyng (*Seyn*)'.

Western thought, according to Heidegger, leads to a civilization devoid of meaning, characterized by machination (*Machenschaft*) and the rule of the 'Man'. *Machenschaft* is a derogatory term describing the active shaping of the environment and the society in the modern age as a criminal activity. The 'Man' is a Heideggerian neologism which he created as an upper-case variant of the lower-case German third-person singular pronoun 'man' which is used to identify an anonymous person (as in 'one takes a pound of butter' in a recipe). He uses it to describe anonymous power structures. For Heidegger, modernism makes the world available, calculable, an object of constant reckoning, purposing and repurposing, explaining, arranging, and planning. The technical transformation of the world leads to an emptiness without perspective, an organized uncertainty as the consummated aimlessness of a dying mankind. Rationalism is a means of rule and must be uncovered and overcome, though Heidegger cannot say how.

He also rejected the political philosophy of Western Enlightenment with its principles of natural law, freedom, autonomy of the individual, and equality before the law. He saw all of these as damaging products of Western metaphysics that he wanted to get rid of. Heidegger also rejected Humanism which he saw as inseparably connected to Western metaphysics. His core argument against Humanism is its supposed starting point. Heidegger thinks that the Western metaphysical grounding of Humanism is its view of the human being as a living organism, so that the metaphysics is tied to the biological existence of man, man's existence as an animal. He believed that this supposed binding to man's life form prevents metaphysical Humanism from accurately characterizing the existence of man, therefore driving us further into forgetfulness of being (*Seinsvergessenheit*).

But Heidegger found no way out of *Seinsvergessenheit*. His attempts to create a new language that would enable us to explore the 'house of being' as he called it, was a philosophical aporia (no-way-out philosophy). A good example can be found in his "Letter on Humanism" written to his French colleague and disciple Jean Baufret in 1947. In this and all his subsequent writings, he served up an esoteric jargon of language that sounded interesting when it was fashionable in the postwar period. It makes no sense, leads nowhere, gives no answers to anything, provides no solutions, but sounds complicated and somehow strangely attractive to the reader who follows Heidegger in his damnation of Western civilization.

With this style of empty, murmuring pseudo-meaning, Heidegger created one of the blueprints of postmodern thinking which massively influenced French postmodernists such as Derrida, Foucault, Lacan, Deleuze, Baudrillard, Lyotard, Badiou, and their disciples down to Žižek and Butler.

Like other postmodernist thinkers, Heidegger also saw a solution in the apocalypse. He had no compassion for human beings, no charity, but thought that a cleansing of mankind of rationalism and metaphysics could only be brought about by means of violence. Despite his constant talk of the 'beying' of humans, he deeply hated human beings and believed that the Holocaust was a failed attempt to achieve a cleansing of Western civilization via the annihilation of the Jews, a people that he saw as a major bearer of the cold rationalism that brought us *Seinsvergessenheit*. In the last years of his life, he wrote to his brother that it was unfortunate that the Nazis had failed in their mission to cleanse the Earth of the Jews. This motif of profound hatred for humans is a core feature of post-modernism which Heidegger shares with the other founders of this ideology of tyranny (according to Preparata).

He also believed that the globalist (he called it 'plane-tarist') machination would lead to the destruction and devas-tation of humankind. He sees this as the only chance of liberation from rationalism and metaphysics and a return to the original form of 'beyng'. He apocalyptically concluded: 'Everything must go through annihilation, that follows an utter devastation of the apparent maintenance of the 'culture'. This is the only way to rock the two-thousand-year-old fabric of metaphysics and to bring it to crumble.' Other postmodernists have similar apocalyptic visions.

One of the most influential thinkers of postmodernism, Michel Foucault, is a follower of Heidegger. For a discus-sion of his work and influence, see the books by Preparata, Scruton, and Hicks.

14

Trans Hype

And if you gaze for long into an abyss, the abyss also gazes into
you.

—FRIEDRICH NIETZSCHE, *Beyond Good and Evil*, 1886

Dr. Miriam Grossman recalls "the good old days" when
parents worried about their children having sex and taking drugs. A child might become infected with a sexually
transmitted disease, or might get sick and die because
of an adulterated opiate. Yes, those were the good old
days!

Today, many parents are worried sick because their
children, manipulated by Wokish schoolteachers, might
start to believe that their true 'gender' is the opposite of
that which they have always believed since babyhood.
And this can easily lead to the compulsory mutilation and
sterilization of the child, with the authorities removing
the child from the parents if they try to oppose this officially sanctioned molestation and abuse.

The story often goes like this. Starting in kindergarten,
the children are told by the teacher that they may be boys
or girls, according to what they would like to be. This message is drummed into the children repeatedly, day after
day. The children may pick up on the message that if they do
choose to change their 'gender' they will become objects of favor-
able attention. Some of the boys express a preference for
being girls and some of the girls express a preference for
being boys. The teacher then explains to them that what

267

they have chosen is their true 'gender'. The kids are told to keep this knowledge from their parents: it's a secret shared by the teacher and the students. The children are encouraged and supported in this belief, and may be given a secret name denoting their 'new' gender.

As this Wokish project proceeds, the child is promised that any confusion and anxiety they experience as they approach puberty can be cured by 'gender-affirming care'. This means drugging the children with puberty blockers, so that their normal development is arrested. Eventually, this gender-affirming care progresses to surgery: including removal of breasts and reproductive organs from the girls and of all genitalia from the boys.

All gender-affirming care leads to irreversible changes: there's no going back, or if the 'care' is halted early enough, there may be some hope of getting back on track in a partial and crippled manner. If the progression is too far advanced, the child can never beget or bear children, nor ever experience orgasm. Now you see why we might long for the return of those good old days.

How did we get into this dreadful nightmare of government-enforced child abuse? Although for most people, the arrival of this situation appears to have been very sudden, and to have occurred only in the last ten to fifteen years, it was being busily prepared much earlier, as Dr. Grossman documents (Grossman 2023).

The expanded use of the term 'gender' was promoted by Dr. John Money, beginning in the 1950s. Money was eventually exposed as a total fraud, but the idea of a 'gender identity' (his coinage, 1956) outlasted him. However, Money contended that sex and 'gender', meaning subjective identification as male or female, were quite separate, the former determined entirely by biology, the latter entirely by social conditioning.

The new gender ideologues preach something different: that gender is always fluid and is ultimately governed by the way the individual person happens to feel. So, you can choose your gender at the age of five. (Yes, there are actually people who believe this, as well as those who pretend to believe it for their own reasons.) And, since these demented ideologues use the word 'gender' in places where people used to say 'sex', we get the conclusion that there is no such thing as objective sex, not even as defined by social conditioning.

Thus we arrive at the position that what 'gender' you are is something that no one except you can possibly know. But then, how can you know it? What does it mean for a child to know that he is really a female or that she is really a male? This is a twofold problem: 1. How can a child gain an understanding of what gender means? And 2. if an apparently male child chooses to be a female, or vice versa, what is this thing called female, or male, that he is choosing to be? (Two and a half thousand years ago, Plato wrote that we should be careful about telling children certain stories about the gods, because children can't possibly understand the context and may therefore be harmed by hearing such stories.)

You may be wondering what you can do to protect your children from these fanatical child molesters, now empowered by the judicial system in some states. In the United States, the first step is obvious: Quit the public school system. Get out, right now! You are incredibly fortunate to live in a country where homeschooling is a legally recognized right (though subject to some degree of regulation, varying state by state). So, either find a private school which you are absolutely convinced is deeply hostile to gender-affirming care, or embark upon the great homeschooling adventure, as laid out by Susanne Gibbs. If you can't conveniently do either of these, start watching closely what goes on in your children's public school, ready to pull the children out if you find anything untoward. If you see dangerous signs, consider moving yourself and your family to another, less Wokish state— but do this abruptly, without warning, and early on, before law enforcement in your state gets brought in to compel the kidnapping of your children, followed by their chemical abuse and surgical mutilation.

Gender Ideology in the Culture

Unremitting propaganda for the new gender ideology is not confined to the educational system. Everywhere we look today we observe intense propaganda for gender ideology, leading with inexorable logic to the government-enforced mutilation of children.

Mass culture such as movies, TV, or books, is now full of characters from the various LGBTQ groups, to a proportion that is nowhere encountered in a real population. Public events to praise sexual deviancy and perversions are regularly held, previously convicted male sexual offenders in drag read fairytales to children in public libraries or schools, educational material for primary schoolchildren is full of damaging sexual content, including a focus on sexual deviance and pathology.

Males self-declaring as women ('trans women') participate in female sports, where normal heterosexual women now face competition from both trans men (women taking male hormones) and males 'identifying' as women. Both groups are superior in physical strength to natural women, thus giving these athletes an unfair advantage. Female sport is being destroyed in the name of diversity. During the 2024 Olympic Games, 'trans woman' boxers beat up hopelessly disadvantaged female fighters in a complete negation of the very idea of the Games.

Convicted male rapists identifying as trans women but with full male sexual equipment have been imprisoned in female prisons where they have, of course, promptly raped the other inmates. It's hard to conceive of a more absurd or nightmarish implementation of criminal justice. And worst of all, there is the monstrous Crime Against Humanity called gender-affirming care.

The transgender ideology victimizes the weakest members of our society, women from the bottom of the social hierarchy (which constitute the vast majority of female prisoners) and underage children, among the weakest of all, without providing benefit to anyone but the felons and the medical institutions performing child mutilation surgery, a vicious and highly lucrative form of organized crime.

What's going on here? How does Trans Hype result in the very opposite of a Humanistic approach to dealing with transsexuals and the weakest members of our society?

Transsexuality Is a Mental Disease

Transsexuality, the fundamental emotional attitude of being born as a mental woman in a male body (or vice versa) and urgently wishing to adapt your outer physical appearance to this psychic experience through medical gender reassignment—a transformation of the chromosomal make-up is physically impossible—is a severe but rare disorder of sexual identity that is always accompanied by a personality disorder.

Transsexuals are usually unable to reproduce normally and start families, and they suffer from being severely disturbed at the core of their identity. Transsexuals have a very high comorbidity with other mental illnesses, especially DSM Axis I disorders (formerly called neurotic disorders), which according to a typical study 71 percent of transsexuals have suffered from, and other personality disorders, which 42 percent of transsexuals are diagnosed with.

These people suffer so much from their condition that suicidality is very high in this group—often they have to be hospitalized in psychiatric hospitals after suicide attempts or because of self-harm (Peterson 2017). The prognosis after 'gender reassignment surgery' is even gloomier. Many continue to suffer under their severe condition after the treatment. This is the typical situation with deep personality disorders, which are notoriously hard to treat.

Among many lay people who have never treated transsexuals and do not know their suffering, it is no longer ideologically correct to regard transsexuals as ill, but their condition—together with hedonistic expressions of normal sexuality in modern, highly individualized society—is taken as just another variant of the new sexuality. This denies these people the disease state, and it is deeply inhumane, as many of them are so ill that they need professional help for life. Suffering transsexuals are human beings who deserve compassion and care. Treating them is very demanding and requires a lot of experience, empathy and patience—a therapy that really eliminates their suffering does not exist in the vast majority of cases, even though partial therapeutic adjustments of the external sex characteristics are the standard treatment today.

In 2013, the American Psychiatric Association renamed this severe illness 'gender dysphoria' in the DSM V in order to avoid the stigmatization by the term 'disorder'. However, the choice of term is unfortunate, because prior to this change in terminology, 'dysphoria' denoted a transient mood—the term does not do justice to the severity and chronic character of the disease.

The current canonical definition of the disorder is also very problematic: DSM defines gender dysphoria as the "distress people feel because of a disagreement between their gender identity and the sex assigned to them at birth." The definition thus assumes that gender is assigned at birth by the gynecologist. But this is only very rarely the case—in about 3–5 out of 100,000 births (the estimates are imprecise): More than 99.99 percent of newborns have a clear biological sex which the doctor does not really 'assign' but establishes by inspection of the newborn. For a tiny minority of newborns with inherited disorders of the sex chromosomes (such as a XXXY genotype) or disorders of embryogenesis it may be difficult to establish the sex, though the presence of a Y chromosome always indicates male sex, even in these individuals.

In a tolerant society with value pluralism, life as a transsexual (also called trans identity) is quite possible if the personality disorder is not too profound. A German trans woman author, a genetic male with a female identity and a condition after 'gender reassignment' treatment writes: "The vast majority of trans people do not want attention. They want to be left alone and live their lives, to drift into normality, so to speak." And so it is. In many sexual perversions such as fetishism, transvestism, voyeurism, sodomy, pedophilia, or sadomasochism, an excessive or misguided sexualization of the general experience is characteristic. This is not the case in sexual identity disorders.

This pinpoints a crucial feature of the whole trans craze. *The few articulate and aggressive people who present themselves as spokesmen for trans people don't represent the vast majority of trans people.* They were not elected by them, and they are very different from them. Most trans people are not a 'community' headed by some trans celebrity. They are rather people who recognize that they have serious personal problems, or as the psychotherapeutic vernacular currently has it, issues. Dave Chappelle says that the trans community hates him. No! It's a handful of attention-grabbing activists who hate him. They can't speak for trans people in general. Most rank and file transsexuals probably find Dave's jokes about trans people and other 'sensitive' issues just as funny as the rest of us do.

To those who feel that they are trapped in the wrong sexual body, we should show compassion and offer help. When a psychotic man actually believes he is a woman, that is a delusion comparable to the patient who believes he is the emperor Napoleon. But it is entirely possible that a rare individual man, undeluded as to fact, believes that he can gain most satisfaction from life by 'identifying' as a woman, behaving as a woman, and generally acting out the role of a woman. In that case, we may be skeptical about what he expects from this course of action, but if he sticks to it, and he is of age, we recognize his right to pursue that course, and hope that it leads him to some measure of happiness.

Classical liberalism advocates a tolerant view towards transsexuals and in that spirit, adults with full ability to consent to medical treatment should have the opportunity to undergo the treatment they desire. They should even get health insurance reimbursement if there is a medical indication for the interventions. But it is a crime to subject children to life-changing treatments which permanently disable their sexual functions and irrevocably prevent them from reproducing. A modern society normatively committed to natural law and the rule of law must be measured by how it deals with transsexuals and accepts these people and provides them with medical and socio-psychiatric care when they are unwell and cannot live permanently in a stable manner, just as it does when dealing with other minorities burdened by nature, such as the physically disabled or schizophrenic. Trans Hype achieves the exact opposite of this.

Transgender Hype

Transgender ideology claims to stand up for transsexuals, but also homosexuals, bisexuals, as well as sexually perverted ('queer') persons. Not only is acceptance of these very different states of sexuality demanded by society, but we are told that special rights or privileges for these groups are additionally required. What can we make of this?

The areas covered by the LGBTQ movement are so heterogeneous that the groups supposedly represented cannot have any common goals at all: homosexuality and bisexuality, which were the focus of the original LBG movement in the 1980s, are non-perverted variants of sexual preference; they are not diseases. Both groups have received full civil equality in Western societies since the mid-1970s.

'Queer' people often (though not necessarily) suffer from sexual perversions. These are mental illnesses in which sexual experience (intentionality, desire, dreams, actions) is directed towards objects that are unsuitable for sexuality, such as shoes or clothes, animals, or children. Perversions can also be characterized by a disturbance of sexual experience which is so severe that sexual acts are accompanied by violence or health risks, such as all forms of direct sexual violence (molestation or rape), intense sado-masochistic practices, for example involving strangulation, or the eating of excrements or drinking of human blood in the course of sexual acts. It also includes voyeurs, exhibitionists, stalkers, and frotteurs, all disorders of sexual experience in which the sexual objects of these perverts suffer. Whenever others suffer from sexual perversion, such criminal behavior must be correctly identified in accordance with the penal law to be prosecuted and punished. Therapies should be offered while the offender is serving his sentence in prison. The prognosis is not very good, unfortunately.

In contrast, transsexuals, as we have seen, are often seriously mentally ill and in any case need the intensive attention of the healthcare and rehabilitation system. They are usually peaceful and do not commit crimes more often than the average citizen, so very rarely.

We see that all the groups lumped together under the LGBTQ umbrella have different needs and society must deal with them differently. Sexual offenders must be removed from society in proportion to their crimes, perverts must be punished when other people suffer from their sexual acts—including consuming child pornography because the production of this material requires crimes to be committed.

Homosexuals and bisexuals, on the other hand, are normal members of society. Transsexuals need care and attention. Therefore, it is nonsensical to make demands for these completely different groups from within one movement. As Dave Chappelle has reminded us, the different letters in LGBTQ don't have common interests. The motives are certainly political, but why has sexuality, the natural expression of the deepest mutual human affection among genetically unrelated adults, been loaded with politics?

Why There Is Sex

Biologically, the emergence of sexual reproduction at least six hundred million years ago is a milestone in evolutionary history, because populations that reproduce sexually have many times higher genetic diversity than those that reproduce asexually (which is called monogony). In monogony, the offspring receive exact copies of the genome of the cell from which they arise through division. This results in populations that—apart from spontaneous mutations—are genetically very homogeneous and stable, but are strongly bound to a narrow habitat to which they are genetically adapted.

Sexual reproduction, on the other hand, has disadvantages, because finding and choosing a mate and the act of reproduction as well as rearing the offspring are extremely costly in terms of energy. However, through meiotic recombination, the offspring of sexual partners not only receive genetic material from both parents, but the material is newly combined for each individual, which can be seen in the difference in genetic characteristics of siblings, such as body morphology, but also differences in inherited mental characteristics. This creates population diversity.

The advantages of this genetic diversity outweigh the disadvantages of sexual reproduction, as becomes evident from the fact that the overwhelming majority of species that have evolved since the Cambrian explosion about five hundred million years ago reproduce sexually. Diversity allows for individuals with differently distributed strengths and weaknesses, resulting in the population as a whole having a mix of characteristics optimized for reproduction and survival. For example, a better resistance of the population to pathogens or a better ability to exploit different habitats.

Without sexual reproduction, evolution would probably never have produced higher species, especially not *Homo sapiens.* What's called 'anisogamous' sexual reproduction depends on two specialized and biologically fundamentally different but complementary sexes. In the animal kingdom, these biological characteristics of the two sexes completely and highly effectively determine their division of labor. In humans, they also have a very great influence on role behavior, even if we can recognize and reflect on its biological roots.

What Happened to Sex

In the West, until the end of the nineteenth century, the division of labor in humans was mainly determined by sex differences. Most of the work required to support families was physical and was done by males. Males also dominated the world of non-physical labor consisting of activities such as trade, administration, law, medicine, theology, and research. Women mostly worked in reproduction and raising the children, with few exceptions. This changed from about 1880, when the basic needs of the population had been met thanks to the Liebig fertilizer, the industrial revolution, artificial lighting, canalization, coal-based urban apartment heating, and running water, which enabled an acceleration of the rate of social change. Women's liberation with political and economic participation was a consequence of the emancipatory movement of the Enlightenment, and a great achievement. The biologically determined division of labor was seemingly overcome. But was it really?

Mary Harrington (2023) summarizes the feminist debates of the first half of the century as follows:

> The feminism of care makes the case for women's interests as bound up with our embodied nature, especially as mothers, and the relational ties and obligations that come with this. The feminism of freedom argued that the best means of securing women's interests is for us to enter the

market on the same terms as men, and where necessary to socialize domestic obligations—for example, via institutional childcare.

According to her, the debate ended at the end of the 1960s, when all industrialized societies (at that time, the West plus the Communist countries) moved to the feminism of freedom. This deep cultural change was enabled by hormonal contraception, which severed the link between sexual activity and reproduction. Previously sexually active women had to give birth and raise children or commit abortion (killing of the unborn child). Once this connection was severed, the feminism of freedom culture prevailed. Shortly thereafter, abortion for non-medical reasons was legalized in most Western countries. *From now on, individuation* (the source of the person's self-realization) of a woman was based far more on individual autonomy than on the social and moral obligations to dependent children.

As Harrington puts it:

Predicating access to 'personhood' on the right to abort an unborn child is about the strongest possible statement a culture can make in favor of freedom over care, where these are seen to be in zero-sum conflict. Making this the centerpiece of 'women's liberation' ended the back-and-forth between the feminisms of freedom and care, and left the field to freedom. This is the 'feminism' we've lived with for over half a century now.

This pseudo-feminism has called for the overcoming of the biological differences between men and women using technology in the name of radical liberation from the bonds of flesh and from the biological foundations of our existence as mammals. To this end, women have to be prevented from pregnancy, and if it occurs despite the pill, the killing of unborn humans is legal to restore the self-actualization of the averted motherhood of the woman. This egocentric, shallow pseudo-self-realization consists in working (producing), consuming, and being consumed as sexual objects of regularly changing male partners who do not see sex as the fulfilment of love resulting in children that are raised together, but as short-term hedonistic, self-centered pleasure.

In heterosexuals, who constitute approximately ninety-five percent of the adult population, the reproduction rate in Western societies drastically declined once the pill was introduced. But besides this demographic effect and the enormous damage done to women's health, the pill has not removed the fundamental biological difference between the sexes. Instead, it has reinforced a culture of hedonistic sex without responsibility and devoid of its onto-logical dimension, the procreation of life. Regularly or fre-quently changing sex partners has led to a vast expansion of the dating and pornography industry. The classical family, on the other hand, which is the institutional foundation of Western societies, has lost importance, to the detriment of the quality of life of the few children who do appear. Those who grow up in state institutions instead of families are dis-advantaged for life.

An empirical proof of these effects is hard to obtain and consensus on the results of empirical studies even harder, but it seems unlikely that human happiness and the sense of a fulfilled life can increase by trying to live against the biological and social wellsprings of our species. Certainly, the culture of hedonist, ontologically void sex and the mas-sive decline of a sense of responsibility among males con-tributes to the high consumption rate of anti-depressants in childless women and single mothers over forty. Thus, the dating and the pornographic industry cash in once, but the pharma industry makes money on the women thrice: By selling the pill over a period of thirty years from age fifteen to forty-five, then selling anti-depressants to women for another thirty years from forty to seventy, and finally, to the unfortunate proportion of women with pill-induced cancer, chemotherapy any time after forty, which is a very lucrative business altogether.

The movement to disembody sexuality is also visible in pseudo-parenthood without sexual reproduction. This is not the (debatable) IVF for couples with reproduction problems, but male homosexual couples buying eggs, fertil-izing them with their sperms (or, if the couple is female, vice-versa) and getting a surrogate mother to produce the child which they buy right after delivery. This is a very big business in the West, and its effect on the offspring is not yet clear as we lack longitudinal comparative studies.

In the context discussed here, the removal from sex of its ontological nature creates the cultural atmosphere in which the trans ideology is urgently campaigning for gender fluidity and gives children, their parents, and young adults the illusion that the biological sex can be changed at will. Trans ideology is the ultimate form of the illusion that natural and genetic bonds can be severed. It is pushing children into mutilating surgery and hormone therapy, which feeds another big business sector, but is the worst of all since its activity is irreversible and utterly destructive. The human suffering it creates is immense, and the cultural fallout of this trend is currently hard to fathom.

The Political Goal of the Ideology

We've seen that the Trans Hype is acting within a context of disembodiment and negation of the biological nature of sex. Furthermore, its main political arm, the LGBTQ movement, does not help the heterogeneous groups collected under its artificial umbrella. But the movement has massive funding from globalist pseudo-philanthropic foundations. Therefore, it must have a political goal. What is it?

The goal of the transgender ideology is neo-Marxist: the overcoming of traditional society founded in the family and private community. Karl Marx, the first modern socialist with a comprehensive theory of overcoming bourgeois society, already called for breaking up the family as the nucleus of society in the *Communist Manifesto* published in 1848. Since then, social engineers who want to design and implement a new society on the drawing board have always tried to overcome the family: Stalin and the states he ruled, Mao in China, but also the US Democrats, or, in Germany, the Greens, the social-democratic SPD, the FDP, once a classical liberal party, and other cultural Marxist-oriented parties. This is also the goal of the LGBTQ activists funded with billions from private foundations and state actors.

If they were concerned with the interests of the groups they claim to represent, they would actually work for them. But instead, as reported on WHO and UN, they advocate early sexualization of children, teaching masturbation around kindergarten age, the 'right' of pedophiles to have sex with children, irreversible gender reassignment of minors without parental consent, unrestricted 'right' to abortion until the end of pregnancy, or imprisonment in women's prisons of so-called "trans women" with fully functional male sexual organs.

All of these demands are contrary to spontaneously evolved social norms of coexistence that have proven essential to living together in urbanized societies. All of them are profoundly inhumane and evil. Children in all societies need taboos to protect their mental development. Parents have custody of their children because they are genetically committed to caring for their offspring. Furthermore, children are not yet ready to be fully autonomous until their brains have reached the full maturity, which is around the age of twenty (hence the age of majority used to be twenty-one). Abortion is considered a criminal offence because it kills a human being. Exceptions to this should be made extremely rarely and after due consideration. Prisons segregate by gender because otherwise women immediately become victims of sexual violence.

The goal of transgender ideology is to overcome the family, which is seen as the stronghold of conservative thinking and the place where 'false consciousness' (Theodor Adorno, one of the originators of post-World-War-I Western Marxism) is formed.

Many LGBTQ activists are also antinatalists, meaning that they want to prevent people from reproducing because they believe, for example, that humans are destroying the Earth. If we imagine a society in which their goals were realized, we would observe the following picture: Most humans do not reproduce but engage in 'gender fluid' sex with changing partners. More and more children are obtained using IVF and surrogate mothers.

Parents no longer have authority, but children 'determine' their own lives, which means that public institutions manned with fanatical activists direct the children's 'choices'. These fanatics severely damage the children psychologically by early sexualization and abuse in a pedophile environment. Any pregnancy can be terminated at will any time, or the baby may even be killed a few weeks after birth if the parents change their mind. Male sex felons are not punished, or are imprisoned in women's jails if that's their choice.

Such a society cannot exist; it would be a perverted nightmare. LBGTQ activists show their true colors by not demanding what transsexuals need: medical and psychosocial treatment, care, and rehabilitation. Rather, their demands are inhumane and destructive. That they get so much attention, promotion, and sympathy indicates the collective pathological mental state of the ruling elites.

III

Hype
in Political
Context

15

Hype and the Permanent State of Emergency

The whole aim of practical politics is to keep the populace alarmed (and hence clamorous to be led to safety) by menacing it with an endless series of hobgoblins, all of them imaginary.

—H.L. MENCKEN

The various Hypes continually flowing through Western societies are mostly cases of Fear Hype. Most of the Hope Hypes are 'antidotes' to a Fear Hype, like the 'vaccines' forced upon billions of people as an 'answer' to the imaginary pandemic.

But not all Hypes are artificially contrived; there are spontaneous Fear Hypes. These can be caused by natural disasters which are out of the control of humans, such as volcanic eruptions, earthquakes, extended drought, or genuine bacterial pandemics such as the plague or cholera which historically were not understood and could not be controlled. Fear Hypes can also come about following invasions by dreadful enemies with superior weapons or tactics—such as the invasions of Europe by the Huns in the fourth and fifth centuries. Observing such events from the perspective of common sense, without Hype, raises justified fear, which can turn into collective panic if such events seem unavoidable.

But looking at the Fear Hypes of this book, we see that none of them are linked to natural events: *Covid* was not a pandemic at all, it was the natural spreading of a typical respiratory virus which moves through mankind in a typical epidemic pattern, killing only the very frail elderly, a natural cause of death. And there is no dangerous man-made *climate emergency* either; what we see is a slowly moving and probably soon self-terminating climate change to which mankind contributes nothing or almost nothing. There is no dangerous or unusual suppression of *homosexuals, transexual minorities or women* in the West, just some resentment against minorities that we find in every society.

There is huge economic inequality, but there is no *systemic racism* in the West either. Similarly, we don't have to be afraid of *Artificial Intelligence* as a potential ruler of the world. All the major Fear Hypes we're confronted with are invented, unnatural, and purely imaginary. Without continuous media bombardment, nobody would be concerned with any of them, because they cannot be observed in reality. Yes, there is contempt and unjust treatment of minorities, and affluent modern societies should try to enable minorities to lead their lives with dignity. But no human society is perfect, and minorities always have some disadvantages; this is due to man's natural attitude towards strangers. To a certain extent, it is the natural consequence of the unequal distribution of capabilities and resources among men. Its perfect mitigation is not practically feasible.

But if we cannot perceive the artificial Hypes listed above in reality, why are they causing so much pain? Where do they come from? *These Hypes are made* by investing huge amounts in propaganda via the media, supported and fueled by a neo-Lysenkoist scientific establishment that we have discussed in the chapters on Medical Hype and Climate Hype. The former has not only produced unscientific Hype models about the pseudo-pandemic to create mass panic, it has also engineered the virus to be more contagious (though not more virulent, thank God) and simultaneously, with some offset, engineered the toxic nucleic acids used as pseudo-vaccines against a virus three to five times less deadly than the regular influenza virus. These nucleic acids protect neither individuals nor the population, but cause nothing but damage and increase the likelihood of infections. In the climate case, the neo-Lysenkoists create unscientific models to support the false claim that we live in a man-made climate emergency.

To create and maintain these and the other artificial Fear Hypes that have been invented and cannot be observed anywhere in reality, NGOs, huge foundations created by globalists such as Soros, Getty, Ford, Gates, or Kellogs, spend astronomical amounts of cash. Furthermore, the public sector of the entire Northern Hemisphere engages in propagating these narratives via the education system, public statements of the executive branch of government, so-called NGOs which are publicly funded but outside the legal sphere of governmental institutions, as well as the public media (such as the BBC in Britain). The Christian churches and many other institutions which are directly or indirectly controlled by governments also support these narratives in speech and deed, for example by financing immigration. If they drop one of the Hype topics, such as HIV or Covid, which was de-emphasized towards the end of 2022, the Fear Hype immediately stops. In contrast, fear of a real natural catastrophe such as a real bacterial pandemic would not subside in the absence of propaganda, but would be able to sustain itself because humans can perceive its consequences with their own eyes.

We've seen that Western societies are running through multiple Hype Cycles overlapping each other. The Fear Hypes are employed to establish a *new form of rule, the rule by interminable states of emergency.* As Giorgio Agamben has recounted, the idea of emergency rule goes back to the Roman republic, but only emerged in its full form with the French Revolution. In medieval political philosophy, rule by emergency was only seen as legitimate as an occasionally appropriate exception. Benjamin Constant was the first to show that with the French Revolution, illegitimate rule by usurpation based on the declaration of emergencies was introduced as a regular political pattern. Napoleon's reign was the first modern rule essentially based on a permanent state of emergency, mostly justified by Napoleon's aggressive wars against the entire European continent. These started as wars to defend the young French republic, but quickly became wars of aggression.

Since the events of September 11th 2001, the United States has been held within a perpetual state of emergency, endowing the state with powers which are incompatible with the limitation of the monopoly on the use of force imposed by the US Constitution. Since 9/11 the rule of law and common law, the main foundations of the US political system of government, have been eroded. Over the last twenty years, rule via state of emergency has intensified in the West, the main Fear Hype topics that have fueled it are: Terrorism Hype, Climate Hype, Pandemic Hype, AI Hype (a type of Technology Hype), and War Hype.

Rule by State of Emergency

Traditionally, rule by state of emergency is a form of temporary, interim dictatorship which is declared by public actors and used to save a society in situations of war (usually, an attack by an external enemy) or natural (or, more recently, technical) disaster. Such situations can cause public unrest, panic, and civil upheaval. They require rapid decisions and a fast mobilization of the resources of a society to defend it against its enemies, which may even include internal enemies in a civil war. Or the state of emergency may be declared to save lives during a natural disaster such as an earthquake or a technical disaster, for example, a major incident at a chemical or a nuclear plant as we witnessed them in the late 1970s and 1980s in Bhopal, Seveso, and Cernobyl. During the state of emergency, the habitual legal and political norms of decision making are suspended, a single dictator or a small group of decision-makers takes over all political power to resolve the situation.

As soon as the actual emergency is over, the state of emergency is ended and the normal political system is restored. This pattern repeatedly worked well during the classic age of the Roman republic before its decline during the first century B.C. *Obviously, there is a contradiction between legal and constitutional norms that usually regulate the political system and the state of emergency, which breaks with the norms.* If the emergency is over and a return to the norms does not occur, tyranny or rule by usurpation begin.

In the nineteenth century and then rapidly intensifying during World War I, rule by state of emergency became habitual and extended over longer periods of time in the West. As Agamben explains, we see it regularly in France under Napoleon III; during World War I in all Western states including Switzerland; in Germany during the

Weimar Republic, and then under Hitler; in France under Daladier from 1938 onwards, and, of course, during World War II in all Western countries, including the United States and the United Kingdom.

During the Cold War, we no longer saw a rule by state of emergency in the West. There were Fear Hypes, the most important of which was Fear of a war with Russia, which was depicted as the stronghold of evil. Without this constant Hyping of the danger facing us from the East, military spending would have been much lower, more wealth would have been available for more benign goals. Consequently, it's likely that less taxpayer money would have been transformed into private wealth for the owners of defense companies.

There has been another important Fear Hype since the 1970s: domestic terrorism, mostly Communist. This Fear was used for the justification of some, rather minor, domestic repression. To some extent, the terror threat was real, but without the Hype, it would have remained meaningless for the average citizen. Another Fear Hype of the time was the Fear of energy production using nuclear fission, which was very common in German-speaking countries and ultimately led to the abandonment of nuclear power.

A global Fear Hype of the 1980s was AIDS, which can be seen as a small prototype of the Hype that was created forty years later with Covid. The main beneficiary of the AIDS/HIV Hype was the pharmaceutical industry. These mild Fear Hypes of the 1970s and 1980s had the effect of increasing the loyalty of Western citizens to their governments, and tended to legitimize a more intrusive role for the state.

A huge gap suddenly opened up when the major justification for an expanded role for the state disappeared with the end of the USSR. *Since then, that gap has been filled by the Hypes discussed in this book.* For the ruling class, this type of rule enables the concealment of the absence of legitimacy by the collective emotions of Hype. It can justify anti-democratic measures against the opposition, and also exerts a divide-and-conquer effect by means of the rift it creates between the believers in the Hype narratives and those who remain composed and intelligently skeptical towards them.

Surveying the history of rule by state of emergency since the French Revolution, *we can see that this rule is a new pattern that paradoxically arose together with the modern democratic state and that currently dominates it more and more.* Why is this so?

How Philosophers See the State of Emergency

In the 1920s, following many predecessors, the political philosopher Carl Schmitt tried to demonstrate that a permanent state of emergency can be regarded as constitutional and therefore legitimate. He also termed it a 'sovereign (permanent) dictatorship' and claimed this state of affairs to be legal even if its essence is the replacement of legal norms by what he called the 'decision' of the sovereign dictator and the state he leads.

Schmitt tried to argue that the state of emergency can be understood as a part of the law, but Schmitt's reasoning has been effectively criticized. The permanent state of emergency is in fact the antithesis of the rule of law and the constitutional order. Schmitt's and his predecessors' attempts to bring them into coherence were based on attempts by the nineteenth-century 'legal positivist' tradition to arrive at a consistent theory of law and state.

The philosopher Giorgio Agamben provides a useful history of the concept of 'state of emergency', and is one of the most cited contemporary authors on the topic, yet even he does not give a fully satisfactory account of it. Agamben calls the law and the norms which are valid under normal circumstances *potestas*, the legitimate power of the state. He believes that this legitimate power depends dialectically on an anomalous, meta-legal influence which he calls *auctoritas*, the raw power-based rule of a charismatic leader (giving Hitler and Mussolini as examples). Agamben maintains that potestas and auctoritas are held together in their dialectical relationship by the state of emergency. This is clearly a postmodern meme, very close to Foucault's apparent view of power as a deep form of visceral force flowing through society. These postmodernist ideas may seem fashionable, but they are nonsensical and in contradiction with the way human societies work.

In urban societies, there's only one form of legitimate power, power rooted in social norms and in respect of the function of the office, which ideally must prevent officials and politicians from abusing their power. In other words, a legitimate state has three core properties in Western political metaphysics, all of which are usually approximated in the political reality during peaceful, equilibrated periods. They are listed here with the main places of their historical origins. Other Western countries, including the USA, France, and Switzerland (let alone Germany), came later.

1. It respects the autonomy of the individual and the rights that follow from it—this is what is meant by the notion of *natural law* which evolved with the slow rise of the bourgeoisie since the twelfth century, starting in England, Scotland, and the Netherlands.

2. It takes into consideration the needs and the political will of all citizens—though always of some more than of others; this is called *participation*, the absence of which was the cause of the seventeenth-century civil wars in England.

3. And its institutions do not systematically treat any group of citizens differently from the others, which we call *isonomy* (equal treatment) and rule of law, another motive that initially evolved in England and the rich towns of Flanders.

A legitimate state abstains as much as possible from abusing the necessary power of the state. As Edmund Burke and many others pointed out, a legitimate state is set up in accordance with the long-term trend of social norms that have evolved spontaneously, and it evolves with social change. Its actors, the administrators and politicians, act accordingly, and there is a complicated and multi-layered web of institutional checks and balances to enforce this.

In a *legitimate state of emergency*, the state can briefly act against these principles to avert a natural disaster or defend against an invading enemy—but it must return to the normal state of affairs characterized by the three properties once the immediate danger is averted. A chronic or permanent state of emergency violates these principles, and it cannot be in accordance with legitimate rule or be legally justified. Of course, it can be brought into accordance with positive law (meaning whatever the law just happens to be at a given time and place), if this law is changed accordingly, as it was in Germany in 1933 and the following years, or in the US after September 2001. *But positive law can be the juridical backbone of an illegitimate state* and is insufficient to enable a peaceful relationship of the state and its citizens if the state turns into a dictatorship and the citizens become subjects.

Taken together, while a temporary state of emergency with an interim dictatorship is often the sole approach to save the political or even cultural continuity of a society, the rule by a permanent state of emergency is always a form of illegitimate usurpation. *We live in such a period of usurpation, and the various Hypes are driving our populations into accepting it out of fear or enthusiasm for positive Hypes.* But why has the permanent state of emergency evolved since Napoleon and how does it differ between the West and parts of the world which lack democratic traditions, such as Russia or China?

Why the State of Emergency and Democracy Belong Together

Societies which lack the traditions of natural law, participation and isonomy/rule of law have forms of government with a different source of legitimacy than Western states. In such societies, the individual is not seen as having the same value as in our culture; the concepts of individual autonomy and dignity, which form the grounding of our political metaphysics, are lacking. Because the perpetual state of emergency is the absence of the three principles derived from the idea of human autonomy listed above, it can only be understood in the context of Western political metaphysics. *China and Russia cannot be understood using that framework* and we do not aim to compare their circumstances to ours.

But what about the West? The cause of the first modern period of permanent state of emergency under Napoleon was the French Revolution. It created a situation of public unrest in France in combination with external threats from opponents of the Revolution, which allowed the legitimate declaration of a state of emergency. But very soon, Napoleon switched from defending France against its inner and outer feudal enemies to a policy of conquering and continental domination. *The state of emergency, that might have seemed legitimate for a short period at the beginning of his reign, became chronic and illegitimate.* France was not on the verge of becoming a democracy at the time, rather the first attempt to introduce democracy on the old continent by force led to a period of usurpation and chronic state of emergency which came about under the inner and outer pressure against the new anti-feudal republic. So what transpired under Napoleon might better be explained by the failed attempt to democratize France than by an inner connection of democracy and permanent state of emergency during his reign.

But later on, with the stabilization of democratic states in the US and Europe, we see this connection throughout the nineteenth century and then during the World Wars, in between them and, since 2001, also in our times. *Why do democracies fall into an illegitimate state of government so regularly?*

Democracy is the rule based on delegation by vote and institutionalized periodic representation. In his epochal work *Power*, Guglielmo Ferrero points out why this principle is so brittle and prone to failure. His arguments were formulated during World War II and are now eighty years old. They may seem very strange to the modern reader in whose eyes there is no alternative to democracy, which has been the Western consensus since 1945.

Ferrero believes that there are four principles of legitimate order, classified by their source and type:

Source of order	Type of order
election	republican
inheritance	feudal

According to Ferrero, these four principles and their combinations are not rationalizable. In other words: *It cannot be determined a priori which is better or more*

legitimate for a city (a political society). There can be an
elected republic, an inherited republic, an elected oli-
garchy, and so forth—all combinations are possible and
have been realized in history with various degrees of legitimacy. Its level does not depend on the particular combination of principles, but on the extent to which the rulers
and their magistrates (the bureaucracy in modern societies) systematically take into account the needs of the
ruled population and to what degree their rule is limited
and divided up between institutions (or powers in the
framework of Montesquieu).

Among Ferrero's four principles, there is neither the
rule of the proletariat nor any other Marxist-inspired principle nor populist fascism, both of which for Ferrero, who
had them vividly before his eyes, were totally unacceptable.
It's only against this astonishing and far-sighted view of
legitimacy that we can grasp Ferrero's understanding of
democracy—which is not anti-democratic at all, but very
shrewd in its identification of the difficulties of this principle of rule.

So why does Ferrero see democracy as vulnerable? First of
all, the basic principle of the equilibrium of power in a
democracy is the balance between majority government
and opposition. But in a legitimate, vital democracy the
parliamentary majority must not be acting in the interests
of a hidden minority; rather, it must really represent the
majority of the population. And the minority represented
by the opposition—often a minority only by a small mar-
gin—must be able to demonstrate real political alternatives
to the majority in an undisturbed and fruitful manner to
prevent big gaps of representation from opening up.
Based on this consideration, Ferrero lists five difficulties in
implementing democratic representation:

1. The necessary fair play of the majority towards the
   minority is only possible if the majority is 'real', as Ferrero
   puts it in his unique way of thinking and not merely an
   'enacted majority' merely representing the interests of a
   minority. In the latter case, only a pseudo-majority has
   no interest in respecting the opposition and will do
   everything to suppress it or to prevent a real alternative
   from rising. This is a very frequent phenomenon even in
   mature democracies; we now see it in Germany, for

example, where the parliamentary majority obviously represents mainly the interests of a tiny minority and seeks to suppress all opposing voices.

2. The majority must not only be real, but also be ready to be replaced by the minority, it must be willing to cede the power to the opposition once the opposition becomes the majority. This also includes the officials who may try to serve the old majority even it if was voted out (as we saw during the presidency of Donald Trump, and also in the opposite direction when Trump refused to concede claiming his 'victory' was 'stolen').

3. The opposition must also be real and represent strong currents of political will formation. It must neither be a uni-party opposition that only mimics an alternative formation of purpose (a phenomenon now very common in the West, we see it in the UK blatantly, where each new government merely intensifies the politics of the previous one); nor must it fundamentally disagree with the rules of democracy: it must truly accept the right of the majority to take decisions, to make laws and must productively subject itself to their validity as long as they are not anti-constitutional. Ferrero says that "nothing is more dangerous for a democracy than small groups consumed by ruthless hatred . . . and whose opposition can only lead to a total subversion of the legitimacy." He gives the French Third Republic (1870–1940) as an example of this, especially its last ten years, which he directly witnessed.

4. Ferrero warns us not to confuse political liberty with philosophical liberty, another of his astonishing thoughts since today we tend to equate the two. But *he reduces political liberty to the sum of the conditions necessary for the opposition to be real and the popular sovereignty adequate.* In his thinking, for example, political liberty must not include the liberty of religion, an unthinkable point of view from today's UN-Charter style political metaphysics. His concept of liberty is thus more restricted than in traditional bourgeois state metaphysics (which he calls philosophical liberty). Even stranger, political liberty in his sense also includes the right to restrain the liberty of those who fundamentally oppose it (to use a modern example: Islamists in the West), which is unthinkable in the version of political freedom officially proposed by the US State Department. Overall, he

describes political liberty as very hard to obtain and maintain, and philosophical liberty as unrealizable.

5. The body of the sovereign. The medieval king had two bodies: His body as a person and his body politic, which expresses his role as the sovereign. But what is the body of the sovereign of a democracy, its population? Its body can only be formed by universal suffrage, to which there is no alternative in the theory of democracy, but this suffrage merely constitutes a metaphysical political body. *In reality, many members of the public are incapable of political will formation, so that*—unlike in the traditional deliberations of a monarch with the institutionalized assembly of the upper nobility in the English or German traditions—*their participation via universal suffrages makes it very hard to form a unified political will and to enact it.* When external or internal instability arises, the popular vote can lead to tremendous instability. This is why all representative democracies (Switzerland to a slightly lesser extent) have attempted to minimize the impact of the suffrage.

From Ferrero's analysis it follows that the fair and legitimate exercise of power in democracies is very demanding and depends on preconditions which are very hard to meet. Most importantly, it needs what he calls real majority and real opposition which embody alternatives to political will formation and in both cases the expression of the political will of the sovereign, the masses of citizens of the democratic state. At the same time, this will formation depends on the existence of a popular body politic of this sovereign.

In reality, the decisions of the parliament and the formation of the political will from the bottom can rarely be brought into coherence; very often democracies show a detachment of the political will that is expressed in legislation and executive government from the political will of the masses. Or, in other words, *it is almost impossible to rule the masses under the metaphysical fiction of their political autonomy and their ability to form a political body.*

The realization of these principles is rare. In reality, democracies have seldom had long phases of political stability with a constantly high degree of the legitimacy of rule. The best period over the last 120 years was from the 1950s until the mid 1990s under the Pax Americana. Before that, Western democracies often resorted to the chronic state of emergency as a principle of government, as we saw at the beginning. *Since the 1990s, we see a rapid decline in the principle of representation, as we witness a legislation and an executive government that obviously acts against the political will of the masses in many areas,* such as migration, foreign policy, taxation, social security systems, the financial system, education, the Woke agenda, or government spending. Rather, it acts in the interest of a tiny minority. The discrepancy between the masses' political will formation and government actions leads to a decline in the legitimacy of the political structure.

This lack of natural legitimacy which results from a lack of coherence between the political will of the masses and the way the parliament and the government act is now compensated using Fear Hype, of which we have seen several examples in this book, as a source of legitimacy. The resulting excitement in the population, but especially among the carrier stratum of society (the top ten to fifteen percent in charge of leading the rest and creating public opinion, the Outer Party), is used to rule in the interest of the hidden minority. And so we have arrived at a post-democratic system we can call neo-feudalism, an unstable system whose legitimacy is shaky.

The ruling neo-feudal minority, unlike the ruling minority of feudalism and absolutism, is hidden; it generates neither politicians nor public servants, but rules indirectly. Because this rule is so fundamentally illegitimate, there is a tendency to utilize the permanent state of emergency as a mode of governance everywhere in the West. This chronic state of emergency is alien to our political traditions and is not compatible with Western political culture. Over time, it must be overcome, to usher in a new phase of truly legitimate government.

Bibliography

A Time of Hype

Arendt, Hannah. *The Origins of Totalitarianism*. Penguin, 2017.
Burnham, James. *The Machiavellians: Defenders of Freedom*. Lune, 2019 [1943].
Canetti, Elias. *Crowds and Power*. Farrar, Straus, and Giroux, 1984.
Desmet, Mattias. *The Psychology of Totalitarianism*. Chelsea Green, 2022.
Eibl-Eibesfeldt, Irenaus. *Human Ethology*. Routledge, 2017.
Feyerabend, Paul. *Against Method*. Verso, 2010 [1975].
Le Bon, Gustave. *The Crowd: A Study of the Popular Mind*. Dover, 2002 [1895].
Ludwig, Max. Review of Mattias Desmet: The Psychology of Totalitarianism
    (Max Ludwig). *Globkult*. https://www.globkult.de/gesellschaft/
    besprehungen-gesellschaft/2226-mattias-desmet-the-psychology-of-
    totalitarianism. 2022.
Mosca, Gaetano. *The Ruling Class*. Babel, 2023 [1896].
Mulligan, Kevin. Foolishness and the Value of Knowledge. In Leo
    Zaibert, ed., *The Theory and Practice of Ontology* (Palgrave
    Macmillan, 2016).
Ortega y Gasset, José. *The Revolt of the Masses*. 2022 [1930].
Orwell, George. *Nineteen Eighty-Four*. Secker and Warburg, 1949.
Popper, Karl R. *The Logic of Scientific Discovery*. Routledge, 1992 [1935].
Scheler, Max. *Formalism in Ethics and Non-Formal Ethics of Values*.
    Northwestern University Press, 1973.
Stove, David Charles. *Popper and After: Four Modern Irrationalists*.
    Pergamon, 1982. Reprinted twice: *Anything Goes: Origins of the Cult
    of Scientific Irrationalism* (1998) and *Scientific Irrationalism* (2017).

1. Artificial Intelligence Hype

Bentham, Jeremy. The Panopticon Writings. Verso, 2011 [1785].
Bostrom, Nick. *Superintelligence: Paths, Dangers, Strategies*. Oxford
    University Press, 2003.
Chalmers, David. The Singularity: A Philosophical Analysis. In *The
    Singularity: Could Artificial Intelligence Really Out-Think Us (and
    Would We Want It To)?* ed., Uziel Awret. Imprint Academic, 2016.

Cohen, Hermann. *Logik der Reinen Erkenntnis.* Bruno Cassirer, 1902.

Kant, Immanuel. *Critique of the Power of Judgement.* Cambridge University Press, 2000 [1790].

Kurzweil, Ray. *The Singularity Is Near: When Humans Transcend Biology.* Viking, 2005.

Landgrebe, Jobst, and Barry Smith. *Why Machines Will Never Rule the World: AI Without Fear.* Second edition. Routledge, 2025 [2023].

Searle, John R. *The Rediscovery of the Mind.* MIT Press, 1992.

Tour, James. We're Still Clueless about the Origin of Life. In: *The Mystery of Life's Origin.* ed., Robert J. Marks and John West. Discovery Institute Press, 2020.

2. Planet Hype

IPCC. *Special Report on global warming of 1.5 degree Celsius above pre-industrial levels and related global greenhouse gas emission pathways.* http://www.ipcc.ch/report/sr15/ (2018).

IPCC. *AR6 Synthsis Report: Climate Change. 2023.* https://www.ipcc.ch/report/sixth-assessment-report-cycle/(2023).

Koonin, Steven E. *Unsettled: What Climate Science Tells Us, What It Doesn't, and WhyIt Matters.* BenBella, 2021.

Landgrebe, Jobst, and Barry Smith. *Why Machines Will Never Rule the World: AI Without Fear.* Second edition. Routledge, 2025 [2023].

May, Andy, and Marcel Crok, eds. *The Frozen Climate Views of the IPCC. An Analysis of AR6.* Amsterdam: clintel.org, 2023.

Peters, E. Kirsten. *The Whole Story of Climate: What Science Reveals about the Nature of Endless Change.* Prometheus, 2012.

Plimer, Ian. *Green Murder: A Life Sentence of Net Zero with No Parole.* Redland Bay, Australia: connorcourt, 2022.

Popitz, Heinrich. *Phenomena of Power.* Columbia University Press, 2017.

Scheffer, Marten, et al. Catastrophic Shifts in Ecosystems. *Nature* 413.6856 (2001).

Steele, David Ramsay. Why Do We See Lysenko-Type Mass Delusions in Western Democracies? In Steele, *The Conquistador with His Pants Down: David Ramsay Steele's Legendary Lost Lectures.* St. Augustine's Press, 2024.

Stéphant, Aurore. *Notre Civilisation au Bord du Gouffre?* https://www.thinkerview.com/aurore-stephant-efforndrement-notre-civilisation-au-bord-du-gouffre/ (2023).

Svensmark, Henrik, and Nigel Calder. *The Chilling Stars: A New Theory of Climate Change.* Icon, 2007.

Vahrenholt, Fritz, and Sebastian Lüning. *The Neglected Sun.* Heartland Institute, 2015.

———. *Unerwünschte Wahrheiten: Was Sie über den Klimawandel Wissen Sollten.* Langen Mueller Herbig, 2020.

Van Wijngaarden, W.A., and W. Happer. 2020. Dependence of Earth's Thermal Radiation on Five Most Abundant Greenhouse Gases. *arXiv:2006.03098* (2020).

3. Transhumanism Hype

Alanis-Lobato, Gregorio, et al. Frequent Loss of Heterozygosity in CRISPR-Cas9–edited early human embryos. *Proceedings of the National Academy of Sciences* 118.22 (2021), e2004832117.

Bataille, Georges. *On Nietzsche*. State University of New York Press, 2015 [1945].

Boyle, Evan A., Yand I. Li, and Jonathan K. Pritchard. An Expanded View of Complex Traits: From Polygenic to Omnigenic. *Cell* 169 (2017).

Gobineau, Joseph-Arthur, Comte de. *Gobineau: Selected Political Writings*. Cape, 1971.

Harari, Yuval Noah. 2016. *Homo Deus: A Brief History of Tomorrow*. Random House, 2016.

Herder, Johann Gottfried von. *Herder: Philosophical Writings*. Cambridge University Press, 2008.

Landgrebe, Jobst, and Barry Smith. *Why Machines Will Never Rule the World: AI Without Fear*. Second edition. Routledge, 2025 [2023].

Laplace, Pierre-Simon. *The System of the World, Volume 1*. Legare Street Press, 2022.

Mettrie, Julien Offray de la. *Man a Machine and Man a Plant*. Hackett, 1994 [1747].

Mirandola, Pico della. *On the Dignity of Man/On Being and the One/Heptaplus*. Hackett, 1998.

Morelly Abbé Étienne-Gabriel. *Code de la Nature*. Chez le Frai Sage, 1755.

Mumford, Lewis. *The City in History: Its Origins, Its Transformations, and Its Prospects*. Harcourt, 1968 [1961].

Rothblatt, Martine. *From Transgender to Transhuman: A Manifesto on the Freedom of Form*. Rothblatt, 2011.

Schwab, Klaus. *The Fourth Industrial Revolution*. Portfolio Penguin, 2017.

Stirner, Max. *The Ego and Its Own*. Cambridge University Press, 2009 [1844].

Taylor, Charles. *The Ethics of Authenticity*. Harvard University Press, 1991.

Tour, James. We're Still Clueless about the Origin of Life. In *The Mystery of Life's Origin*. ed., Robert J. Marks and John West. Discovery Institute Press, 2020.

Vico, Giambattista. *New Science*. Penguin, 2000 [1725].

4. Food Hype

Barakat, Shima, et al. Emerging Technologies that Will Impact on the UK Food System: Rapid Evidence Assessment. University of Cambridge, 2021.

Van Eenennaam, Alison L., et al. Genetic Engineering of Livestock: The Opportunity Cost of Regulatory Delay. *Annual Review of Animal Biosciences* 9:1 (2021).

He, Rui, et al. Perspectives on the Management of Synthetic Biological and Gene Edited Foods. *Biosafety and Health* 2:4 (2020).

Martinez-Steele, Euridice, et al. Best Practices for Applying the Nova Food Classification System. *Nature Food* 4:6 (2023).

Means, Casey, with Calley Means. 2024. *Good Energy: The Surprising Connection between Metabolism and Limitless Health.* Avery.

Pixley, Kevin V., et al. Genome Editing, Gene Drives, and Synthetic Biology: Will They Contribute to Disease-Resistant Crops, and Who will Benefit? *Annual Review of Phytopathology* 57:1 (2019).

Teicholz, Nina. *The Big Fat Surprise: Why Butter, Meat, and Cheese Belong in a Healthy Diet.* Simon and Schuster, 2015 [2014].

———. A Short History of Saturated Fat: The Making and Unmaking of a Scientific Consensus. *Current Opinion in Endocrinology, Diabetes, and Obesity* 30:1 (February 2023).

5. Medical Hype

COVID

Bentham, Jeremy. *The Panopticon Writings.* Verso, 1995 [1787].

Berenson, Alex. *Pandemia: How Coronavirus Hysteria Took Over Our Government, Rights, and Lives.* Regnery, 2021.

Bhakdi, Sucharit, et al. *mRNA Vaccine Toxicity.* https://d4ce.org/mRNA vaccine-toxicity/ (2023).

Bhakdi, Sucharit, Karina Reiss, and Michael Palmer. Gene-Based Vaccination—Quo Vadis? *Doctors for COVID Ethics.* htpps://doctors4Covidethics.org/gene-based-vaccination-quo-vadis/ (2022).

Bruttel, Valentin, Alex Washburne, and Antonius VanDongen. Endonuclease Fingerprint Indicates a Synthetic Origin of SARS-CoV-2. *bioRxiv* (2022).

Chien-Te Tseng, et al. Immunization with SARS Coronavirus Vaccines Leads to Pulmonary Immunopathology on Challenge with the SARS Virus. *PloS one* 7:4 (2012).

Illich, Ivan. *Medical Nemesis.* Pantheon, 1982.

Ioannidis, John P.A. A Fiasco in the Making? As the Coronavirus Pandemic Takes Hold, We Are Making Decisions without Reliable Evidence Data. STAT. https://www.statnews.com/2020/03/17/a-fiasco-in-the-making-as-the-coronavirus-pandemic-takes-hold-we-are-making-decisions-without-reliable-data/ (2020).

———. Global Perspective of COVID-19 Epidemiology for a Full-cycle Pandemic. *European Journal of Clinical Investigation* 50:12 (2020).

Joravsky, David. *The Lysenko Affair.* University of Chicago Press, 1970.

Kelly, Amy. *Pfizer Documents Analysis Volunteers' Reports: Find Out What Pfizer, FDA Tried to Conceal,* ed. Naomi Wolf. DailyClout, 2023.

Kennedy, Robert Francis, Jr. *The Real Anthony Fauci: Bill Gates, Big Pharma, and the Global War on Democracy and Public Health.* Skyhorse, 2021.

Kuhbandner, Christof, and Matthias Reitzner. Estimation of Excess Mortality in Germany During 2020–2022. *Cureus* 15:5 (2023).

Kulldorff, Martin, Sunetra Gupta, and Jay Bhattacharya. *Great Barrington Declaration.* htpps://gbdeclaration.org (2020).

Malhotra,Aseem. Curing the Pandemic of Misinformation on Covid-19 mRNA Vaccines through Real Evidence-Based Medicine. *Journal of Immune Deficiency*, 2022.

Malone, Robert W. *Lies My Gov't Told Me: And the Better Future Coming.* Skyhorse, 2022.

Meslé, M. et al. Estimated Number of Lives Directly Saved by COVID19-Vaccination Programmes. *The Lancet Respiratory Medicine* 12:9 (2024).

Montagnier, Luc. *Virus: The Co-Discoverer of HIV Tracks Its Rampage and Charts the Future.* Norton, 1999.

Qart, S.Q.U., et al. *Covid 19 and Anthony Fauci Dossier.* Amazon Digital Services LLC - KDP Print US, 2021. htpps://booksgoogle.de/books?id=KppZzgEACAAJ.

Saltelli, Andrea et al. What did COVID-19 Really Teach Us about Science, Evidence, and Society? *Journal of Evaluation in Clinical Practice* (2023). https://doi.org/ 10.1111/jep.13876.

Scheler, Max. *Formalism in Ethics and Non-Formal Ethics of Values.* Northwestern University Press, 1973.

Sheng-Fan Wang et al. Antibody-Dependent SARS Coronavirus Infection Is Mediated by Antibodies Against Spike Proteins. *Biochemical and Biophysical Research Communications* 451:2 (2014).

Steele, David Ramsay. Why Do We See Lysenko-Type Mass Delusions in Western Democracies? In Steele, *The Conquistador with His Pants Down: David Ramsay Steele's Legendary Lost Lectures.* St. Augustine's Press, 2024.

Stéphant, Aurore. *Notre Civilisation au Bord du Gouffre?*

Uversky, Vladimir N., et al. IgG4 Antibodies Induced by Repeated Vaccination May Generate Immune Tolerance to the SARS-CoV-2 Spike Protein. *Vaccines* 11:5 (2023).

Willis, Mikki. 2021. *Plandemic: Fear Is the Virus. Truth Is the Cure.* Simon and Schuster, 2021.

Woods, Thomas E. *Diary of a Psychosis: How Public Health Disgraced Itself During Covid Mania.* Libertarian Institute, 2023.

HIV/AIDS

Doitsh, Gilad, and Warner C. Greene. Dissecting How CD4 T Cells Are Lost during HIV Infection. *Cell Host and Microbe* 19:3 (2016).

Duesberg, Peter, Claus Koehnlein, and David Rasnick. The Chemical Bases of the Various AIDS Epidemics: Recreational Drugs, Anti-Viral Chemotherapy, and Malnutrition. *Journal of Biosciences* 28:4 (2003).

Kalichman, Seth C. The Psychology of AIDS Denialism: Pseudoscience, Conspiracy Thinking, and Medical Mistrust. *European Psychologist* 19:1 (2014).

Kennedy, Robert Francis, Jr. *The Real Anthony Fauci: Bill Gates, Big Pharma, and the Global War on Democracy and Public Health.* Skyhorse, 2021.

Weber, Max. *Gesammelte Aufsätze zur Wissenschaftslehre.* J.C.B. Mohr, 1988.

6. Quantum Hype

Aaronson, Scott. How Much Structure Is Needed for Huge Quantum Speedups? In *arXiv:2209.06930* (2022).

Comte, August. *Introduction to Positive Philosophy*. Hackett, 1988.

Degen, Christian L., Reinhard Friedemann, and Paola Cappellaro. Quantum Sensing. *Reviews of Modern Physics* 89:3 (2017).

Deutsch, David. *The Fabric of Reality: The Science of Parallel Universes and Its Implications*. Penguin, 1998.

Dyakonov, Mikhail I. *Will We Ever Have a Quantum Computer?* Springer, 2020.

Eibl-Eibesfeldt, Irenaus. *Human Ethology*. Routledge, 2017.

Freeborn, David, Marian Gilton, and Chris Mitsch. How Haag-tied Is QFT, Really? arXiv: 2212.06977. Routledge, 2022.

Gehlen, Arnold. *Man: His Nature and Place in the World*. Columbia University Press, 1988 [1940].

Hauke, Philipp, et al. Perspectives of Quantum Annealing: Methods and Implementations. *Reports on Progress in Physics* 83:5 (2020).

Horton, Robin. Tradition and Modernity Revisited. In Martin Hollis and Steven Lukes, eds., *Rationality and Relativism*. MIT Press, 1982.

Kaku, Michio. *Quantum Supremacy: How the Quantum Computer Revolution Will Change Everything*. Doubleday, 2023.

Landauer, Rolf. 1996. The Physical Nature of Information. *Physics Letters A* 217.4–5 (1996).

Landgrebe, Jobst, and Barry Smith. *Why Machines Will Never Rule the World: AI Without Fear*. Second edition. Routledge, 2025 [2023].

Nielsen, Michael, and Isaac Chuang. *Quantum Computation and Quantum Information*. Cambridge University Press, 2010.

Ravetz, Jerome R. *Scientific Knowledge and Its Social Problems*. Transaction, 1971.

Shor, Peter W. 1994. Algorithms for Quantum Computation: Discrete Logarithms and Factoring. *Proceedings 35th Annual Symposium on Foundations of Computer Science*. 1994.

Williams, Richard N., and Daniel N. Robinson. *Scientism: The New Orthodoxy*. Bloomsbury, 2014.

7. Globalism Hype

Fisher, Irving. *The Debt-Deflation Theory of Great Depressions*. Martino, 2011.

Hayek, Friedrich August. *Studies in Philosophy, Politics, and Economics*. Touchstone, 1996.

———. *Denationalisation of Money: The Argument Refined*. Ludwig von Mises Institute, 2009.

Hersh, Seymour. How America Took Out the Nord Stream Pipeline. https://seymourhersh.substack.com/p/how/america-took-out-the-nord-stream (2023).

Hudson, Michael. *The Destiny of Civilization*. Dresden: Islet Verlag, 2022.

Marx, Karl, and Friedrich Engels. *The Communist Manifesto*. Penguin Classics, 2002 [1848].

Mises, Ludwig von. *Socialism: An Economic and Sociological Analysis*. Jonathan Cape, 1936.

Morelly, Abbé Étienne-Gabriel. *Code de la Nature*. Chez le Frai Sage, 1755.

Nitzan, Jonathan, and Shimshon Bichler. *Capital as Power: A Study of Order and Creorder*. Routledge, 2009.

Piketty, Thomas. About Capital in the Twenty-First Century. *American Economic Review* 105:5 (2015).

Rothbard, Murray N. *Man, Economy, and State*. Ludwig von Mises Institute, 2009.

Scheidler, Fabian. Seymour Hersh: The US Destroyed the Nord Stream Pipeline. Interview with Hersh. *Jacobin* (February 2023).

Veblen, Thorstein. *Absentee Ownership: Business Enterprise in Recent Times: The Case of America*. Routledge, 2017 [1924].

———. *The Theory of Business Enterprise*. MJP, 2023 [1904].

Webb, David Rogers. *The Great Taking*. Lulu, 2023.

———. The Great Taking. https://thegreattaking.com/ (2023).

8. War Hype

Aftergood, Steven. The Costs of War: Obstacles to Public Understanding. Watson Institute, 2018,

Amoghli, Parviz, and Alexander Meschnig. *Siegen: Oder vom Verlust der Selbstbehauptung*. Tumult Werkreihe, 2018.

Diesen, Glenn. *The Ukraine War and the Eurasian World Order*. Clarity, 2024.

Horton, Scott. *Provoked: How Washington Started the New Cold War with Russia and the Catastrophe in Ukraine*. Libertarian Institute, 2024.

Mearsheimer, John. 2022. Playing with Fire in Ukraine. *Foreign Affairs* (August 17th 2022).

———. John Mearsheimer's Substack. https://mearsheimer.substack.com (2023).

Wikipedia Author Collective. List of wars involving the United States (2023). https://en.wikipedia.org/wiki/List_of_wars_involving_the_United_States#20th-century_wars.

9. Multicultural Hype

Collier, Paul. *Exodus: How Migration Is Changing Our World*. Oxford University Press, 2013.

Mackinder, Halford J. *Heartland: Three Essays on Geopolitics*. Spinebill, 2022 [1904].

Nagel, Tilman. *Angst vor Allah? Auseinandersetzungen mit dem Islam.* Duncker und Humblot, 2014.

Said, Edward W. *Orientalism.* Vintage, 1979 [1978].

Senior, Jayne. *Broken and Betrayed: The True Story of the Rotherham Abuse Scandal by the Woman Who Fought to Expose It.* Pan, 2016.

Spencer, Robert. *The Politically Incorrect Guide to Islam (and the Crusades).* Regnery, 2005.

10. Death Hype

Benatar, David. *Better Never to Have Been: The Harm of Coming into Existence.* Oxford University Press, 2006.

Dalferth, Ingo. *Das Böse: Essay über die Denkform des Unbegreiflichen.* Mohr Siebeck, 2010.

Department of Justice Canada. Canada's Medical Assistance in Dying (MAID) Law. https://www.justice.gc.ca/eng/cj-jp/ad-am/bk-di.html (2024).

Herms, Eilert. Zwei-Reiche-Lehre/Zwei-Regimenten-Lehre. In Betz, Hans D., et al., eds. *Religion in Geschichte und Gegenwart.* Mohr Siebeck, 2005.

Hershenov, David B., and Rose J. Hershenov. If Abortion, then Infanticide. *Theoretical Medicine and Bioethics* 38 (2017).

Keller, Carl-A., et al. Das Böse. In Betz, Hans D., et al., eds. *Religion in Geschichte und Gegenwart.* Mohr Siebeck, 2005.

Knight, Les. Experience: I Campaign for the Extinction of the Human Race. *The Guardian* (January 10th, 2020).

Krainer, Alex. The 21st Century Opium War. https://alexkrainer.substack.com/p/the-21st-century-opium-war (2023).

Lorenz, Konrad,. *On Aggression.* Harcourt, 1974 [1963].

11. Gender Hype

Asimov, Isaac. *The Gods Themselves.* Neha, 2022 [1972].

Comte, August. *Introduction to Positive Philosophy.* Hackett, 1988.

Creveld, Martin van. *The Privileged Sex.* DLVC Enterprises, 2013.

Eller, Cynthia. *The Myth of Matriarchal Prehistory: Why an Invented Past Won't Give Women a Future.* Beacon, 2001.

Goldberg, Steven. *Why Men Rule: A Theory of Male Dominance.* Open Court, 1999.

Graglia, F. Carolyn. *Domestic Tranquility: A Brief Against Feminism.* Spence, 1998.

Grossman, Miriam. *Lost in Trans Nation: A Child Psychiatrist's Guide Out of the Madness.* Skyhorse, 2023.

———. *You're Teaching My Child What? A Physician Exposes the Lies of Sex Education and How They Harm Your Child.* Regnery, 2023 [2009].

Morelly, Abbé Étienne-Gabriel. *Code de la Nature.* Chez le Frai Sage, 1755.

Orwell, George. *Nineteen Eighty-Four*. Secker and Warburg, 1949.

Diane Ravitch. *The Language Police: How Pressure Groups Restrict What Students Learn*. Vintage, 2004.

Ross, Kelley L. *Against the Theory of 'Sexist Language'*. https://www.friesian.com/language.htm (2023).

Klemperer, Victor. *The Language of the Third Reich:LTI—Lingua Tertii Imperii, a Philologist's Notebook*. Bloomsbury Academic, 2013 [1957].

Sapir, Edward. *Language: An Introduction to the Study of Speech*. Ishi, 2014 [1921].

Whorf, Benjamin Lee. *Language, Thought, and Reality: Selected Writings of Benjamin Lee Whorf*. Dead Authors Society, 1955.

12. Race Hype

Boyle, Evan A., Yand I. Li, and Jonathan K. Pritchard. An Expanded View of Complex Traits: From Polygenic to Omnigenic. *Cell* 169 (2017).

Clarke, Laura, et al. The International Genome Sample Resource (IGSR): A Worldwide Collection of Genome Variation Incorporating the 1,000 Genomes Project Data. *Nucleic Acids Research* 45:D1 (2017).

Edwards, Anthony William Fairbank. Human Genetic Diversity: Lewontin's Fallacy. *BioEssays* 25:8 (2003).

Eibl-Eibesfeldt, Irenaus. *Human Ethology*. Routledge, 2017.

Guess, Teresa J. The Social Construction of Whiteness: Racism by Intent, Racism by Consequence. *Critical Sociology* 32:4 (2006).

German Zoological Society. Jena Declaration. https://www.dzg-ey.dr/akt-nelles/dzg2019-jenaer-erklaerung/.2019.

Heidegger, Martin. *Gesamtausgabe Bd. 9: Wegmarken/Brief über den Humanismus*. Klostermann, 2005.

Herrnstein, Richard J., and Charles Murray. *The Bell Curve: Intelligence and Class Structure in American Life*. Free Press, 1994.

Himmelfarb, Gertrude. 1994. *On Looking into the Abyss: Untimely Thoughts on Culture and Society*. Knopf.

Jorde, Lynn B., and Stephen P. Wooding. Genetic Variation, Classification, and Race. *Nature Genetics* 36: Suppl 11 (2004).

Levin, Michael. *Why Race Matters*. New Century, 2005 [1997].

Morelly, Abbé Étienne-Gabriel. *Code de la Nature*. Chez le Frai Sage, 1755.

Murray, Charles. *Facing Reality: Two Truths about Race in America*. Encounter Books, 2021.

Oakeshott, Michael. *Rationalism in Politics*. Basic Books, 1962.

Scheler, Max. *Die Wissensformen und die Gesellschaft, Gesammelte Werke, VIII*. Francke, 1960.

Witherspoon, David J., et al. Genetic Similarities within and between Human Populations. *Genetics* 176:1 (2007).

13. Diversity Hype

Elias, Norbert. *The Civilizing Process: Sociogenetic and Psychogenetic Investigations.* Blackwell, 2000 [1939].

Forsthoff, Ernst. Rechtsstaatlichkeit und Sozialstaatlichkeit: Aufsätze und Essays. In *Wege der Forschung* 118 (1968).

Foucault, Michel. *The Order of Things: An Archeology of the Human Sciences.* Vintage, 1984 [1966].

Gehlen, Arnold. *Moral und Hypermoral: Eine Pluralisitische Ethik.* Klostermann, 1969.

Heidegger, Martin. *Basic Writings.* Harper, 2008.

Hicks, Stephen R.C. *Explaining Postmodernism: Skepticism and Socialism from Rousseau to Foucault.* Scholargy, 2004.

Jünger, Ernst. *Eumeswil.* 2015 [1977].

Kolnai, Aurel. *Politics, Values, and National Socialism.* Transaction, 2013.

Mahoney, Daniel J. *The Idol of Our Age: How the Religion of Humanity Subverts Christianity.* Encounter, 2020.

Marx, Karl, and Friedrich Engels. *The Communist Manifesto.* Penguin Classics, 2002 [1848].

Morelly, Abbé Étienne-Gabriel. *Code de la Nature.* Chez le Frai Sage, 1755.

Mulligan, Kevin. Foolishness and the Value of Knowledge. In Leo Zaibert, ed., *The Theory and Practice of Ontology.* Palgrave Macmillan, 2016.

Orwell, George. *Animal Farm: A Fairy Story.* Secker and Warburg, 1945.
———. *Nineteen Eighty-Four.* Secker and Warburg, 1949.

Parsons, Talcott. *The Structure of Social Action, Volume 1.* Free Press, 1967 [1937].

Popitz, Heinrich. *Phenomena of Power.* Columbia University Press, 2017.

Preparata, Guido. 2007. *The Ideology of Tyranny: Bataille, Foucault, and the Postmodern Corruption of Political Dissent.* Springer, 2007.

Rawls, John. *A Theory of Justice.* Harvard University Press, 1999 [1971].

Max Scheler. *Formalism in Ethics and Non-Formal Ethics of Values.* Northwestern University Press, 1973.

Scruton, Roger. *Fools, Frauds, and Firebrands: Thinkers of the New Left.* Bloomsbury, 2015.

Simmel, Georg. *Grundfrage der Sociologie.* Goschen, 1917.

Sölter, Arpad. Heideggers Kulturkritische Theorie des Gegenwärtigen Zeitalters. In Alfred Denker and Holger Zaborowski, eds., *Heidegger-Jahrbuch 12: Jenseits von Polemik und Apologie.* Alber, 2020.

Stirner, Max. *The Ego and Its Own.* Cambridge University Press, 2009 [1844].

University of Washington. *Diversity, Equity, and Inclusion.* www.washington.edu/research/or/office-of-research-diversity-equity-and-inclusion/dei-definitions (2024).

Weber, Max. *Economy and Society: A New Translation.* Harvard University Press, 2019.

14. Trans Hype

Eberstadt, Mary. *Adam and Eve after the Pill, Revisited*. Ignatius Press, 2023.

Gibbs, Susanne. *Homeschooling Quick Start: What You Need to Know*. Open Universe, 2024.

Grossman, Miriam. *You're Teaching My Child What? A Physician Exposes the Lies of Sex Education and How They Harm Your Child*. Regnery, 2009.

———. *Lost in Trans Nation: A Child Psychiatrist's Guide Out of the Madness*. Skyhorse, 2023.

Harrington, Mary. *The Three Principles of Reactionary Feminism*. https://www.thepublicdiscourse.com/2023/04/88473/ (2023).

Otto, Katharina B. Psychopathen, Dummies, Verirrte? Gedanken einer Transfrau. www.achgut.com/artikel/psychopathen_dummies_verirrte_gedanken_einer_transfrau (2023).

Peterson, Claire M., et al. Suicidality, Self-Harm, and Body Dissatisfaction in Transgender and Emerging Adults with Gender Dysphoria. *Suicide and Life-Threatening Behavior* 47:4 (2017).

15. Hype and the Permanent State of Emergency

Agamben, Giorgio. *State of Exception*. University of Chicago Press, 2008

Ferrero, Guglielmo. *Pouvoir: Les Génies Invisibles de la Cité*. Paris: Plon, 1942.

Foucault. Michel. *Power: The Essential Works of Michel Foucault, 1954–1984*. Penguin, 2020.

Popitz, Heinrich. *Phenomena of Power*. Columbia University Press, 2017.

Schmitt, Carl. *Dictatorship: From the Beginning of the Modern Concept of Sovereignty to Proletarian Class Struggle*. Polity, 2014 [1921].

Veblen, Thorstein. *Absentee Ownership: Business Enterprise in Recent Times: The Case of America*. Routledge, 2017 (1924).

Index